Western Frontiersmen Series, XXI

James F. Milligan in Later Life
Tintype in possession of Milligan Family

John C. Frémont
From Bigelow's *Life of Frémont*
(New York, 1856)

JAMES F. MILLIGAN

His Journal of Fremont's Fifth Expedition, 1853-1854; his adventurous life on land and sea.

by
MARK J. STEGMAIER
and
DAVID H. MILLER

THE ARTHUR H. CLARK COMPANY
Glendale, California 1988

LIBRARY OF CONGRESS CATALOG CARD NUMBER 88-71007
ISBN 0-87062-189-0

For

Diane and Sylvia

Contents

Maps and Illustrations

Introduction

The name James Fisher Milligan is not a household word today, and never was. In fact, the name is not even familiar to historians at all, except for those who have specialized in researching military signals in the Civil War era. He was a nineteenth-century man whose life touched upon some of the important events during that epoch of American history. It was a life filled with more adventure than most men are permitted to encounter — a boyhood on a frontier farm in Missouri; midshipman in the U.S. Navy, first on the Gulf Coast of Mexico in the Mexican War and then in the Africa Squadron; a series of occupations and diversions in St. Louis, including service as a U.S. mail carrier to Utah, a deputy marshal, and a volunteer fireman; member of Frémont's fifth expedition in 1853-1854 and buffalo robe trader at Bent's Fort; lieutenant on several U.S. revenue cutters, mainly at Norfolk; newspaper correspondent; Confederate signal officer in the James River area in the Civil War; postwar newspaperman in Norfolk.

Despite the adventurous life he led, it would be easy to question the desire to write as full a biography of James Milligan as the following book entails. The reason is simply that Milligan left enough records of his life, not only enough to piece together a narrative of his life, but also enough and of such a nature that we can reasonably well portray the man's character as he struggled through the vicissitudes of life. Certainly the most important of these records is the daily journal which Milligan kept while a member of Frémont's fifth expedition and as a buffalo robe trader at Bent's Fort in 1853-1854. It is the only day-by-day journal of that last and least-known Frémont expedition. Most importantly, it is a nearly unique frontier journal in its honest and often caustic commentary on Frémont and the other personnel of the expedition and in its forthright account of the social mores of the buffalo robe traders. His journal is more than a mere narrative of places and events; it is a telling character study of Milligan himself and of the expedition leader whom he grew to dislike intensely — John Charles Frémont. The significance of Milligan's journal of the Frémont expedition has dictated the structure of this biography. The annotated journal forms the central chapter of the book, preceded and followed by narrative chapters covering the other events of Milligan's life.

Editorial Procedures

In preparing James F. Milligan's journal for publication, we have followed the editorial model used by Donald Jackson and Mary Lee Spence in *The Expeditions of John Charles Frémont*.

Milligan kept his journal in a leather-bound volume with pages measuring 7½ x 9¼ inches. It has remained in the possession of the Milligan family to this day. Regular entries begin on April 14, 1853, and run through July 25. There are no entries from that date until September 6, the day Milligan started out with the Frémont expedition. The portion of the journal reproduced herein is ninety-four pages long in the original holograph. It runs from September 6, 1853, through April 28, 1854. It covers the entire time that Milligan was associated with the fifth expedition as well as his subsequent adventures at Bent's New Fort. Milligan continued to make occasional journal entries after his return to St. Louis. These, along with drafts of letters, poetry, and newspaper clippings fill the remainder of his journal and are not reproduced herein. Milligan also kept a midshipman's journal of his experiences in the Mexican War covering the years from 1846 to 1848. His decision to keep a daily journal of the fifth expedition was undoubtedly based upon his experience in keeping a midshipman's journal. We have used his Mexican War journal in preparing our chapter on his experiences in the war, but have made only limited quotations from it.

The original holograph text is followed as closely as possible. Departures from the original text are based upon common sense, current scholarly convention, readability, and the editors' desire to achieve a measure of uniformity. Milligan was inconsistent in placing the month, day and year at the head of each daily entry. He often abbreviated the month. Sometimes he provided the year, but often he did not. There are six instances where he mistakenly wrote the year 1854 instead of 1853. These are the entries for September 13, 14, 15, and 19; October 1; and December 9. These errors in dating raise the distinct possibility that he recopied his journal sometime in 1854. For the sake of uniformity we have placed all date headings near the left margin. We have spelled out the month, provided the year, and have corrected the year for the six entries mentioned above.

We have followed Milligan's capitalization except in cases where his intent is not clearly evident. We have followed modern capitalization in these few instances.

We have adhered to the punctuation of the original. However, we have provided periods where necessary, and replaced dashes at the end of sentences with periods. We have added missing punctuation in those instances where the sentences otherwise would be difficult to understand. Words which were underscored in the original are italicized.

We have followed Milligan's spelling except in a few cases where the word might otherwise be unintelligible. We have retained his spelling of proper names. Where necessary we have provided the correct spelling in the notes. Since Milligan and most of his nineteeth-century contemporaries did not use the acute accent mark over the *e* in Frémont's name, it does not appear here in his published journal. We have used the accent mark in our narrative chapters. We have retained his variant spellings for Indian tribes, such as Arrapahoe and Arapahoe. He consistently spelled village as "villiage." For the sake of modern readers we have used the correct spelling. He usually spelled plurals such as luxuries, wolves, and bellies as "luxurys," "wolfs" and "bellys." These spellings have been retained.

In the case of doubles, e.g. "was was," or "and and ," we have deleted the word duplicated.

The authors owe an immense debt of gratitude to numerous individuals and institutions across the country for their assistance in our research:

Col. Robert M. Stegmaier (Ret.), Sun City, AZ — originally brought James Fisher Milligan's journal to attention, and offered helpful suggestions throughout project.

Robert Fisher Milligan, Sun City, AZ — grandson of JFM, possessor of JFM journals, gave kind assistance and information throughout the project.

National Archives and Records Service — especially staffs of Navy and Old Army Branch and the Judicial and Fiscal Branch — JFM career records from Navy, Revenue Marine, and Confederate Army.

Mary Lee Spence freely shared her intimate knowledge of

obscure Frémont materials as well as her insight and empathy for John C. Frémont. Her help has been invaluable in preparing annotations.

Anthony R. Crawford and his staff at the Library and Archives of Missouri Historical Society, St. Louis.

Lucile B. Portlock at Sergeant Memorial Room of Norfolk Public Library.

David Winfred Gaddy of New Carrollton, MD — Civil War.

Brenton Karhoff of Knox County Historical Society, Edina, MO — Early life of Milligan.

Staffs of County Courthouses in Knox County (Edina), Lewis County (Monticello), and Scotland County (Memphis), MO — legal records of Milligan Family.

Prof. Dan Hawk Moon Alford, Dept. of Linguistics, University of California, Berkeley — Cheyenne Indian words.

Wayne Leman, Busby, MT — Cheyenne Indian words.

Lance Henson, Calumet, OK — Cheyenne Indian words.

D.C. Allard and Staff of Naval Historical Center, Washington Navy Yard — information relating to JFM in Mexican War.

Staff, Library of Congress, Newspaper Section.

Staff, Bureau of Vital Statistics, St. Louis, MO.

Staff, Jefferson Medical College, Philadelphia, PA.

Staff, Manuscripts Division, Oklahoma Historical Society, Oklahoma City, OK.

Dr. K. Jack Bauer, Prof. of History at Rensselaer Polytechnic Institute, Troy, NY — JFM in Mexican War.

Staff, St. Louis Public Library, St. Louis, MO.

Staff, Kansas State Historical Society, Topeka — Frontier newspapers, 1850-1854.

Staff, William Perkins Library, Duke University, Durham, NC — Mexican War.

Dr. Seymour Conner, Lubbock, TX — Mexican War.

Staff, Bancroft Library, University of California, Berkeley — Frontier records, Frémont Papers.

Mary Mewes, Ref. Librarian, St. Louis Mercantile Library Assn.

Staff, Marriage License Bureau, City Hall, St. Louis, MO.

Staff, St. Louis Society for Medical and Scientific Education.

Staff, Circuit Court of City of Norfolk, VA.

Cameron University Research Committee for research grants.

C.U. Division of Social Sciences, for grant of released time for research.

Connie Dillon, Cameron University Media Services.

C.U. Library, Interlibrary Loan Dept. — Sharon Kauanui — excellent service in acquiring little-known sources from distant libraries.

Paula Raney, Sally Soelle, and Susan Brinson — research assistance.

C.U. Division of Social Sciences secretaries — typing: Azie Notzke, Mary Zumwalt, Colleen Longacre, Nancy Alexander, Nina Sloan-Perry, Kathleen Glenn, and Sue Wilson.

Prof. Sherry Newell, Dept. of Language Arts, C.U., and life member of Santa Fé Trail Historical Society — Manuscript editing.

Little, Brown and Co. — permission to publish Mexican War map from Morison, *Old Bruin.*

Johns Hopkins University Press — permission to reprint material from Anderson, ed., *Centennial Ed. of Works of Sidney Lanier.*

National Historical Publications and Records Commission.

JAMES F. MILLIGAN
His Adventurous Life on Land and Sea

1

James F. Milligan, 1829-1846 Background and Early Life

While there is a paucity of details concerning the early life of James Fisher Milligan, there exists enough information to enable us to piece together a general account of his youth. He was born in Philadelphia on March 15, 1829,[1] son of Edward Milligan and his wife Louisa F. Milligan.[2] Little information can be found concerning Edward Milligan prior to 1840. He was born in Ireland, but his date of birth and his date of immigration to the United States are unknown.[3] One source mentions that he had married his wife in Boston, but that cannot be corroborated by other records.[4] An Edward Milligan is recorded in the census of 1830 for Philadelphia; this listing shows a male child under five years old in his household, the correct category for a son born the year before. This entry also shows Edward to be in his twenties at that time,

---

[1] This date is given in two records: his record of marriage in 1856, Marriage Register I, p.8, line 24, Circuit Court of the City of Norfolk, VA; and a notation in the Milligan family Bible, attested to in a written statement of W. L. Prieur, Jr., Clerk of Courts in Norfolk, dated Oct. 31, 1940, in possession of Mr. Robert F. Milligan, Sun City, AZ.

[2] While there are any number of records of Edward Milligan, the only mention of the name of James Milligan's mother is in a revocation document from Knox Co., MO, in 1849. Land Records, Book A, p. 405, Knox Co. Courthouse, Edina, MO.

[3] Ireland is given as his birthplace in the 1850 census. "Popuation Schedules of the Seventh Census of the United States, 1850," Microfilm M432, reel 416, p. 283, Record Group 29 — Records of the Bureau of the Census, National Archives and Records Service (hereafter cited as "U.S. Census"). A search of immigration records at the National Archives failed to locate any immigration record for this Edward Milligan.

which corresponds to his age given later in the census of 1850 as 45.[5] Other records indicate that Edward Milligan was possibly a printer by trade.[6] Whatever his trade, he was undoubtedly a man of some education, judging from the command of English found in his letters.

Edward Milligan was an ambitious man who sensed better opportunities for himself farther west. Sometime in the late 1830s he moved his family to St. Louis. By 1840 [7] he had secured himself a clerk's position in the post office there, possibly through the influence of another emigré from Philadelphia, newspaper editor and frontier politician William Gilpin, whom Milligan later described as "an old personal & political friend."[8] But while Edward Milligan continued himself to live and work in St. Louis, he purchased land in the northeast corner of Missouri and established his family in residence on a farm there. Milligan began purchasing parcels for his farm early in 1840. On February 26, 1840, Edward Milligan paid three hundred dollars to Thomas Hannay and John Hunsicker for 240 acres in Colony Township in what was then Lewis County.[9] Later that year, in October, Thomas Hannay executed a will in which he left his property in the area and one hundred dollars to Edward Milligan, as he stated, "in consideration of the friendship I bear him."[10] Since these

---

[4] *History of Lewis, Clark, Knox, and Scotland Counties, Missouri* (St. Louis, 1887), 556. Hereafter cited as *Knox County History*.

[5] "5th U.S. Census, 1830," M19, reel 159, p. 208, RG 29, NARS. Philadelphia directories do not list Edward Milligan.

[6] Later, when he was county judge in Missouri, Knox Co. paid Edward Milligan "for press and seal for county court, $33; for county map, $8." *Knox County History,* 559. And in the census of 1850 he gave his occupation as "printer." "7th U.S. Census, 1850," reel 416, p.283.

[7] *Keemle's St. Louis Directory for 1840-1841* (St. Louis, 1840), 41.

[8] On Gilpin, *see* James F. Willard, "William Gilpin" in Allen Johnson and Dumas Malone, eds., *Dictionary of American Biography,* 12 vols. (New York, 1958), IV,316; Karnes, *William Gilpin,* 31-71; and Edward Milligan to William Gilpin, Dec. 6, 1844, "County Court Papers, 1844" (MS, Missouri Hist. Soc., St. Louis).

[9] Land Records, Book D, p. 470, Lewis Co. Courthouse, Monticello, MO.

[10] Land Records, Book A, p. 90, Scotland Co. Courthouse, Memphis, MO.

were lands which Hannay and Hunsicker had purchased jointly from the Federal Government, a court-appointed commission, following Hannay's death, was assigned the task in 1843 of partitioning the property between Hunsicker and Edward Milligan. Milligan received four hundred acres in the partition, lands contiguous to the property he already held.[11] Edward Milligan bought an additional 80-acre parcel from the Federal Government for one hundred dollars on November 6, 1840. In 1842, he assigned this last parcel to his eldest son, Edward William Milligan, who held it until his death a few years later.[12] The various parcels together constituted a 720-acre farm, which Edward Milligan named "Oak Ridge." Located about seven miles northeast of the town of Edina in Township 63 North (Colony Township), Range 10 West, lying in portions of Sections 29-32, it is part of present-day Knox County.

It was at Oak Ridge that James Milligan spent most of his early teen-age years in the period from 1840 to 1846. The area was still in the frontier stage of development and still part of Lewis County when the Milligans moved there in 1840. It was an area of rolling hills with stands of timber near the many streams. Agriculture there was not commercial yet but subsistence; and the Milligans, like most families in the area, probably relied heavily upon corn for their food staple, cultivated flax to provide homespun

---

[11] *Ibid.*, p. 318

[12] "Land Entry Papers of the General Land Office" — Palmyra, MO., cash certificate 22398, vol. 44, p. 346, Record Group 49 — Records of the Bureau of Land Management, NARS. This certificate is the source of an error in the only history of Knox Co., although the authors of that history recognized their account was probably in error. Edward Milligan is recorded in that work as having made the earliest land entry in Knox Co., on Nov. 6, 1830, which is exactly ten years prior to his purchase from the government. Someone simply misread the date and copied it wrongly at some point in time. *Knox County History*, 556, 577; Edward William Milligan's death is referred to in later deeds. Land Records, Book B, p.227; and Book C, p.118, Knox Co. Courthouse, Edina, MO.

clothing, and grazed a flock of sheep on their farm. Undoubtedly the Milligans enjoyed all the rustic pleasures associated with farm life, as well as the many deprivations of that existence.[13]

Although the Milligans apparently did not own slaves, slavery was an established institution in Missouri. Many settlers in Lewis County owned slaves, and even those who did not own slaves appear to have supported the "peculiar institution." The Lewis County census of 1840 shows a total population of 6040, of whom 4966 were white and 1074 were black. Occasional disturbances in the early 1840s by abolitionists from Illinois seeking to induce slaves to escape from northeast Missouri forced the whites to confront the rising abolitionist agitation over the slavery issue, but abolitionist arguments and efforts did not shake the belief of most whites in northeast Missouri that slavery was a righteous institution. James Milligan, even though he would never own a slave, grew up strongly supportive of the right to hold slaves and inveterately prejudiced against blacks.[14]

Since their father was busy at his post office job in St. Louis, and made only occasional visits to Oak Ridge, the work of running the farm fell to Mrs. Milligan and her brood of growing children. Edward William was the eldest son, followed by James, brother Francis, and their sisters Isabelle and Mary. Certainly not all of James' life at Oak Ridge was hard work. He cultivated friendships as well as crops, and, according to an entry in one of his journals, even had a boyhood sweetheart named Zarilda. James also managed to acquire a basic education. Possibly some of his schooling took place in one of the transitory one-room cabins that were occasionally established on that frontier,[15]

[13] *Knox County History,* 580-84.

[14] *Ibid.,* 62-63.

[15] *Ibid.,* 584-85. Edina had its first schoolhouse in 1839 or 1840.

but one account also indicated that James Milligan received some of his education at a school in St. Louis.[16] Just where he may have gone to school in St. Louis or what the nature of his studies there were remains unknown. However, it is apparent from his journals that he learned to write well, was well-versed in literature and poetry, and enjoyed the theatre.

Edward Milligan would have liked to join his family at Oak Ridge permanently, but his position in St. Louis provided the security of a steady income — an important consideration for a man with family obligations and debts which required repayment. It was not until late in 1844 that Milligan saw an opportunity to leave his job in St. Louis. The Missouri legislature was carving up old Lewis County into three new counties. Clark County had been established in 1838, Scotland County in 1841, and now the legislature was in the process of establishing Knox County in the area where Milligan's farm lay.[17] Realizing that there would be patronage involved in the organization of a new county, Edward Milligan utilized what influence he could muster in order to secure an interim appointment as county judge until regular elections were held for these offices. Receiving such an appointment would offset the economic loss of his post office clerkship and allow him to rejoin his family.

In December, 1844, Milligan not only applied for the judgeship to Governor John Edwards, but also requested his friend William Gilpin to employ his influence with the governor to secure Milligan the patronage plum. Milligan followed these requests with another letter to Governor Edwards on February 13, 1845, stating that he would need time to train someone to take over as distribution clerk if

[16] This information is from a later obituary notice. Norfolk *Landmark*, Mar. 23, 1899.

[17] *Knox County History*, 62, 555.

the judgeship were granted. On February 26, 1845, Edward Milligan was appointed one of the three judges for Knox County.[18] Later in his own life, James Milligan would employ procedures similar to those of his father in attempts to secure patronage appointments and increased status for himself.

The Missouri state legislature passed the act to fully organize Knox County and a number of other counties on February 14, 1845. The act provided that the county court judges of Knox County should meet at Edina on Monday, April 7, 1845, to establish the political machinery of the county. Edward Milligan and the two other county judges were present, and Judge Melker Baker was selected as presiding judge. Edward Milligan's position as a judge undoubtedly increased the social status of his family in the county. Yet, apparently, Judge Milligan still felt unable to take up permanent residence there, because as one source relates, he continued to live in St. Louis most of the time and came up to Knox County only when court was in session. Despite his absences, he helped to oversee the early development of the legal and political system of the county during its first year or so of organization.

The Knox County phase of the Milligan family history did not endure. Circumstances soon intervened which made continued actual occupancy of the farm impractical. Judge Milligan's eldest son, Edward William, died sometime during this mid-40s period, and Louisa Milligan, the judge's wife, died soon thereafter. His son James joined the Navy with the outbreak of the Mexican War in 1846, and his younger brother Francis went off to study medicine in Philadelphia. With no one left to run the farm, Edward

[18] Edward Milligan to William Gilpin, Dec. 6, 1844; and Edward Milligan to Governor John Edwards, Dec. 7, 1844, "Co. Court Papers, 1844"; and E. Milligan to Edwards, Feb. 13., 1845, "Co. Court Papers, 1845" (MS, Missouri Hist. Soc., St. Louis).

Milligan apparently did not stand for re-election in the general election of August, 1846,[19] and took his two daughters to live in St. Louis. Legal title to Oak Ridge farm remained in the Milligan family until the late 1850s.

---

19 *Knox County History,* 555-57, 567, 659.

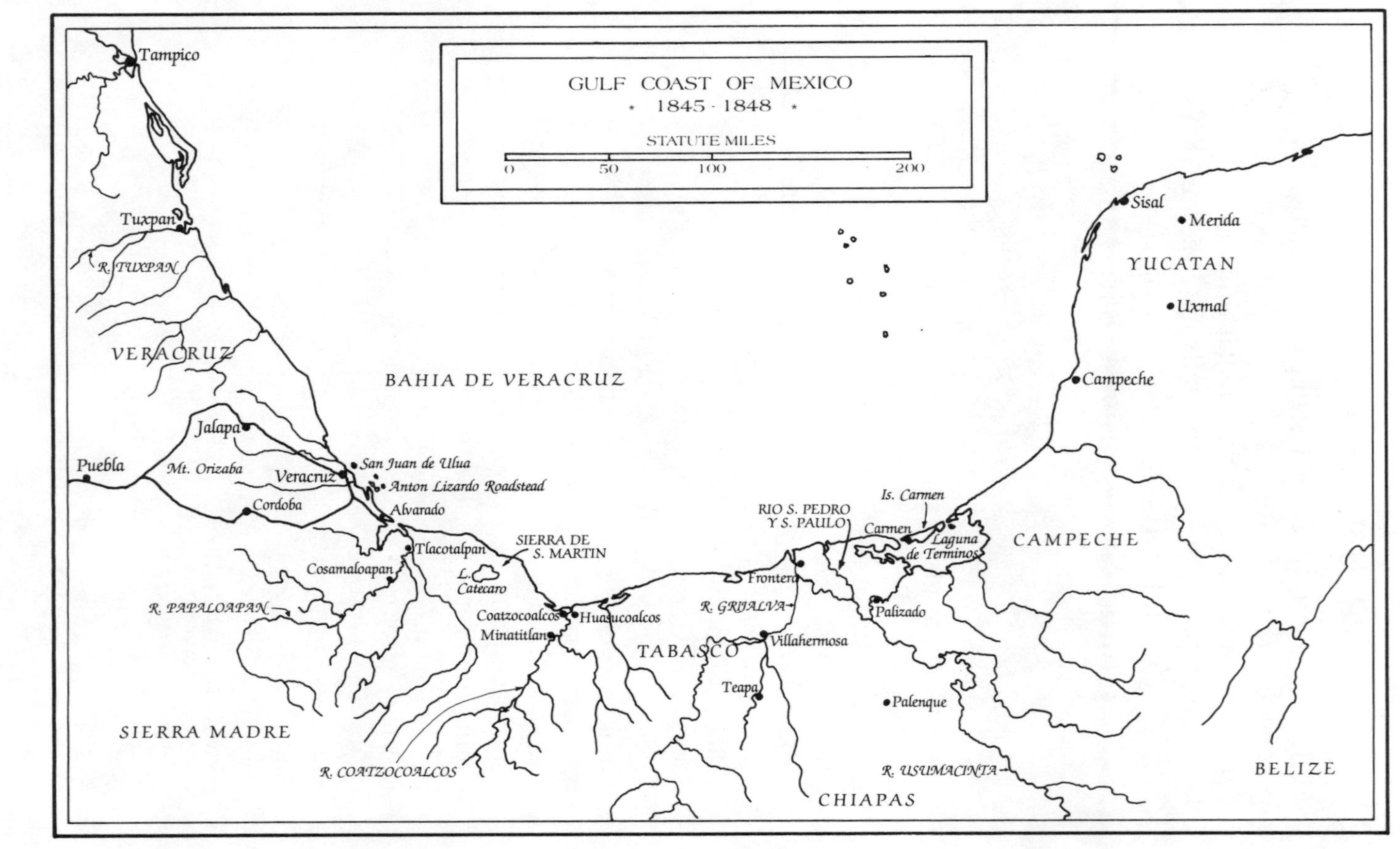
GULF COAST OF MEXICO
* 1845 - 1848 *
STATUTE MILES
0
50
100
200
Tampico
Tuxpan
R. TUXPAN
VERACRUZ
Jalapa
Puebla
Mt. Orizaba
Veracruz
Cordoba
San Juan de Ulua
Anton Lizardo Roadstead
Alvarado
BAHIA DE VERACRUZ
Tlacotalpan
Cosamaloapan
R. PAPALOAPAN
SIERRA DE
S. MARTIN
L.
Catecaro
Coatzocoalcos
Huasucoalcos
Minatitlan
SIERRA MADRE
R. COATZOCOALCOS
TABASCO
Frontera
R. GRIJALVA
Villahermosa
Teapa
CHIAPAS
RIO S. PEDRO
Y S. PAULO
Is. Carmen
Carmen
Laguna
de Terminos
Palizado
Palenque
R. USUMACINTA
CAMPECHE
Campeche
Sisal
Merida
YUCATAN
Uxmal
BELIZE

2

Midshipman Milligan of the United States Navy, 1846-1850

On March 15, 1846, on his 17th birthday, James Milligan wrote a letter applying for an appointment to the Navy as a midshipman.[1] The war with Mexico had not yet begun, but talk of war was certainly in the air. President Polk's efforts to convince the Mexican government to sell California to the United States and to recognize the Rio Grande as the legitimate southern boundary of Texas had come to nought. When diplomacy had failed, Polk ordered General Zachary Taylor to march his army to the Rio Grande. Taylor's army was still on the march when young James Milligan applied for a Navy appointment. Why he chose this particular service is unknown. At any rate, he was probably hoping at least to have his application for appointment on file before a war started, thus avoiding competition for appointments once hostilities began.

The war finally came in May, following news of a skirmish between Taylor's army and Mexican troops north of the Rio Grande. Congress officially declared war on May 12. Through the efforts of Congressman James H. Relfe of Missouri, James Milligan received his appointment, dated July 28. Milligan did not take his oath of office, however, until September 2, 1846, when he was sworn in

[1] Milligan to Sec. of the Navy George Bancroft, Mar. 15, 1846, "Index to Letters Received, 1823-1866," Letters, Mar. 1846 to Aug. 1846, No. 35, RG 45-Naval Records Coll. of the Office of Naval Records and Lib., NARS.

by his father, Judge Milligan of Knox County. Judge Milligan explained in a letter to Secretary of the Navy George Bancroft that the delay in his son's acceptance of the appointment was due to James' absence in St. Louis when the appointment arrived at Oak Ridge. On October 21 the new midshipman was ordered to proceed to New York and report for duty on the U.S. sloop of war *Albany.*[2]

Leaving family, friends, and home in northeast Missouri for an unknown new life on far-away seas would have been hard enough under any circumstances, but this leave-taking was especially heart-rending for James Milligan. His mother, Louisa, was on her deathbed. Milligan later commemorated the scene in a poem he wrote in the back of his journal in 1855, verses entitled "Reminiscences of Youth."

> The scenes of my childhood come fresh to my mind,
> Of parting from "Loved ones" & a mother so kind
> For the oceans a wanderer to roam
> In distant lands away from my home.
> Oh well I remember the last fond embrace,
> My dear mother's tears as she kissed my young face
> When I knelt for a blessing beside her sick bed.
> She raised with exertion, placed her hand on my head
> With her eyes heavenward turned, o'er flowing with tears
> And with the anguish of a mother's fears.
> She prayed fervently to He that rules above
> To watch, guard & cherish the boy of her love.
> As she sank back on the pillow o'er powered with pain
> I kissed her pale cheek and embraced her again.
> And with a sad heart I drew a deep sigh,
> As I kissed all the loved ones and bid them good bye.
> Deep, deep was my sorrow, when months had passed o'er
> To learn the sad tidings I had a mother no more . . .

[2] Appointment No. 4838, "Register of Applications for Appointment as Midshipmen, 1840-1857," RG 45, NARS; Milligan to Bancroft, Sept. 2, 1846, "Letters from Officers Acknowledging Receipt of Commissions and Warrants and Enclosing Oaths of Allegiance, 1804-64," Acceptances, 1845-1846, no. 160, RG 45, NARS; and Biographical File — James F. Milligan, Operational Archives Branch, Naval Historical Center, Wash. Navy Yard.

The *Albany*, the ship to which Milligan reported, was a new first class sloop of war displacing 1042 tons, armed with four 8-inch shell guns and eighteen solid shot-firing 32 pounders, and manned by a crew of 210 men. Her commander was a twenty-year veteran of the Navy, Captain Samuel L. Breese. The *Albany* was to be used to reinforce the Home Squadron of Commodore David Conner operating in the Gulf of Mexico.[3]

The activities of the Home Squadron are usually lost sight of in the Mexican War in contrast to the Army campaigns of General Zachary Taylor and Winfield Scott. But the Home Squadron nonetheless performed a crucial function in the conflict. The Navy's main duty, as outlined in Secretary of the Navy George Bancroft's instructions to Commodore Conner, was to blockade the Mexican ports, seize Mexican vessels, capture coastal towns, and assist the Army if possible. With the exception of neutral vessels and British mail steamers, the blockade was to be strictly enforced. The Home Squadron was supposed to enforce this blockade of roughly a thousand miles of coastline, from the Rio Grande to Campeche, with a few frigates, sloops of war, steamers, and schooners. Actually the task was not as difficult as it appears on paper. For one thing, there were only a handful of Mexican ports on the Gulf to blockade, Vera Cruz being by far the most important. Moreover, the Mexicans never mounted even a slight challenge to U.S. naval supremacy because Mexico had no navy at all. In fact, the severest challenges to the efficiency of naval operations came, not from the Mexicans, but from the severe gales called "northers," which raged in the Gulf from October to April, and from the yellow fever known as the "vomito," which took its toll from April to October.[4]

---

[3] On the *Albany*, *see* Bauer, *Surfboats and Horse Marines*, 18, 62, 253. On Breese, *see* Hamersly, comp., *The Records of Living Officers*, 21; and the extensive collection of Breese's writings. Samuel Breese Papers (MS, Perkins Lib., Duke Univ., Durham, NC).

Commodore Conner was nearing the end of his tour of duty, and the men of the Home Squadron were anxious to see that day come. Conner was a man of vast experience and usually good judgment, but the course of events so far had conspired with his extreme sense of caution and his bad health to make him rather unpopular amidst younger officers and men hungry for action. Conner's bad luck in his futile attempts to capture the port town of Alvarado did nothing to help the sagging morale of the squadron. One rumor among the junior officers was that Conner was really a member of the Peace Society and that members of that group had adopted the Navy uniform as their own.[5]

Secretary Bancroft, aware of the problem, sent Conner's replacement to be on hand when Conner finally decided to relinquish his command. The replacement was Matthew C. Perry, a decisive man of action. So as to avoid personal conflict with Conner, Perry was given the rank of Vice Commodore, and was thus subordinate. Therefore Perry flew a red pennant at the foremast in the first-class steamer *Mississippi,* while Conner flew a blue pennant at the mainmast as commander in chief of the Home Squadron in the first-class frigate *Potomac.*[6]

It is doubtful that Midshipman Milligan paid too much attention to these larger questions of command. He was too busy being initiated into the ways of naval life. The main duty of a midshipman was to learn practical seamanship, mathematics, and whatever else was necessary to transform him into an officer and gentleman. Much of the training was done on the job itself, such as learning how to stand watch. One duty of a midshipman was to keep a journal, in order to train him in how to keep a ship's log. James

[4] Bauer, *Surfboats,* 19-20, 24; Morison, *Perry,* 186-87; and Conner, *The Home Squadron...,* 12-13.

[5] Bauer, *Surfboats,* 87; Morison, *Perry,* 188-89; and Ellicott, *John Ancrum Winslow,* 39.

[6] Bauer, *Surfboats,* 44-45; Morison, *Perry,* 187-88; and Connor, *Home Squadron,* 12.

Milligan's journal has survived, being now in the possession of his grandson, Robert F. Milligan, and this journal provides us with the best glimpse of his cruises during the Mexican War. Since the journal was a training exercise, the pages have almost no personal information, especially at the beginning. The journal reads like a ship's log, full of details about rigging and sails and the ship's position. In fact, a comparison of Milligan's journal with the actual log of the *Albany* reveals that his entries are nearly identical with the official log in many instances.[7]

Midshipman Milligan began his journal on November 4, 1846, just after reporting for duty. Most of that month was spent taking on provisions at New York and getting the new vessel ready to sail for the war zone in the Gulf. The *Albany* finally set sail southward at the end of November, arriving at Havana on December 8 and remaining there for a week. From Havana the *Albany* set course north and west for the naval base at Pensacola. After spending nearly a week at Pensacola, the ship was under way again, this time for Mexico. The towering eminence of Mt. Orizaba, west of Vera Cruz, was sighted on January 7, 1847, and the *Albany* anchored at Green Island (Isla Verde), just a few miles east of Vera Cruz, on the 8th.

Green Island was one of the several small islands and reefs near Vera Cruz. Closer to shore, to the southwest, was another small island called Sacrificios. This area was sometimes used as an anchorage by the American ships, since it did afford some protection from "northers" when they suddenly struck. But a much safer anchorage, and the main one utilized by the squadron, lay another ten miles or so southeast at Antón Lizardo. The reefs and Salmedina Island provided adequate shelter for the fleet at Anton Lizardo even in strong "northers."[8]

---

[7] Ship's Log, U.S.S. *Albany*, RG 24-Records of the Bureau of Naval Personnel, NARS.

[8] Bauer, *Surfboats*, 19, 28; and Parker, *Recollections of a Naval Officer, 1841-1865*, 49, 76.

Upon joining the squadron, the *Albany* immediately took up cruising on blockade duty north and south of Vera Cruz. This primarily involved checking out any suspicious ships and taking control of those merchant vessels which attempted to run the blockade into Vera Cruz. Blockade duty was an important part of the war effort, but it was also excruciatingly boring. Only the pursuit of a suspicious vessel, the onset of a "norther," or the momentary flash of excitement caused by temporarily running aground, as happened to the *Albany* in early March, seemed to break the monotony. The tedium inevitably led to discipline problems, and one seaman of the squadron had already been executed for striking an officer on the sloop of war *St. Mary's*.[9] Judging from the number of floggings for drunkenness or insubordination which James Milligan mentions in his journal, the *Albany* was certainly not spared the discipline problems inherent in blockade duty. The only more boring thing which sailors experienced was confinement to ship at Antón Lizardo for an extended period. Crowded conditions, poor ventilation below decks, and bad food only added to the misery.[10]

It is no wonder, then, that the men of the Home Squadron were anxious to see some action, and they were about to have their wish. The administration in Washington had decided to open a second major front in Mexico commanded by General Winfield Scott. While Taylor continued the conduct of operations in northern Mexico, Scott planned to make an amphibious landing at Vera Cruz, capture that crucial port, and then march overland to Mexico City itself. The army and its transports arrived at Antón Lizardo and were fully assembled by the first week in March, 1847 — some 10,000 men and nearly 100

[9] Bauer, *Surfboats,* 42. A good description of this incident and the execution is in Taylor, *The Broad Pennant,* 263-83.

[10] Bauer, *Surfboats,* 24, 42; Morison, *Perry,* 189-90; and Semmes, *Service Afloat,* 76.

ships, an awe-inspiring sight, to say the least. It was to be the largest amphibious landing operation by the United States prior to World War II.

The naval aspects of the invasion were handled by Commodore Conner, an efficient planner. Perry was temporarily absent in the United States while the steamer *Mississippi* was being repaired, but he was hurrying back to Vera Cruz as fast as possible to get in on the action. General Scott and Commodore Conner reconnoitered the area south of and out of range of the Mexican artillery at Vera Cruz and the offshore castle of San Juan de Ulúa. They decided on Collado Beach as the landing site, just opposite Sacrificios Island. Since the anchorage between the island and the beach was too small to accommodate the transports, Conner suggested that the troops be transferred to naval vessels and five Army steamers at Antón Lizardo and shuttled to the embarkation point off Collado Beach. At that point surfboats, commanded by midshipmen or petty officers and manned by a coxswain and six seamen, would take the troops to the beach.[11]

The surfboats, the first amphibious landing craft ever specially contracted for by the Navy, were admirably suited for this operation. They were built in three sizes so that they could be efficiently stowed as a set, one inside the other. The boats were double-ended, flat-bottomed, and made of white oak and pine. Their respective lengths were 40 feet; 37 feet, 9 inches; and 35 feet, 9 inches, while their respective breadths measured 12 feet; 11 feet; and 10 feet. The largest could transport 45 or more men, in addition to crew, while the smallest size accommodated fewer than 40. A set of three boats weighed almost 16,000 pounds. While 141 surfboats were ordered, only 65 were actually on hand by the time of the Vera Cruz landings. Although it is not

[11] The best account of the planning is in Bauer, *Surfboats,* 63-77.

clear from his journal, it is very likely that Midshipman James Milligan commanded a surfboat at Vera Cruz, ten of which were manned by the *Albany.*[12]

On March 7, the *Albany's* men were busily employed getting their surfboats from the transport *America* and storing them on Salmedina Island. The landing at Collado Beach was first ordered for March 8, but the possible threat of a "norther," which never materialized, forced a postponement until March 9. That day commenced with beautiful weather, or as Milligan put it, "with light airs and pleasant." The sea was calm. While surfboat crews went to Salmedina Island at 5 A.M. to prepare their craft, troops aboard the Army transports made ready to transfer to the Navy vessels or Army steamers which would take them from Antón Lizardo to the channel between Sacrificios Island and Collado Beach. The assault was to be made in three waves, and the *Albany* was one of six ships designated to transport the reserves, or third wave, commanded by General David Twiggs. Therefore, the first task which the *Albany's* surfboats engaged in was the transfer of about 900 reserves — the Brigade of Mounted Riflemen and battalions of the 2nd and 3rd Infantry Regiments — from the transports to the *Albany.* These ten surfboats were then made fast behind two steamers, the *Petrita* and the *Eudora,* for towing to the landing area.

Before 10 A.M. the five schooner-gunboats, which were to supply close-in fire support for the invasion force, got underway from Antón Lizardo. The other vessels made preparation to sail, and at about 11 A.M. Commodore Conner on the frigate *Raritan* and General Scott in the steamer *Massachusetts* began leading the other ships single file out of the Antón Lizardo anchorage. *Albany* set sail

[12] A detailed description of the surfboats is in Temple, "Memoir of the Landing of the United States Troops" in Conner, *Home Squadron,* 60-62.

about 11:45 A.M. The short trip up the coast went as planned, and the whole fleet was in place off Collado Beach by 3 P.M. As soon as the steamers arrived, they cut loose the surfboats, which were then rowed to the troop-carrying ships. While the five schooner-gunboats and the steamers *Spitfire* and *Vixen* moved closer to shore to give covering fire if needed, the army troops climbed down into the surfboats. Getting the surfboats into some sort of orderly lines for the final landing took some time, but by 5:30 P.M. General Scott gave the signal to land. The surfboats dashed the last few hundred yards into shore, dropping 130-150-pound kedge anchors out beyond the breakers and paying out their hawsers as the boats approached the beach. The troops piled out of the boats into a shallow surf and got a bit wet, but in this way the fragile surfboats did not have to come all the way ashore and could easily return to the ships to bring more troops to land. The operation continued without difficulty until 10 P.M., when all the troops — over 8600 of them — had been safely landed. It was a magnificent achievement, thanks mainly to Commodore Conner's planning. As for the Mexicans, they did not contest the landing at all.[13]

Within four days the Army was able to encircle the city, still without any Mexican resistance. Surfboats were soon bringing supplies and the siege artillery ashore, and the Army began building emplacements for the batteries of cannon and mortars. A big "norther" came up and disrupted operations temporarily, but the battered fleet rode it out without having too many ships driven ashore, and the Army shoveled the blown sand out of its installations. The Navy even got a chance to contribute to the

[13] The best accounts of the landing are in *ibid.*, 64-68; and Bauer, *Surfboats*, 78-82. Besides Milligan's own journal, the journal of Captain Breese has some information about the *Albany's* role, as does the ship's log. Breese Papers, Duke Univ.; and Ship's Log, U.S.S. *Albany*, RG 24, NARS.

bombardment of the city. Scott's artillery was not heavy enough to breach the soft coral walls of Vera Cruz as easily as the heavier naval artillery, especially the new Paixhan guns which, with their explosive shells, could batter gaps in them. Commodore Conner suggested their use to Scott, but Conner was no longer in command when Scott decided to use them. Commodore Perry arrived in the *Mississippi* on March 20, bringing with him orders finally to replace Conner as Commander of the Home Squadron. Perry worked out with Scott the establishment of a six-gun Naval Battery on shore, to be serviced by naval officers and men, who were delighted to have the opportunity for more action. The bombardment began on March 22, conducted by Army batteries ashore and Commander Josiah Tattnall's pesky fleet of steamers and schooners firing from off shore. The Naval Battery guns — three 32-pounders and three 8-inch Paixhan shell guns — were set up and joined the barrage on Vera Cruz on the afternoon of March 23. After exchanges of artillery duels for two days, during which the Naval Battery wreaked havoc on the beleaguered city, the Mexicans decided to surrender both the city and the powerful, almost untouched Castle of San Juan de Ulúa. The articles of surrender were agreed to on March 27 and the official ceremonies took place on the 29th. The Naval Battery had proven the decisive factor. American casualties in the entire siege totalled only 14 killed and 59 wounded.[14]

Midshipman Milligan observed the action from the *Albany* and made record of it in his journal. He makes no personal comments and does not even say what he himself was doing. He mentions the surfboats several times, either landing troops or provisions, and gives a detailed account of the items sent ashore for the *Albany's* shell gun at the

[14] Bauer, *Surfboats*, 85-97; Morison, *Perry*, 215-22; Semmes, *Service Afloat*, 126-47; Parker, *Recollections*, 86-100; and Griffis, *Matthew Calbraith Perry*, 221-38.

Naval Battery. It is clear that Milligan was not one of the *Albany's* men to serve in the squadron's rotating shifts at the battery. Such was the competition to service those guns that junior officers drew lots to see who the lucky participants would be and James Milligan apparently lost out.[15] Captain Breese sent three thirty-man shifts, plus officers, to the Naval Battery during the bombardment and Breese himself commanded the battery at the time of the surrender.[16] Midshipman Milligan was forced to content himself with duties aboard the *Albany* and probably also in the surfboats.

The invasion at Vera Cruz was by far the most significant military action in which the Navy took part during the war, but Commodore Perry had no intention of making it the last such operation for his men. There were still several small Mexican ports in enemy hands, such as Alvarado, Tuxpan, Coatzacoalcos, and Tabasco, and the best way to prevent Mexico from receiving any military supplies through those ports, and thereby greatly tighten the blockade, was to capture those positions. Perry intended to do just that, by organizing his own naval personnel into the first infantry brigade in American naval history to assault and seize the ports.

Perry's first such effort immediately followed the surrender of Vera Cruz, and he organized an attack on Alvarado, the well-fortified port twenty miles southeast of Antón Lizardo which had frustrated Commodore Conner's two attempts to capture it. Perry wanted also to secure the beef and horses near the port for Scott's army. But when Perry's fleet, *Albany* included, arrived off Alvarado on April 1, Perry learned that the Mexicans had scattered the livestock, evacuated their soldiers, and had already sur-

[15] Griffis, *Perry*, 226.

[16] Breese's journal at Duke Univ. gives an excellent account of this.

rendered Alvarado to Lieutenant Charles Hunter of the one-gun steamer *Scourge.* With Alvarado having fallen into his hands, probably because the Mexicans thought it untenable after the fall of Vera Cruz, Commodore Perry turned to Tuxpan, 180 miles north of Vera Cruz and six miles from the mouth of the Tuxpan River. There he intended to test the combat capabilities of his men. Perry gathered a force of 1519 officers and sailors from his ships and spent time organizing them as an assault force to be commanded by Captain Breese of the *Albany,* but Midshipman Milligan does not appear to have been part of the force. When all was ready, the fleet sailed north and rendezvoused off Lobos Island, north of Tuxpan, on April 13-14. On the 17th, while the *Albany* and the bigger ships remained at sea, the steamers and schooner-gunboats, towing thirty surfboats with the landing force, crossed the bar of the Tuxpan River and proceeded toward the town. The Mexicans put up a half-hearted fight from a few fortified positions on the river, but this action did not impede the expedition, and Tuxpan was captured that afternoon. After destroying anything of military use in the town, Perry evacuated his troops but left the *Albany* and the schooner *Reefer* to guard the mouth of the river. Because of this duty, the *Albany* did not participate in Perry's next venture, the capture of Coatzacoalcos. Perry again organized a large naval assault on this port 100 miles southeast of Alvardo, but the effort proved unnecessary; when Perry's ships arrived off Coatzacoalcos on May 12, the Commodore found that the Mexicans had already abandoned their fortifications. The *Albany* soon rejoined the squadron for a trip along the Gulf Coast all the way to the port town of Sisal on the northwest coast of Yucatán.[17]

[17]These actions can be traced in Bauer, *Surfboats,* 99-109; and Morison, *Perry,* 222-29.

The last major operation for Perry's fleet and naval brigade was the capture of Tabasco, also known as San Juan Bautista de Villahermosa. This port town lies 72 miles up the old Tabasco River (now known as the Grijalva River), the mouth of which empties into the Gulf some sixty miles west of the port of Carmen and the entrance to the body of water known as Laguna de Terminos. While the mouth of the Tabasco River was guarded by blockade vessels of the Home Squadron to prevent military supplies from reaching the Mexican Army through Tabasco, some materials were still filtering through the town from more easterly ports like Campeche. The Americans permitted non-military trade on this part of the Gulf Coast to be conducted as usual, and inevitably some military supplies were smuggled into these ports and then smuggled through Tabasco.[18]

Perry had raided Tabasco once before in October, 1846, but had not permanently occupied it. The Mexicans, meanwhile, had strengthened the fortifications and established breastworks and other obstacles along the river from which they could ambush any force approaching Tabasco. Perry's naval infantry brigade had not yet been seriously challenged, except briefly at Tuxpan, and the Mexican defenders of Tabasco prepared to contest vigorously the Commodore's attack.

The various ships of the Squadron, including the *Albany*, gathered near the mouth of the Tabasco River on June 12-13, 1847. On the morning of June 14, the small steamers towed various brigs and schooners across the rough waters of the river bar, and then they steamed back out to the bigger vessels still beyond the bar. Perry transferred his flag from the *Mississippi* to the steamer *Scorpion* and the assault force climbed into the surfboats.

[18] Bauer, *Surfboats*, 111; and Morison, *Perry*, 202-03, 230.

Midshipman Milligan was among several *Albany* officers, in addition to 135 seamen, and twenty marines, and one piece of artillery from that ship, whose surfboats were taken in tow by the steamer *Spitfire* for the trip over the bar. Altogether the assault force consisted of over 1100 men. By 2 P.M. all were safely across the bar and anchored off the small coastal town of Frontera. At sunset Commodore Perry ordered the entire flotilla to proceed upriver. The *Spitfire,* towing not only the *Albany's* surfboats but also the bomb brig *Stromboli* and the schooner *Bonita,* was unable to make headway against the strong current and was forced to anchor after a half-hour's effort. Not until 3 A.M. on June 15 did the strength of the current ease because of flood tide, and permit the *Spitfire* to proceed. By 11 A.M. the steamer and its dependents caught up with the rest of the expedition, which had thus far encountered no opposition. Not until later that afternoon did Mexican troops commanded by Colonel Miguel Bruno ambush the leading ships of the group from the river bank, but return fire from the ships silenced that attack. By sunset on the 15th, every vessel had passed the treacherous S-shaped turn in the river known as Devil's Bend, only a few miles below the town of Tabasco. Just above Devil's Bend the Mexicans had obstructed the river with pilings driven into the bottom, which could not be negotiated at night, and Perry decided to anchor for that night about a hundred yards from the obstructions. The men slept that night on the decks of the ships with their firearms next to them, protected from potential Mexican attack only by a flimsy barricade of hammocks stretched between logs on the decks of the vessels. Luckily for the uneasy sleepers, the Mexicans did not attack that night.[19]

[19] Milligan's own journal only mentions his participation in the landing force. The Samuel L. Breese Papers at Duke Univ. give a good account of the *Albany's* men in the operation. Two excellent accounts of the expedition are Bauer, *Surfboats,* 111-16; and Morison, *Perry,* 230-33.

At dawn on the morning of June 16, Perry sent two survey officers to reconnoiter the river obstacles. The Mexicans fired on them, wounding one. They reported the river impassable, so Perry decided to effect a landing where they were and attack overland. The landing site was near a steep embankment just below a site known as Seven Palms. The landing force got back aboard the surfboats, and, as several ships provided covering fire, quickly began the landing. In ten minutes time, over 1100 men and seven pieces of artillery were ashore. The men climbed the embankment, laboriously dragged the six-pounders up with them and formed their line of march. The "Pioneers" led the way, followed successively by marines, Perry and his staff, the artillery, the two divisions of infantry, and a field ambulance. Mid-shipman Milligan was in the first division of infantry, commanded by Captain Breese, and was later listed in Perry's official report.[20] The landing had been accomplished without opposition, and the brigade was ready to march by 8:30 A.M.[21]

The advance to Tabasco went smoothly. The "Pioneers" felled trees to provide a corduroy road ensuring that the artillery pieces did not get bogged down in the dirt path the brigade followed. The American force by-passed the first Mexican breastwork and launched an all-out charge against the next one they encountered. But the three hundred Mexicans simply fled from that position. The landing force continued to advance, albeit slowly in the heat and humidity. When finally they arrived at the town's main defenses, the Americans discovered their own flag flying over the town. What had happened was that the men near the landing site had placed powder drums at the base of the river obstructions, detonated them by using electric batteries, and made a channel through the obstructions.

[20] U.S. Cong., 30th Cong., 2nd sess., *House Executive Documents,* No. 1, 1212.

[21] On the landing *see* Bauer, *Surfboats,* 116-17; and Morison, *Perry,* 233-35.

Then the *Scorpion,* the *Spitfire,* the *Scourge,* and the *Vixen* advanced upriver past occasional Mexican fire, attacked and captured a defensive work called Ft. Itúrbide, and secured the unconditional surrender of the town. Perry's brigade entered the town at 3:30 P.M. in a heavy rain and sought shelter in the government buildings on the plaza. The following day most of the seamen were sent back aboard the ships, while others dismantled and destroyed whatever of military significance could be found in Tabasco. The *Spitfire* transported most of the *Albany's* officers — Milligan included — and 86 men back to their ship. Captain Breese returned on the 19th. Commodore Perry remained at Tabasco for five days and stationed troops there for another month, but guerilla tactics by the Mexican troops in the area and yellow fever wore down the garrison until the decision was made to evacuate it in late July. After that, ships stationed at the mouth of the river were left to guard against any trade with Tabasco.[22]

One reason that Perry had decided to attack Tabasco when he did was that the *Albany* and some other ships were soon to be sent home for repairs. The *Albany's* copper-plated bottom had been damaged when the ship had run aground back in March. In order to maintain naval personnel strength in the Home Squadron, some of the *Albany's* crew were transferred to other ships before the *Albany* sailed home in July from Antón Lizardo. Midshipman James Milligan was one of these, and he was ordered to Perry's flagship *Mississippi* on July 6. That move proved to be only a temporary expedient while Perry reorganized his squadron. On August 6, Milligan was transferred to the steamer *Scorpion,* captained by Commander Abraham Bigelow. The *Mississippi* itself, badly infected with yellow fever and malaria, was dispatched a few days later to

[22] Breese Papers, Duke Univ.; Bauer, *Surfboats,* 117-22; and Morison, *Perry,* 235-38.

Pensacola to be fumigated. Thus Perry's squadron became rather depleted after the Tabasco operation.

James Milligan's journal becomes a bit more interesting to read after his transfer to the *Scorpion.* His comments became somewhat more personal on occasion, although generally the entries are not terribly dissimilar from earlier entries. It is possible that he was no longer being required to keep the journal as a matter of training but continued to do so for his own reasons.

Apparently Midshipman Milligan had proven himself to be a competent junior officer and conscientious trainee. Otherwise he probably would not have been transferred to the *Scorpion,* the most active single vessel of the Gulf Squadron. Wherever there was an operation of significance, particularly on the rivers, the *Scorpion* was there. The U.S.S. *Scorpion* was the largest of the squadron's thirdclass steamers, weighing over 300 tons, serviced by a crew of 61, mounting two 8-inch shell guns and two 18-pounders, and capable of making a speed of 7.5 knots with her twin side wheels.[23] Given the missions upon which the *Scorpion* was often sent, Milligan would not have been assigned to her if he had shown himself to be a laggard. And, in fact, Milligan received his warrant as a midshipman in September, 1847; no longer was he simply an "acting" midshipman.[24]

Since the squadron had become depleted by the departure of several larger vessels, the job of the remaining vessels was much more demanding. While there really was no further need of offensive operations by the squadron, Perry's ships still had to enforce the blockade and maintain control over the various captured ports against the threat of Mexican guerillas. The Mexicans sensed that the American position had become more vulnerable because,

[23] Bauer, *Surfboats,* 258.

[24] Biographical file, James F. Milligan, Naval Historical Center.

as the fleet had diminished in size, the level of Mexican guerilla activity had increased. This might have appeared to be a sideshow anyway — after all, General Winfield Scott's army was at the gates of Mexico City itself and would capture it in mid-September, 1847 — but the necessity remained for the Home Squadron to keep order on the Gulf Coast.

The U.S.S. *Scorpion* continued to be one of Commodore Perry's favorite vessels to call on for action. In response to a rumored Mexican threat against Alvarado in August, Perry ordered the *Scorpion* and the small steamers *Vixen* and *Spitfire* to cruise up the Alvarado River (now the Papaloapan River) as far as Tlacotalpan in a show of force. This demonstration had the desired effect; whatever Mexican threat existed to Alvarado simply evaporated. In October the *Scorpion* was again cruising the river between Avarado and Tlacotalpan, and also the Coatzacoalcos River inland as far as Minatitlán. In November Commodore Perry had the steamers *Scorpion* and *Water Witch* accompany his flagship *Mississippi* as Perry visited the Gulf ports from Alvarado to Campeche. After that, until March, 1848, the *Scorpion* usually operated from Laguna de Terminos near the port of Carmen.

In his journal entries from these months, Milligan mentions himself more often than before, possibly because he had more responsibility now. On November 7, 1847, Milligan writes of being sent to get a schooner towed over a river bar. Almost two weeks later, after the *Scorpion* had run aground in the Alvarado River, Midshipman Milligan was dispatched in a schooner to Tlacotalpan to fetch the assistance of the *Spitfire* in pulling the *Scorpion* off. At Coatzacoalcos, on December 15, Milligan was put in charge of a cutter to secure a drifting canoe. On January 8, 1848, he was entrusted to take various messages to the squadron at Frontera. Milligan even records one instance of his own misconduct. He apparently got drunk while ashore at Carmen in late January. According to his entry of January 27, "The Captain informed me that I was not to be sent on shore anymore." Milligan added in verse:

> Oh isn't it hard, that a fellow should be,
> Quarantined, for taking a spree.

This was all a prelude to the most interesting action of Midshipman Milligan's Mexican War career. It began with Commodore Perry's last visit to Carmen and Yucatán in March, 1848. The wartime situation in that region was very complex and gave Perry no end of frustration and worry. Yucatán at that time comprised the present states of Yucatán, Campeche and Quintana Roo.[25] Carmen and Laguna de Terminos, now part of Campeche, were therefore at the extreme western end of Yucatán, near the border with the neighboring Tabasco province. In this remote area, Commodore Perry really had two different wars going on at the same time. One war was between the Yucatecos and the Mexicans, the other between the Yucatecos and the Maya Indians. Yucatán's loyalty to Mexico never seemed more than tenuous at best, and during the U.S.-Mexican hostilities, Yucatán, "La Repûblica Chica" — or tiny republic, as it was called — declared its independence from Mexico. After the Navy occupied Carmen and Laguna in December, 1846, the people of the region readily collaborated with the American authorities and profited from trading with them. However, these policies earned the collaborators the bitter enmity of the Mexican authorities in Tabasco, particularly General Miguel Bruno, and Mexican soldiers conducted a number of raids into western Yucatán. But the most potent threat

[25] Morison, *Perry*, 202.

to the tranquility of Yucatán was not from Mexican raids; rather, it was from the Maya Indians of Yucatán itself. The Indians rose in rebellion against the white Yucatecos in the "Caste War," conducting a campaign of wholesale slaughter wherever they went. The white Yucatecos fled by the thousands to the coastal towns like Carmen and Campeche, and demanded U.S. military protection. In fact, many of the whites were asking the United States to annex Yucatán, and their chief agent in Washington, Don Justo Sierra O'Reilly, lobbied mightily for military assistance.[26]

There was not really very much that Commodore Perry could do to stop the conflicts in Yucatán. His depleted Home Squadron could protect the white refugees on the coast to some extent and could patrol some of the rivers in western Yucatán, but that was about all. Perry would have liked to have been able to have done more, knowing how desperately the Yucatecos depended on his assistance, but he simply did not have the resources to restore peace in Yucatán. Besides, he was extremely contemptuous of the Yucatecos themselves and blamed most of their failure to defeat the Indians on their own cowardice. So Perry's visit to Yucatán in March, 1848, was designed to instill some measure of resolve in the Yucatecos themselves and hopefully scare the Mexicans and Mayas into halting their depredations. Perry had orders from the administration in Washington to avoid much more involvement than this, since the Mexican War was all but over.[27]

Midshipman Milligan of the *Scorpion* did not see action in the conflict between the whites and the Mayas. Instead,

[26] On all the aspects of the Caste War, *see* Reed, *The Caste War of Yucatan.*

[27] On Perry's role concerning Yucatán, *see* Morison, *Perry,* 242-49. Much of Perry's correspondence and other items about Yucatán are in U.S. Cong., 30th Cong., 1st sess., *Senate Executive Documents* No. 43, 4-30; No. 45, 3-4; and No. 49, 2-10. Hereafter cited as *Sen. Ex. Docs.,* 30th Cong., 1st sess.

his role concerned Perry's attempts to protect the people of western Yucatán from the Mexican threat. More particularly, Milligan became one of the participants in the temporary occupation of a village called Palizada, an action which is almost totally unknown to historians, except for an extremely brief mention by Perry's biographer.[28]

While Palizada had always been on the periphery of American concern, Perry's forces had maintained an occasional presence there since December, 1846, when Laguna had been occupied. The little town lay about forty miles inland from Laguna on the Palizada River, very near the border with Tabasco. Upon capturing Laguna, the Americans established a regular patrol by small ships in the bay and up the river as far as the town of Palizada. The purpose was to cut communications and transit of military supplies which could reach Tabasco from the ports of Yucatán and British Honduras.[29] In April, 1847, after rumors had circulated that General Santa Anna, following his defeat by General Scott's army at Cerro Gordo, was planning to escape from Mexico via the Gulf Coast, Commodore Perry dispersed his forces to various points to intercept and capture the fugitive. One version of the rumor was that Santa Anna might flee through the Palizada area to Honduras. Pursuant to that, the commander of the brig *Porpoise,* which was on guard near Carmen, sent Lieutenant Augustus L. Case, Midshipman F. K. Murray, and 25 men in a large canoe called a bungo to occupy Palizada. They mounted one of the *Porpoise's* 24-pounders on the boat for added effectiveness. This group remained at the town for two weeks, constantly on alert against rumored Mexican cavalry attacks.[30]

[28] Morison, *Perry,* 247.

[29] Semmes, *Service Afloat,* 83-84.

[30] Bauer, *Surfboats,* 106; and the biographical sketch of Augustus L. Case in *A Naval Encyclopedia, 116.*

Even after Lieutenant Case's troops had departed, the military governor at Carmen, Commander Bigelow of the *Scorpion*, continued to maintain surveillance in the Palizada area. The vessel mostly used for this patrol duty upriver was a small schooner previously captured from the Mexicans by Commodore Perry on his first visit to Tabasco in late 1846, and renamed by him the U.S.S. *Morris* in honor of a young naval officer killed in that operation.[31]

Palizada was still of concern to Perry during his trip to Yucatán in March, 1848, although the dominant item preying on his mind then was the Indian massacre of whites in Yucatán. The problem was that Tabasco's military chief, General Miguel Bruno, refused to acknowledge that Mexico had been defeated, even at that late date when all that was lacking was the ratification of a treaty ending the war.[32] Bruno was simply a proud, stubborn fighter. As part of Commodore Perry's trip, he journeyed inland on March 16, hoping to visit the ancient ruins of Palenque. According to one report, he had an interview with General Bruno while traveling toward Palenque.[33] What they discussed is not certain, but Perry decided to forego his visit to the ruins, returned to Carmen, and left on March 24. Possibly he gave up the archaeological excursion because he learned that it would take a difficult trek through the jungles actually to reach the ruins,[34] but maybe another factor in his decision to return was that he found out in his interview with Bruno that the

---

[31] Bauer, *Surfboats,* 52, 256; and Morison, *Perry,* 197. *See* also Commander Abraham Bigelow to Commodore Matthew Perry, Mar. 25, 1848, "Letters from Officers Commanding Squadrons, 1841-1866," Home Squadron, Jan.-May, 1848, M89, reel 88, item 60, RG 45, NARS. Hereafter cited as "Squadron Letters." This letter is also printed in *Sen. Ex. Docs.,* 30th Cong., 1st sess., No. 43, 26-27.

[32] There is a good deal of information about Miguel Bruno, although not directly relating to his threat to Palizada, in Ghigliazza, *Invasión Norteamericana.*

[33] New Orleans *Bee,* Apr. 6, 1848; and Charleston *Mercury,* Apr. 12, 1848. *See* also New Orleans *Daily Picayune,* Apr. 4, 1848; and Charleston *Mercury,* Apr. 10, 1848.

[34] Morison, *Perry,* 247.

Mexican general had no intention of ending hostilities yet. Or at least he had no intentions of sparing the collaborating populace of western Yucatán whatever measure of vengeance he could wreak upon them.

Perry wanted at least to provide some protection for the people of Carmen, and they were constantly portraying for him the horrors to which they would be subjected by the Indians and/or Mexicans if the Americans left. They even wanted U.S. ships and marines to remain after a peace treaty between the U.S. and Mexico was agreed to.[35] As Perry admitted, the protection he could give extended no farther than the range of the guns on a few ships,[36] but the desperate Yucatecos wanted it if that was all that could be had. General Bruno certainly understood Perry's situation, for no sooner had Perry left Laguna on March 24 than Bruno led a plundering raid on Palizada.[37] He chose the time for his raid carefully, not only to coincide with Perry's departure, but also just after Commander Bigelow had ordered the schooner *Morris* back to Laguna from Palizada in order to shore up his defenses there.[38] Bigelow responded by sending "a small armed sloop," probably the *Morris*, back to Palizada, at which time Bruno and his men retreated.[39] Commodore Perry notified Secretary of the Navy John Y. Mason about the raid and sent him a newspaper account of it, commenting that: "As the misfortunes of the people of Yucatán increase, the military authorities of the adjoining Mexican state — Tabasco —

[35] New Orleans *Daily Picayune*, Apr. 4, 1848; and Charleston *Mercury*, Apr. 10, 1848.

[36] Perry to Sec. of the Navy John Y. Mason, Mar. 13, 1848, *Sen. Ex. Docs.*, 30th Cong., 1st sess., No. 43, 7-9.

[37] Mexico City *Daily American Star*, Apr. 11, 1848; New Orleans *Daily Picayune*, Apr. 14, 1848; Norfolk *Daily Southern Argus*, May 15, 1848.

[38] Bigelow to Perry, Mar. 25, 1848, "Squadron Letters," M89, reel 88, item 60, RG 45, NARS.

[39] Perry to Mason, Apr. 15, 1848, "Squadron Letters," M89, reel 88, item 70, RG 45, NARS.

seem to be disposed to take advantage of their troubles, and to enter the frontier of the district of Carmen for purposes of plunder."[40] Perry dispatched sixty marines to Bigelow[41] and sent the steamer *Scorpion* back to Laguna.

Commander Bigelow decided to make another show of force against Bruno in April by sending the schooner *Morris* back upriver with a small force to occupy Palizada for a while. The *Scorpion* provided a crew for the *Morris*, with Midshipman James F. Milligan assigned as second in command to Passed Midshipman William H. Reily. Milligan proceeded to keep his journal on each day of the expedition to Palizada, and it is the only record of this operation which exists.

After transferring men and supplies from the *Scorpion* to the *Morris* on the morning of April 18, the crew of the *Morris* sailed to the Palizada River mouth that afternoon, guided by a few local inhabitants. They navigated upriver until 9 P.M. that evening and then continued on the next day. Again they labored all day and anchored in the middle of the river that night. Finally, the *Morris* arrived at Palizada at 10 A.M. on April 20.

Following the arrival of thirty marines under Lieutenant Edmund Jenkins,[42] the marines and sailors spent the afternoon of April 21 landing supplies, small arms, and a field piece, and establishing themselves in a barracks. Next the officers and some of the men displayed a show of good public relations by joining the local villagers in a religious procession to commemorate the burial of Christ.

As in all military operations, life in this one soon

[40] Perry to Mason, Apr. 8, 1848, *ibid*, item 64.

[41] *Ibid*. The newspaper account which Perry sent was almost certainly the Apr. 6 issue of the Vera Cruz *Free American*. It is referred to in the New Orleans *Daily Picayune*, Apr. 14, 1848. Copies of that issue of the Vera Cruz paper apparently no longer exist. *See* Bodson, "A Description of the United States Occupation of Mexico...," 11.

[42] Jenkins' men had left the *Scorpion* the day before. Ship's log, U.S.S. *Scorpion*, RG 24, NARS.

established a rather regular pattern. The officers kept the men busy with various chores, such as painting a gun carriage, procuring supplies of wood, and constructing a platform for troops to sleep on. Also, the troops practiced with small arms and the field piece nearly every day, in order to be prepared for any attack.

The main difficulties on this operation appear to have been sickness and occasional lack of discipline among the troops. During the 22 days Milligan spent at Palizada, the numbers of men reported sick gradually climbed to an average of five or six a day, roughly 10% of the total U.S. force. Milligan records that the sick were given extra rations of sugar to bolster their strength. Maintenance of discipline among the troops amidst the usually boring routine of the operation was another problem. Midshipman Milligan's journal mentions fourteen occasions when sailors or marines were flogged at Palizada, nearly all of them for drunkenness. A local Negro who attempted to smuggle liquor into the barracks was also flogged. On two separate occasions, a search for a thief and stolen money was conducted, and one thief, a corporal, deserted.

On one occasion, at least, the troops got excited about General Bruno, the Mexican leader from whom they were to protect Palizada. On the night of May 3-4, information arrived indicating that Bruno was planning to descend upon Palizada and its American defenders with "200 men assisted by 150 rebellious citizens." Milligan continued in his May 4, 1848, journal entry to state that the Americans "made every preparation to give him a cool reception." They loaded the *Morris'* artillery piece and the marines' field piece with grape and canister, and at 1 A.M. on May 4, the marines practiced skirmishing tactics through the town. Whether the threat of the attack by Bruno was real or simply a rumor, it never came, and the troops returned to their various routine duties.

As with other parts of Midshipman Milligan's journal, it is difficult to tell exactly what role he himself played in the operation. It is certain, however, that, since there were so few officers present, Milligan's responsibilities must have been considerably greater than at any earlier time in his naval career. It is obvious that his journal served as the ship's log of the *Morris* during that Palizada expedition since the commanding officer, Passed Midshipman Reily, regularly examined the journal and signed it.

Milligan's duties at Palizada lasted until May 12 when orders arrived for Jenkins and Milligan to return to Laguna. At 5 P.M., the two officers, fourteen marines and all the sick boarded a bungo and proceeded downriver. They arrived at Laguna at 6 A.M. on May 15, and Midshipman Milligan again reported for duty on the *Scorpion.*

The *Scorpion* soon steamed back to Vera Cruz, and Commodore Perry signaled the news on May 28 that the Treaty of Guadalupe Hidalgo had been ratified, as Milligan recorded in his journal. Midshipman Milligan had become ill by that time and was recuperating in the military hospital at Salmedina Island. Meanwhile, the *Scorpion* returned to Laguna, to which Passed Midshipman Reily finally brought the *Morris* back from duty at Palizada on June 5. The die-hard General Bruno had apparently quit causing trouble for Palizada but had been refusing to give up his command in Tabasco to the appointee of the newly installed government in Mexico City.[43] Just to be sure that things remained tranquil, Perry kept a garrison of marines and some armed schooners at Carmen under Bigelow's command until the final evacuation of that place on July 30.[44] Yucatán returned to the Mexican fold, and later that year the Indians were defeated by the Mexicans.

[43] Mexico City *Daily American Star,* May 4 and 16, 1848.

[44] Morison, *Perry,* 250.

James Milligan reported back for duty from the hospital to the *Scorpion* on June 9 and a few days later was transferred to the frigate U.S.S. *Cumberland,* Perry's flagship at the time, for the final voyage home. On June 15, just after Milligan reported to the *Cumberland,* she sailed north from Mexico. The voyage, by way of Pensacola and Havana, was uneventful except for the epidemic of sickness on board. This epidemic, mostly malaria, had broken out before the homeward voyage. Milligan was probably still sick at the time, probably suffering from malaria. Anyway, the ship arrived at New York on July 22. On July 28, Milligan requested a leave of absence for as long as proper, and on August 11 he received notice that his leave would be granted as soon as other midshipmen could be ordered to the *Cumberland.* Midshipman Milligan remained on duty at the Brooklyn Navy Yard until his orders for two-months' leave, dated September 30, arrived.[45] Secretary Mason also notified Edward Milligan, who had been requesting leave for his son, that the leave had been granted.[46] Midshipman Milligan finally headed for home. The last entry in his Mexican War journal was dated October 3.

Milligan spent his leave in St. Louis. He wrote from there to Secretary Mason on December 6 stating that he had been studying mathematics under a Professor Stewart while on leave and requesting that he be permitted to continue these studies until wanted for active service.[47] After spending Christmas with his family, Milligan notified the Navy Department on January 8, 1849, that his leave

[45] Milligan to Mason, July 28, 1848, "Letters from Officers of Rank Below That of Commander, 1802-1884," M148, reel 185, July letters, item 266, RG 45, NARS (hereafter cited as "Officers' Letters"); and Mason to Milligan, Sept. 30, 1848, "Letters to Officers, 1798-1886," M149, reel 44, vol. 42, p. 118, RG 45, NARS.

[46] Mason to E. Milligan, Sept. 30, 1848, "Miscellaneous Letters Sent, 1798-1886," M209, reel 15, p. 405, RG 45, NARS (hereafter cited as "Misc. Letters Sent").

[47] Milligan to Mason, Dec. 6, 1848, "Officers' Letters," M148, reel 187, Dec. letters, item 47, RG 45, NARS.

had expired, that he was reporting for duty, and that he was requesting assignment to either the Mediterranean or Pacific Squadrons.[48] On January 20, the Navy ordered Midshipman Milligan to report for sea duty at Norfolk, and he acknowledged receipt of the orders.[49] He reported to Commodore Sloat on February 22 and remained attached to U.S. Receiving Ship *Pennsylvania* at Gosport, Virgina, until ordered to the second-class sloop of war *John Adams,* a somewhat smaller warship than the *Albany,* on May 24, 1849.[50] This assignment began one of the most disappointing and frustrating episodes of James Milligan's life, for the *John Adams,* rather than being part of one of the more glamorous squadrons, was a component of the Africa Squadron; and the Africa Squadron was considered to be one of the worst duty stations in the naval service.

The Africa Squadron's purpose was to cruise the West African Coast, intercept slave ships attempting to smuggle slaves to the Americas, and otherwise maintain peace along the coast. While the British squadrons were larger and more aggressive in disrupting the overall trade, the small American squadron of fewer than ten ships based at Porto Praya in the Cape Verde Islands had the responsibility for policing vessels flying the American flag. The United States was traditionally wary of British naval personnel boarding ships flying the U.S. flag, and so the Africa Squadron had been provided by the American government under provisions of the Webster-Ashburton Treaty of 1842.[51]

[48] Milligan to Mason, Jan. 8, 1849, "Officers' Letters," M148, reel 188, Jan. letters, item 46, RG 45, NARS.

[49] Mason to Milligan, Jan. 20, 1849, "Letters Sent Relating to Officers' Appointments, Orders, and Resignations, 1842-1895," vol. 24, p. 31, RG 24, NARS (hereafter cited as "Letters — Orders"); and Milligan to Mason, Feb. 6, 1849, "Officers' Letters," M148, reel 188, Feb. letters, item 44, RG 45, NARS.

[50] Milligan to Sec. of the Navy William B. Preston, May 8, 1849, "Officers' Letters," M148, reel 189, May letters, item 76, RG 45, NARS; and Preston to Milligan, May 24, 1849, "Letters — Orders," vol. 24, p. 137, RG 24, NARS.

[51] A good work on the actual workings of the squadron is Foote's *Africa and the American Flag.*

A combination of factors made the Africa Squadron a miserable place to serve. The task itself was frustrating. For one thing, the American squadron was supposed to maintain friendly relations with the coastal tribes, paradoxically the very tribes who lived on the slave trade which the Navy was trying to supress.[52] Then there was the catand-mouse game to play with the slave ships. Slave ships would slip into ports on the coast bearing one flag and crew, and then come out loaded with slaves and sporting a different flag and crew.[53] Sometimes slavers sent decoy ships out of port first, and then the loaded slave ship would sneak out after the squadron had gone in pursuit of the decoy.[54] All these tactics were designed to confuse whatever cruisers were around. But the squadron developed some tricks of its own, such as chasing a ship without showing the flag on the cruiser in order to confuse the slaver. However, not many slavers were caught, certainly not enough to dissuade those enamored of the high profits of the trade from engaging in it. Even though slaving was declared to be piracy, few slavers suffered severe penalties. And even though a few cargoes might be lost, the ship owners would then collect insurance to cover the losses.[55] Thus it is not surprising that many who served in the Africa Squadron considered their efforts to be largely wasted.

But much worse in their effect upon the officers and men of the squadron were the climate, diseases, and lack of communication with home on this duty station. Officers spoke of the Africa station as one of almost unrelieved misery. One commander had written in 1843: "Scorching sun and drenching rains with numerous privations &

[52] Sands, *From Reefer to Rear Admiral,* 206.

[53] Foote, *Africa,* 261-62.

[54] Griffis, *Perry,* 195.

[55] *Ibid.,* 194-95.

disagreeable circumstances is one's common lot, to say nothing of a good chance of dying."[56] Another officer felt that "one year of that climate is equivalent to half a dozen of a more temperate one, in its effect upon the constitution."[57] Unlike other duty stations, this one had few opportunities for relaxation and pleasure, or interesting ports of call.[58] Constant efforts to maintain the health of the squadron were necessary. Smudge pots were regularly burned below decks to dry out the interior and to drive out vermin and insects; the ships were regularly cleaned in the "scrub and broom" drill, and the men were brought up on deck, washed down, dried off, and then clothed with absorbent flannel next to the person.[59] Even with these constant precautions, some men of the squadron died of yellow fever and other diseases, and the health of many others was broken on the Africa Squadron, despite certain attempts in government documents to show that mortality in that squadron was not higher than in other squadrons.[60] Given the difficulties and hardship of this particular tour of duty, it is not surprising that drinking was a monumental problem on these ships. As one veteran of the Africa Squadron put it, "These trying cruises break down so many officers, John Barleycorn and brandy generally ruling supreme, — being resorted to at the beginning as a preventative for the dreaded fevers on the coast, and gradually becoming a fascination."[61]

It is not evident exactly what difficulties Midshipman

[56] Quoted in Morison, *Perry,* 164.

[57] Bridge, *African Cruiser,* 166-67. An officer in the squadron in a June 1850 letter equated a year of service there to five years anywhere else. *See* Wash., (D.C.) *National Intelligencer,* July 12, 1850.

[58] Jones, *Commodore Josiah Tattnall,* 53.

[59] Griffis, *Perry,* 187; and Bridge, *African Cruiser,* 12.

[60] Norfolk *American Beacon and Norfolk and Portsmouth Daily Advertiser,* Mar. 26, 1850. Hereafter cited as Norfolk *American Beacon. See* also Wash., (D.C.) *National Intelligencer,* July 12, 1850.

[61] Sands, *Reefer,* 206.

Milligan encountered on the *John Adams.* He may have been fearful of disease and perhaps was still suffering from his earlier fever, if it was malaria. Possibly he succumbed to alcohol, as others did to relieve their woes. In any case, Milligan clearly disliked the Africa Squadron. On October 20, 1849, he wrote from Rio de Janeiro to Secretary William G. Preston asking for a transfer to the Pacific Squadron as a "great favour."[62] Preston apparently paid no attention to Milligan's request. What happened next is a matter of conjecture, but Milligan was not the type to keep his dissatisfaction with the squadron a secret. He may have complained too much, and possibly have drunk too much. Whatever it was, his frustration ultimately led to a confrontation with a fellow officer, Acting Lieutenant James A. Higgins. They probably argued and possibly got into a fight, but there is no specific record of what the nature of the confrontation was. Milligan may simply have refused to obey a particular order. Acting Lieutenant Higgins decided to press charges against Midshipman Milligan. It appears that Milligan was given the choice between facing the charges or resigning without a court-martial.[63] And Midshipman Milligan chose to resign.

Milligan submitted his resignation at Porto Praya on February 5, 1850. The letter simply stated: "Herewith I enclose my warrant as Midshipman, being no longer fit for the service as an officer. I respectfully beg leave to resign." The squadron commander, Commodore Francis H. Gregory, forwarded the resignation to the Navy department with his own recommendation that the Navy consider Milligan unfit for further service, "having frequently and

---

[62] Milligan to Preston, Oct. 20, 1849, "Officers' Letters," M148, reel 192, Oct. letters, item 181, RG 45, NARS.

[63] Edward Milligan later referred to his son's resignation as having been "in a great degree coerced." E. Milligan to Isaac H. Sturgeon, Mar. 14, 1853, "Applications for Positions in the Revenue Cutter Service, 1844-1880," RG 26-Records of the United States Coast Guard, NARS. Hereafter cited as "Applications — R.C.S."

irretrievably committed himself." Gregory's comment indicates that Milligan had made his disenchantment with the squadron well-known to his superiors. Milligan's immediate superior, Commander Levin M. Powell of the *John Adams,* added his recommendation that the resignation be accepted. Upon receiving these communications, Secretary Preston accepted the resignation on April 4, 1850.[64]

On February 5, the day he resigned, ex-Midshipman Milligan transferred from the *John Adams* to the squadron flagship *Portsmouth* at Porto Praya. The *Portmouth's* log says he came aboard as a "supernumerary." Milligan remained there until the brig U.S.S. *Porpoise,* on its way back to Norfolk, anchored nearby on February 20. Milligan then transferred to the *Porpoise* for his passage home. Commodore Gregory transmitted Milligan's resignation on that vessel also. The log of the *Porpoise* does not mention Milligan's coming aboard, but he was on the ship when it sailed from Porto Praya on February 28. The *Porpoise* conducted the schooner *Taney* to St. Thomas in the West Indies for repairs and then continued on to Norfolk, arriving on April 2. Norfolk newspapers listed Milligan as a passenger on the *Porpoise.*[65]

Milligan had had time to think over his action during the long voyage, and by the time he reached Norfolk he regretted having chosen to resign. As soon as the *Porpoise* arrived at Norfolk, he rushed a letter off to Secretary Preston requesting that he be reinstated.[66] However, Secre-

[64] Milligan to Preston, Feb. 5, 1850, "Letters of Resignation from Officers, 1803-1877," Resignations of Officers of the U.S. Navy, 1841-50, no. 320, RG 45, NARS.

[65] Ships logs, U.S.S. *John Adams,* U.S.S. *Portsmouth,* U.S.S. *Porpoise,* RG 24, NARS; Commodore Francis H. Gregory to Preston, Feb. 26, 1850, "Squadron Letters," Africa Squadron, M89, reel 105, item 54, RG 45, NARS; Norfolk *American Beacon,* Apr. 4, 1850; and Norfolk *Southern Argus,* Apr. 4, 1850.

[66] Milligan to Preston, Apr. 2, 1850, "Index to Letters Received, 1823-1866," Letters, July 19, 1849-Apr. 20, 1850, no. 722, RG 45, NARS.

tary Preston refused to reinstate Milligan "under the circumstances of . . . (his) resignation."[67] Upon learning of his son's resignation, Edward Milligan wrote to Preston also, asking for permission for James to withdraw the resignation, but Preston again refused.[68] The Milligans suspected that Preston, being a Whig, refused to reinstate Democrat James Milligan on purely political grounds so that the Whig administration of President Taylor could fill his position with one of their own.[69] Whatever the reasons for Preston's obstinacy, James Milligan's career in the U.S. Navy was over.

[67] Preston to Milligan, Apr. 4, 1850, "Misc. Letters Sent," M209, reel 16, p. 221, RG 45, NARS.

[68] E. Milligan to Preston, Apr. 11, 1850, "Misc. Letters Received, 1801-1884," M124, reel 252, item 79, RG 45, NARS; and Preston to E. Milligan, Apr. 20, 1850, "Misc. Letters Sent," M209, reel 16, p. 264, RG 45, NARS.

[69] E. Milligan to Sturgeon, Mar. 14, 1853, "Applications — R.C.S.," RG 26, NARS.

3

Interim: Milligan on the Salt Lake City and in St. Louis, 1850-1853

Records of James Milligan's activities from 1850 to 1853 are for the most part rather sparse. From Norfolk he returned to St. Louis, and no information about him has been uncovered for the April-September 1850 period. At some time during those months, however, Milligan was hired to run the mail to the Mormon settlement of Salt Lake City.

It was in 1850 that the U.S. Post Office Department first contracted to provide mail service to Salt Lake. James Brown and Samuel Woodson formed Brown, Woodson & Company, and got the contract to transport mail each month from Independence to Salt Lake City and back again. Service commenced on August 1, 1850, when Thomas D. Scroggins led a small party with mule-drawn wagons out of Independence. The route followed the Oregon Trail via the Platte River and through South Pass. The trip usually took more than the officially-allotted thirty days, especially in late fall and winter. And there were no mail stations along the route at first to provide rest and shelter for weary mail carriers.[1]

James Milligan became a participant in this pioneering mail venture. The contractors were possibly acquainted

[1] Hafen, *The Overland Mail,* 57; and Barry, *The Beginning of the West,* 956-57.

with Edward Milligan of the post office in St. Louis, and this may have been the means through which James Milligan got his job of guiding the second regular mail run in September. On September 1, 1850, Milligan's party started from Independence. They passed the Scroggins mail party returning from Salt Lake City on September 28, some 65 miles beyond Ft. Laramie, and finally arrived in Salt Lake City themselves on October 15. The news they brought delighted the Mormons. The *Deseret News* reported that, based on an August 11 issue of the New York *Herald,* Congress had just passed the act to organize the Utah territory. Actually, only the U.S. Senate had passed the Utah bill at that stage, but the bill was fully enacted in early September.[2]

For eight days James Milligan and his three men remained at Salt Lake City before heading back to Independence. When Milligan's party left Salt Lake with the mail for the East on October 22, they did so in company with eleven other men. This latter group included three merchants from St. Joseph, who had found trading with the Mormons profitable and who were carrying back \$75,000-\$80,000 in gold and government drafts. The merchants, representing Middleton & Riley in St. Joseph, were Oscar Middleton; W.E. Horner, a Mormon himself; and Capt. Jeff Thompson, later a Confederate leader in Missouri. Joining them were two Salt Lake merchants headed for Council Bluffs, James M. Livingstone and Charles A. Kincaid; a citizen from Independence, Cogswell or Cogsdale; a Dr. Barnes of St. Louis; and four others — Homer, Waldon, Sledge, and Selman.[3]

---

[2] Barry, *Beginning of the West,* 972; Salt Lake City *Deseret News,* Oct. 19, 1850; and "Early Utah Records" (MS, Bancroft Lib., Univ. of Calif. at Berkeley), 115.

[3] St. Joseph *Adventure,* Dec. 20, 1850; and St. Joseph *Gazette,* Dec. 25, 1850. On Livingstone and Kincaid, *see* Walker, *The Wagonmasters,* 158-66; and Lass, *From the Missouri to the Great Salt Lake,* 6, 51-52, 54, 71-73, 77.

By the time the party began this return trip, the weather had taken a turn for the worse. Snow began falling nearly as soon as the journey commenced but really became heavy just after the group had struggled through South Pass. For three straight days and nights it snowed as the men passed such ominously named landmarks as Hell's Gate, Devil's Gate, and Devil's Backbone. Even after they had reached the open prairies beyond the mountains, deep snow on the ground hindered their progress for several days. A period of fine weather then followed, during which the merchants and others pushed ahead of Milligan's U.S. mail party, separating from them at Scott's Bluff in present-day far-western Nebraska. Since dangerous weather no longer threatened, it seemed unnecessary to remain together. The merchants traveled to within 25 miles of Ft. Kearny without incident, but there the good weather ended. A ferocious snowstorm suddenly descended on them and, even though they were able to reach Ft. Kearny safely, seven of their mules were frozen to death. Before the merchants left Ft. Kearny, Milligan and his men had also reached the fort. The usual route to Independence along the Blue River being impassable because of heavy snow, Milligan's group was forced to travel eastward to St. Joseph along the Ft. Kearny road before heading down to Independence, at which place the mail party arrived on December 26.[4]

After the grueling experiences of the return trip from Salt Lake City, James Milligan apparently lost interest in this sort of endeavor.[5] The next mention of his name is in a city directory for St. Louis in 1852, showing him employed as a steamboat clerk. His father's residence and his are

[4] Salt Lake City *Deseret News*, Nov. 2, 1850; Kanesville, IA, *Frontier Guardian*, Dec. 25, 1850; and Barry, *Beginning of the West*, 976.

[5] Barry noted all the mail trips in 1850-1851 and Milligan is mentioned only in connection with the one journey. Barry, *Beginning of the West*, 976.

listed as being on the north side of Myrtle Street and James probably was residing with his father, who is described as a land agent in the directory.[6]

Apparently James Milligan seriously considered acquiring some land and becoming a farmer. Land warrants were made available by Congress to Mexican War veterans, and Milligan first applied for one of these in spring, 1852. His application was rejected, possibly due to the circumstances of Milligan's resignation from the Navy. Since the commissioner of pensions in 1852 was a Whig, politics may have had a role in it. Milligan would apply again in July 1853, when the Democrats were back in power, but he did not actually receive a warrant for 160 acres in Wisconsin until May 1856. By that time, he had lost interest in the bounty land and immediately sold it.[7]

Milligan began keeping a journal again sometime between 1851 and 1853, a journal that he would continue to keep right through the Frémont expedition of 1853-1854. What possessed him to resume journal writing, in which he had gotten considerable practice as a midshipman, is unclear. Certainly nothing very momentous seems to have been happening to Milligan in St. Louis to have inspired him to take pen in hand almost daily.

The journal begins in April 1853, with James Milligan

[6] *Morrison's St. Louis Directory for 1852,* 176. Edward Milligan, James' father, is listed in most directories from 1840 to 1850 and in 1854 as a post office clerk. In the 1852 directory and from 1857 to 1869 he is listed as a real estate agent. After the death of his first wife, he married Maria Murray in St. Louis on Aug. 29, 1847; Edward was 42, and she was 15 at that time using their ages as given in the census of 1850. Marriage Record 05-431, City Hall, St. Louis. In that census of 1850, which Edward helped to take, his occupation is listed as printer. "7th U.S. Census, 1850," M432, reel 416, p. 283, RG 29, NARS. Edward Milligan died on Nov. 26, 1869 of pneumonia at age 63, survived by his widow Maria. St. Louis *Missouri Democrat,* Nov. 27, 1869; and Death Certificate —Edward Milligan, Bureau of Vital Statistics, St. Louis.

[7] Milligan to U.S. Commissioner of Pensions, Sept. 1, 1853, in possession of Robert F. Milligan; and "Military Bounty Land Warrants and Related Papers — Warrants Issued Under Act of March 3, 1855," certificate no. 27821, vol. 159, p. 107, RG 49, NARS.

employed in St. Louis as a deputy for the U.S. Marshal, Hiram Baber. Exactly how and when Milligan got this position is unclear. Since Baber was a Whig and had been appointed by President Fillmore to the vacancy in September, 1852, it is likely that Milligan began work in the Marshal's office before that date.[8] Among Milligan's duties as related in the journal were collecting court judgments, serving various documents on people, getting juries empanelled, assisting Marshal Baber with arrests, and whipping Negroes for various offenses by order of the court. Apparently he found the work rather boring, according to journal entries on April 26 and May 9, 1853. The only prisoner whom Milligan relates any personal interest in was a girl he visited in jail, one Ginny Burke. As he writes on May 26, "Had a long talk with her about her future course. She promises well but I have my doubts." The only notable event with which Milligan had any official connection as a law officer was the execution of two notorious murderers, Dodge and Schoen, in July 1853.

In July 1852, Joseph Dodge and John Schoen, along with two other deserters from an army post, had fallen in with a young Delaware Indian trader and his sister near Ft. Mackay in the yet unorganized territory west of Missouri. The Indians had thirteen mules, many skins, and plenty of supplies. After traveling together for several days, the party encamped one morning. Suddenly, Schoen started beating the young Indian with a gunstock while Dodge struck the Delaware's sister with a frying pan. After the man had died, Schoen got a razor and slashed the woman's thoat. The whites then took the Indians' property and traveled to Independence to sell it and divide the proceeds. But they made a mistake. The woman, although severely injured, was not dead. She recovered her strength enough to travel on foot for several days. A party of Caw Indians

[8] Hiram H. Baber, "Sketch of His Life, 1795-1873" (MS, MO. Hist. Soc., St. Louis).

gave her a mule and provisions, and the woman's report to authorities in Missouri led to the apprehension, trial, and conviction of Dodge and Schoen.[9]

Originally scheduled to be executed on June 1, 1853, Dodge and Schoen received a respite from President Pierce, which arrived by telegraph the day before the execution. The respite was to postpone the execution until July 22. This was undoubtedly disappointing to some in St. Louis, such as the German whom Milligan recorded having hounded the Marshal on May 30 for seats at the execution for him and his family. No circumstances arose before July 22 which would provide grounds for a pardon. Dodge and Schoen exhibited no particular anguish when their death warrants were read to them on July 18. The two convicts received many calls from their friends during the final days and also the religious consolation provided by two Catholic priests. On the day of execution Marshal Baber led Dodge and Schoen, attended by the priests, to the gallows, which had been set up away from the public view of the large crowd gathered in the vicinity. James Milligan went down to witness the execution. Both Dodge and Schoen made final statements on the scaffold, acknowledging the justice of their execution and thanking their friends for their kindness in previous days. Then the nooses were fixed about their necks and their heads covered. A spring loosed the platform on which they sat, and the two men fell about four feet to their deaths. Milligan states that they "appeared to be perfectly resigned to their fate. Dodge died with a smile on his countenance and apparently happy." Thus were two infamous murderers of the early Kansas frontier "launched into eternity," as a St. Louis reporter put it.[10]

---

[9] St. Louis *Missouri Republican,* Aug. 18, 1852.

[10] *Ibid.,* July 19, 21, and 23, 1853; and St. Louis *Missouri Democrat,* June 1, July 19 and 23, 1853.

If Milligan's official duties usually bored him, his activities apart from work added some variety and excitement to his life. He was a member of the Missouri Fire Company, one of several volunteer fire fighting units in St. Louis. Known as the "Earthquake Rangers," this group not only fought fires but also brawled occasionally with other fire companies. Milligan cites one fight on May 20, 1853, between his rowdies and another fire company in which one member of the opposing side was killed. When Milligan, with his chivalrous spirit, was the only man of his company to attend the funeral the next day, he "raised hell because... (his group's) members would not turn out," as stated in his journal. Milligan wrote several songs to inspire his group, a copy of one of them being preserved in his journal. This song, which is included here, fairly well captures the spirit of the fire fighters of that day. He printed it under the nickname "Bricks, the Reefer," reefer being a slang term for a midshipman.

"The Old No. 5"
(Air — I'm Afloat)
Dedicated to the Missouri Fire Company,
By "Bricks, The Reefer."

Come fill up your glasses, fill, fill to the brim,
United we'll be, as we always have been;
To-night we'll be merry and happy withal,
Good cheer be the sentiment, and honor our call;
We will christen our House with a hearty good cheer,
And ne'er be found wanting when danger is near.

"Press on," is our motto, to conquer our aim,
Our actions give lustre to herald our fame,
Which by deed we have gained from friends fast and true,
Who have ever our interest and welfare in view;
So at the tap of the bell, let us all strive,
To be second to none with the Old No. Five!

Quick! quick! man your brakes and work with a will —
Not by vain "blowing," but "steady and still,"
Strive to save, not destroy, for the public good,
And stand by your friends as firemen should;
When duty will call, "turn out" with a desire
To excel in your actions, and vanquish the fire.

Obey with a will when orders are passed,
And be at your stations and work to the last.
So here's to our friends, God bless them forever,
Their kindness to us old time ne'r can sever.
May grateful remembrance in our hearts live
For the patrons and friends of the Old No. 5.

The ladies, sweet creatures, though last not the least,
Our aim is to please them at party or feast;
And may their bright smiles our actions approve,
Which shall always be worthy of those that we love;
Their love we will cherish with feelings as warm
As that of our motto, which is to "Press On."

James Milligan added to his income by working off and on at the Varieties Theatre on Market Street. The Varieties, established by Joseph M. Field, a pioneer theatre manager in the South who had earlier managed theatrical productions in Mobile, had opened May 10, 1852. The first season of the Varieties had ended with a loss, and Field was destined to leave the Varieties to return to Mobile late in 1853. Milligan appears to have worked as a carpenter and general stagehand at this theatre. He also attended the offerings there and at other theatres in St. Louis quite often.[11]

Milligan found some time for his family too. His thirteen-year-old sister, Mary, was a boarder at the Convent of St. Joseph in Carondelet,[12] and James records

[11] On Joseph M. Field and the Varieties Theatre, *see* Coad, "Joseph M. Field"; Ludlow, *Dramatic Life as I Found It,* 716-17, 729. For an account of St. Louis' early theatres in general, *see* Carson, *The Theatre on the Frontier.*

[12] "7th U.S. Census, 1850," M432, reel 414, p. 284, RG 29, NARS.

two visits to her, on May 22 and July 16, 1853. Her residence at a Catholic convent indicates the probability that her family was at least nominally Catholic. But Edward Milligan's second marriage was not in the church, and James Milligan, neither by statements nor behavior, appears to have taken much interest in any particular religion at this stage in his life. James' younger brother Frank arrived from Philadelphia in May 1853, to set up medical practice in St. Louis. He had graduated from Jefferson Medical College in Philadelphia in 1851. James did not like Frank's tendency to write preachy letters to him, as he states in a journal entry of May 11, 1853: "Rec'd one of Frank's damned foolish letters on attempted moralizing." Despite this, James helped Frank hunt for an office after he arrived on May 23.[13]

Judging from Milligan's journal entries in 1853, some preaching may have been in order. His social life was rather hedonistic. Besides brawling with his friends in the fire company, he reports on one occasion: "choked the saucy clerk of the Law Commissioners Court for putting on 'airs'." Young Milligan was very touchy about anyone who thought he was better than him, and he was always ready to prove himself and get his way by fisticuffs if necessary. His young friends apparently shared this view. Milligan records that on one fishing trip, his friend "Monkey" threw a Frenchman in the lake for supposedly scaring the fish away. Milligan and his fellow hooligans spent much time drinking, gambling, playing billiards, fishing, and chasing loose women of the lower classes.

James Milligan wrote in his journal quite frankly about the dalliances which he and his friends enjoyed with young

[13] A record of Dr. Francis H. Milligan's graduation in 1851 is in the archives at Jefferson Medical College, Philadelphia. He became a member of the medical soc. in St. Louis in Aug. 1853. Typescript record of early membership, St. Louis Soc. for Medical and Scientific Education.

women in St. Louis in 1853. None of these activities seems to have concerned Milligan as a moral issue, but appears to have been just another form of recreation. On one excursion with three friends in April, Milligan's companion Buck "hung a damsel & took her to a retired part of the forest and sounded her bowels." Three days later Milligan himself tried to seduce the "over the river gal" but "she wouldn't take." However, there were some women whom Milligan just would not sleep with, as he relates on May 29: "Stayed all night at Carly's. Buck slept with her and I with Ellen. All safe. I thought too much of myself to have connection with her." Sometimes, though, he did not resist for too long the feminine advances of the girls he did not like. After returning from a visit to the old and now deserted Oak Ridge homestead in July, he "could not talk Ginger-head out of a little horizontal refreshment. She won't do." On July 15 and 17 Milligan made attempts to seduce some "Pot Stewers" at some restaurants. In the incident of the 15th, he struck up a conversation with a "Pot Stewer" who asked him "to treat." As he puts it, "I had an idea she wanted something else but was unable to succeed in my design notwithstanding the temptation of a $5 bill." Apparently, Milligan's sexual adventures were just another facet of his attempts to escape the boring routine of most of his deputy work.

He was planning a more permanent escape from boredom during these months, however. Milligan had loved life on the sea and was anxious to return to it. And if he could not re-enter the U.S. Navy, there might be a chance, with the help of his father's political friends, to land a commission in the U.S. Revenue Marine Service. Also known as the Revenue Cutter Service, this forerunner of the U.S. Coast Guard functioned under the auspices of the Secretary of the Treasury. After the election of Democrat

Franklin Pierce to the White House in 1852, the Treasury post was held by James Guthrie, who would be inclined as a matter of partisanship to assist Democrats seeking government jobs or commissions.

Even before the Whigs left office on March 4, 1853, the political wheels were turning to get Milligan a commission. After one Missourian turned down a commission in the revenue service, Congressmen John S. Phelps and Thomas Hart Benton of Missouri, the state's most famous personality of that time, offered Milligan's name as a replacement in January 1853.[14] But the Whig Secretary of the Treasury, Thomas Corwin, would not make the appointment. The next effort came in March, as soon as the Pierce administration took office. James Milligan renewed his application to Secretary James Guthrie on March 8, citing his naval record in the war and promising faithful service. Other letters followed in support. On March 14, B. Gratz Brown, a leading Missouri Democrat, wrote to Guthrie, praising Milligan's abilities. Another St. Louis Democrat, Isaac H. Sturgeon, wrote a similar letter to Guthrie on the 15th after Edward Milligan had informed him about the circumstances of his son's earlier resignation from the Navy and inability to get reinstated due to the presence of the Whig administration in Washington in 1850.[15]

Milligan's journal during this year mentions nothing about the application. His journal entries run from April 14 to July 25, 1853, and then do not pick up again until his departure on the Frémont expedition on September 6. It is not clear why action on his application, with such powerful political support behind it, was not acted on more quickly by Secretary Guthrie.

---

[14] Thomas Hart Benton and John S. Phelps to Sec. of the Treas. Thomas Corwin, Jan. 14, 1853, "Applications — R.C.S.," RG 26, NARS.

[15] Milligan to Sec. of the Treas. James Guthrie, Mar. 8, 1853; B. Gratz Brown to Guthrie, Mar. 14, 1853; E. Milligan to Sturgeon, Mar. 14, 1853; and Sturgeon to Guthrie, Mar. 15, 1853, "Applications — R.C.S.," RG 26, NARS.

The delay prompted Milligan to do two things in September. First, on September 4, 1853, he wrote to James S. Green, sometime member of Missouri's Congressional delegation in Washington, to bring pressure on Guthrie to act. Milligan again explained his desire to return to sea and expressed the belief that his "act of youthful indiscretion in resigning was too harshly and hastily acted upon by the then Secretary of the Navy (Wm. B. Preston)."[16]

The second thing Milligan did was to decide to accompany John C. Frémont's expedition to search for a feasible central route to the Pacific. Milligan's decision to journey with Frémont appears to have been hasty. There is no mention of it in the letter to Green on September 4. But on September 6, the very day the expedition left, Milligan sent a letter to Secretary Guthrie reminding him of his application. In the letter he states, "I have just volunteered to accompany Col. Fremont on his Noble and Patriotic Survey of a Route to the Pacific." Undoubtedly, in telling Guthrie this, Milligan hoped to impress the Secretary with his staunch loyalty to the Democratic Party by having volunteered to assist the efforts of one of the most prominent Democrats in the country. Whatever other reasons Milligan may have had for joining Frémont, his desire to enhance his chances for getting a commission in the revenue marine was apparently foremost, as he later indicated in his expedition journal entry on October 25, 1853. What is not clear is whether Edward Milligan, with his ever-present sense of politics, may have originally suggested the trip to his son. Wherever the idea originated, Milligan reassured Secretary Guthrie of his desire for a commission and for an assignment to a cutter on the Pacific Coast.[17] In a subsequent letter of October 5, Edward

[16] Milligan to James S. Green, Sept. 4, 1853, "Letters Received — Revenue Cutter Service, 1836-1910," RG 26, NARS. Hereafter cited as "Letters Received — R.C.S."

[17] Milligan to Guthrie, Sept. 6, 1853, "Letters Received — R.C.S.," RG 26, NARS.

Milligan reiterated these same sentiments to Assistant Secretary of the Treasury Peter G. Washington.[18]

Milligan's journal of Frémont's fifth expedition was to become the only day-by-day account of that venture. If Milligan had not decided to go with Frémont, no such account would exist. And if Milligan had not been anxious to impress the Democratic administration in Washington in order to get a commission on a Pacific Coast revenue cutter, he might not have gone with Frémont. But the fact is that he did go and wrote a colorful journal of the expedition as far as Bent's Fort and of his own subsequent activities as a buffalo-robe trader for William Bent.

---

[18] E. Milligan to Asst. Sec. of the Treas. Peter G. Washington, Oct. 5, 1853, "Applications — R.C.S.," RG 26, NARS.

4

James F. Milligan, John C. Frémont and the Central Route to the Pacific

It may have been because of his Irish temperament, or it may have been due to the circumstances of his upbringing, but for whatever reason, James F. Milligan had trouble dealing with authority. So when John C. Frémont attempted to confiscate journals kept by his men during his fifth expedition in the West, Milligan refused to comply; he continued to record his candid, salty observations in daily entries in a large leather-bound folio which he probably made no attempt to conceal. Frémont intended to publish his own account of the expedition, and he did not want competing — and perhaps conflicting — records being kept by his men. However, Frémont never published his account of the expedition. It is only because of Milligan's journal, written in direct defiance of Frémont's orders banning the keeping of diaries, that we have a first-hand account of Frémont's fifth expedition and life at Bent's New Fort.

Until his journal came to light, Milligan was virtually unknown to history as a member of Frémont's fifth expedition. Heretofore, the only published reference to Milligan as a member of that expedition was in Solomon Carvalho's passing observation that Frémont had left "a Mr. Mulligan from St. Louis" at Bent's Fort.[1]

Milligan's early life was punctuated with episodes of insubordination, pugnacity, and impulsiveness. Milligan

---

[1] Carvalho, *Incidents of Travel,* 72.

himself was well aware that these traits often worked to his disadvantage. In fact, he and Frémont shared several personality traits. Both sought out the support of powerful and influential men to further their careers. Both had trouble dealing with authority, and both suffered career reversals as a result. Both at times were arrogant and vain. Both had trouble admitting their mistakes, and both found compromise difficult. Milligan had much to gain by participating in such a bold enterprise. "Many of my future prospects depend upon the success of the expedition," he confided to his diary. But he found it impossible to court Frémont's favor, and when it became clear that the two men could not work together, Milligan was forced to withdraw from the expedition.[2]

"The expedition" to which Milligan referred was the last of John C. Frémont's five expeditions in the West. Frémont's fifth expedition, like his fourth, was undertaken to demonstrate the feasibility of Senator Thomas Hart Benton's proposed "central," or 38th parallel, railroad route to the Pacific. Frémont's purpose was to prove that the southern Rockies could be crossed in winter, that they did not pose an insurmountable barrier for the proposed transcontinental railroad. Like the fourth expedition, his fifth expedition floundered in the mountains and left a legacy of death and suffering.

The construction of a transcontinental railroad was an urgent matter. After the United States' acquisition of California and the settling of the Oregon boundary question, a heated debate ensued in Washington regarding the most feasible route for a railroad to the Pacific.[3] The city chosen as the eastern terminus of the railroad would

[2] We have relied on Rolle's "Psychohistory and John Charles Frémont," 135-63, for a profile of Frémont's personality.

[3] Russel, *Improvement of Communication,* 34-53, 95-109, and 168-86.

benefit economically. By 1853, four major railroad routes were under serious consideration: a northern route from St. Paul to Puget Sound; two central routes, to run up the Arkansas River along the 38th parallel to San Francisco, or along the 35th parallel from Arkansas to Los Angeles; and a southern route to California along the 32nd parallel.

Southerners claimed that the central route was not an all-weather route; mountain snows, it was feared, would block the railroad during the winter months. Frémont and his father-in-law, Senator Thomas Hart Benton of Missouri, championed the central route because of the political advantage of having the railroad originate in Missouri.

In March 1853, Congress funded the Pacific railroad surveys, authorizing Secretary of War Jefferson Davis to organize the reconnaissance of several possible routes.[4] In so doing Congress hoped to remove the decision from the political arena and base the ultimate decision on engineering and cost considerations. Senator Benton applied considerable political pressure to have his son-in-law, Frémont, and his friend Edward Fitzgerald Beale appointed jointly to command the central route survey. But Davis appointed Captain John W. Gunnison instead. Beale was under orders from the Secretary of the Interior to proceed to California to assume his new duties as head of the California Indian Superintendency. With Benton's blessing he decided to travel overland to California via the central route with his cousin, Gwinn Harris Heap, a newspaper reporter, thereby carrying out a hurried reconnaissance using government travel funds.[5]

---

[4] Davis' instructions as well as elaborate reports on the surveys are found in House Ex. Docs, No. 91, 33rd Cong., 2nd Sess., *Reports of Explorations and Surveys.*

[5] Edward Beale's and Gwinn Harris Heap's letters received much attention in the nation's press. Heap's *Central Route to the Pacific* provides a daily record of the expedition. It is reprinted with supporting documentation as volume VII of Hafen's *The Far West and the Rockies Historical Series, 1820-1875.*

When Congress funded the Pacific railway surveys, Frémont was in Europe tending to legal and business matters.[6] By the time he reached Washington in late June 1853, Beale was halfway across the continent, and Gunnison was in Kansas heading west along the Santa Fé Trail. Frémont was still determined to conduct a survey of the central route, for he believed that neither Beale's nor Gunnison's party could settle the essential question posed by the central route: Could mountain passes be negotiated in winter?

Much could be said about Frémont's dogged determination to cross the mountains which had defeated him in 1849. A winter crossing was the kind of sensational feat of endurance which Frémont relished. By challenging the mountains in winter, he could settle an old score growing out of his disastrous fourth expedition, and could also lay to rest the Southern assertion that the Rocky Mountains were impassable in winter. But he had little to gain by conducting another warm weather reconnaissance along Gunnison's wagon tracks. Thus, as the *Missouri Democrat* reported on July 1, "Fremont proposes to start in November, and thus to test the practicability of the route during the seasons of snows."[7]

Frémont did not intend to repeat the mistakes of his fourth expedition by attempting a mid-winter crossing. Although it was too late to organize a summer expedition, he could easily have a small party in the field by early fall. Although he talked to the press about a winter crossing, he had no intention of getting stuck in mountain snows. He quietly made plans for an autumn departure, and by September 2 he was in St. Louis making final preparations.

[6] Frémont's activities in Europe are found in Spence, "David Hoffman," 379-403.

[7] St. Louis *Daily Missouri Democrat,* July 1, 1853.

The St. Louis *Intelligencer* summed up Frémont's final plans for a twofold assault of the Rockies:

> He... will go over the route which he proposed in 1848-9, when he was stopped by deep snows. Believing in a practicable pass through the mountains, and a good route that way, he means to solve the question to his own satisfaction. For that purpose he proposed to make a double expedition, one in the autumn and one in the winter — going out before the snows fall, to see the face of the country, and returning after the snows, and in them, to ascertain their depth and prevalence.[8]

Frémont's plan was to avoid the full brunt of winter weather while making what could still be called a "winter crossing." By traveling with pack animals instead of wagons, and by living off the land, he and his men could move rapidly across the plains into the high mountain country before the first heavy snows. He had arranged with Beale to have fresh animals awaiting him in California for the return journey. If all went according to plan, he would be back in the high mountain country by early March, in time "to test the depth of snows," but late enough in the season to avoid the full force of winter.

However, Frémont was unable to keep to his timetable. A bout of debilitating inflammation in his sciatic nerves forced a six-week delay. A less determined man might have given up the quest, but Frémont, fighting what Andrew Rolle termed "a lifelong battle for self-validation," pressed on to challenge the mountains. Once again he was to be thwarted by severe winter snows.[9]

When Frémont's party left Westport on September 19, Milligan was under the impression that they would be on the shores of the Pacific within sixty days. This, of course, was a totally unrealistic expectation. It had taken Beale's

[8] St. Louis *Intelligencer,* Aug. 31, 1853.

[9] Rolle, "Frémont," 163.

party three and a half months to make a similar journey. Nevertheless, Milligan's journal makes it clear that Frémont intended to make a rapid excursion.

Frémont's expedition was spartan. There was no longer any possibility of government funding. It appears that Frémont may have financed his expedition from the proceeds of a £13,000 loan which he had negotiated in England just prior to his departure for the United States.[10]

Most of the twelve men who set out with him from Westport were raw recruits and adventurers. William H. Palmer of San Francisco was along for a junket. He belonged to a prominent San Francisco banking family with which Frémont had numerous dealings. Frémont placed him in command when he returned to St. Louis for medical advice.

Frémont's "scientific corps" consisted of three men: Frémont; photographer Solomon Carvalho; and topographer Frederick von Egloffstein. Neither Carvalho nor Egloffstein had been in the Far West. Carvalho was the quintessential tenderfoot, who joined the expedition on a wild impulse. Egloffstein was a partner in a St. Louis surveying firm. Although he nearly perished in the mountains of Utah, he went on to become an intrepid explorer in his own right.

Egloffstein was assisted by Oliver Fuller, a young man from St. Louis who had been to California. Fuller was regarded as the strongest man on the expedition; he froze to death in the mountains of Utah.

Frémont's servant was a free mulatto named Albert Lea. Lea's family had worked in the Benton household for years. In 1861, Lea was hanged in San Francisco for murdering his wife.

Max Strobel, who had recently left Isaac Stevens' 49th

[10] *See* Spence, "David Hoffman," 397.

parallel railroad survey, joined the expedition at his own expense. He later replaced Egloffstein as Frémont's topographer.

Frémont's retinue also included four Wyandot Indians and a Mexican named Frank Dickson. In addition, Frémont hired ten Delaware Indians near present-day Topeka. The Delawares were employed as hunters to maintain a full larder of game, thereby reducing the necessity of packing large quantities of food. The Indians' contract was for a round-trip journey.

Although we do not know the terms of his employment, we know that Milligan worked as a general camp helper and roustabout. Frémont provided him with arms, ammunition, a mule, and probably paid him modest wages.

Milligan served only eleven weeks with Frémont's party. During more than half of that time Frémont was convalescing in St. Louis while Milligan and other expedition members were encamped on the Saline River in central Kansas. The two men spent less than a month traveling together. That was more than sufficient time for them to realize that they were totally incompatible.

Milligan's journal provides a needed counterpoint to Solomon Carvalho's effusive account of the fifth expedition entitled *Incidents of Travel and Adventure in the Far West with Col. Frémont's Last Expedition.* Although Carvalho initially had serious misgivings concerning Frémont's leadership qualities, he became one of Frémont's most enthusiastic supporters during the election of 1856, a change of heart apparently brought about by the prospects of gaining a government patronage position if Frémont were elected President of the United States. Unlike Milligan, Carvalho did not keep a daily entry diary of the expedition. He wrote his account in 1856 from memory, utilizing a series of letters he had written home to his wife.

Excerpts from Carvalho's account appeared in John Bigelow's campaign biography of Frémont, published by Derby and Jackson in 1856.[11] The same firm published Carvalho's full narrative in an 1856 English, and an 1857 American edition. Unfortunately, neither Carvalho's account nor Milligan's diary provides a complete record of the expedition, since neither man remained with Frémont for the entire journey. Frémont left Milligan behind at Bent's Fort. Carvalho, suffering from exhaustion and exposure, withdrew from the expedition in Utah.

Solomon Carvalho was once thought to have been the first official photographer on an exploring expedition in the United States.[12] Although we now know that expedition photography predated the fifth expedition, Carvalho is still regarded as one of the great pioneers of field photography. Frémont was well aware of the difficulties posed by the use of daguerreotype equipment in the field, for he had failed in his own efforts to photograph landmarks along the Oregon Trail in 1842.[13] When he decided to utilize photography on the fifth expedition he went to great lengths to acquire the latest equipment and to employ the most competent photographer he could find. He made an excellent choice in selecting Carvalho, an artist skilled in the daguerreotype process.

Carvalho was delayed in reaching St. Louis and almost missed the expedition. While awaiting Carvalho, Frémont hired a back-up photographer named Bomer. Bomer was a recent German immigrant who utilized a photographic process which produced a talbotype or paper print.

[11] John Bigelow, *Memoir of the Life and Public Services of John C. Frémont* (New York, 1856), 430-42.

[12] *See* MacNamara, "The First Official Photographer," 68-74.

[13] Charles Preuss recorded Frémont's first efforts at photography. *See* Gudde, *Exploring with Frémont*, 32-54.

Frémont was hedging his bets by utilizing both daguerreotypes and talbotypes, seeking to assure satisfactory results under difficult field conditions.[14]

Carvalho tells us that before starting west Frémont ordered a contest near Westport, Missouri, for the purpose of determining which process could produce the better photograph under field conditions. Carvalho claimed that his daguerreotype was ready within half an hour, while Bomer's print "could not be seen until the next day."[15] Carvalho insinuated that the long delay was the result of Bomer's inferior technical process which required that his print remain in a developing solution throughout the night. This was an implausible argument, since no process then in use required such a long developing time.[16] We now know from Milligan's humorous account that Bomer had no portable darkroom and was forced to await the darkness of nightfall to begin developing his pictures. He withdrew from the expedition when it became clear that Frémont would be unable to provide him with a portable darkroom.

Milligan took great interest in Carvalho's work. He noted nine different occasions when Carvalho unpacked his camera equipment to make "Daguerreotype views." Milligan's tantalizing account of the scope of Carvalho's photographic activities is especially significant, since none of the original daguerreotypes is known to have survived. Since these missing daguerreotypes were used to produce many of the engravings in Frémont's autobiographical *Memoirs of My Life,* Milligan's journal entries help identify

[14] Newhall, *The Daguerreotype in America,* 88-89; and Taft, *Photography and the American Scene,* 102-108, provide a good backround about the daguerreotype and talbotype. *See* also Jessie Benton Frémont, "Some Account of the Plates," in Frémont, *Memoirs of My Life,* xv-xvi.

[15] Carvalho, *Incidents of Travel,* 24.

[16] *See* Rudisill, *Mirror Image,* 103.

the locale and the conditions under which these photographs were made.[17]

After final preparations at Westport, Frémont's party headed west into Kansas. During a brief stop at the Shawnee Methodist Mission, Frémont became ill and was forced to return to Westport. He ordered his men to proceed west along the Kansas River to a rendezvous point at the Potawatomi Baptist Mission near Uniontown, an Indian village situated a few miles west of modern Topeka. Frémont had arranged to meet his ten Delaware hunters at Uniontown, and hoped to join his men there within a few days.

Shortly after his men reached Uniontown, Frémont sent word that his indisposition had forced him to continue on to St. Louis to seek medical attention. He instructed his men to proceed west "as far as [the] buffalo," since he expected to be detained for several days. Once they were in the buffalo country his men could feast on buffalo meat while saving other provisions for the anticipated crossing of the Rockies. A Delaware hunter named Solomon Everett served as guide. Everett had been with Frémont on his third expedition in 1845, and now led the party west from Uniontown over the same road which Frémont had used in 1845. Frémont's men passed the newly constructed Fort Riley, situated on the opposite side of the Kansas. Near the fort they reached the junction of the Republican and Smoky Hill rivers. They headed south up the Smoky Hill River until they reached its confluence with the Saline River, near Salina, Kansas. They traveled up the Saline a short distance and set up camp.

Frémont's men remained on the Saline during the month

[17] Walt Wheelock has advanced the plausible argument that many of Carvalho's photographs still exist in the form of engravings in Frémont's *Memoirs of My Life*. *See* Walt Wheelock, "Frémont's Lost Plates," 48-53.

of October. Buffalo and wolves were numerous around the camp. The Delawares spent their time hunting buffalo and curing meat. Milligan noted that the camp soon took on the appearance of a "game depot." Since their camp was only fifty miles southwest of Fort Riley, they were able to send occasional riders to the post to purchase supplies and to obtain the latest news about Frémont's condition.

Writing from the perspective of a hired hand, Milligan tells us about the day-to-day operations and about the anxieties the men suffered while they camped in Kansas awaiting Frémont's return from St. Louis. The waiting preyed heavily on the men's minds. And although they occupied themselves by hunting buffalo and curing meat for the anticipated mountain crossing, they could not help speculating about the expedition's dimming prospects and worrying about the approaching cold weather.

Frémont reached the Saline River camp on the evening of October 31. He was accompanied by Alexander Lea and an obese German physician, Dr. A. Ebers, whom Frémont had brought along from St. Louis. Ebers created quite a sensation. He rode a large mule, perched on a huge feather bed which he used in lieu of a saddle.

On November 1 they started west, skirting an immense prairie fire, the result of their own carelessness with their camp fire. Pushing hard on forced marches which averaged over twenty miles per day, they hurried up the Smoky Hill River.

They left the Smoky Hill at a point about twenty-five miles north of the Great Bend of the Arkansas. They traveled in a southwesterly direction for about sixty miles, striking the Pawnee Fork of the Arkansas a few miles west of Fort Larned. They traveled west up the Pawnee River for several days.

On November 11, they left the Pawnee River, headed

southwest to reach the Arkansas River and the "mountain branch" of the Santa Fé Trail just west of the Cimarron Cutoff. That night Milligan complained of having to sleep under wet blankets while Frémont slept "snug in his little tent."

Many of Frémont's pack mules had gone lame by the time his party reached the Arkansas. Since there were no longer enough healthy animals in the mulada to carry the expedition's baggage, Frémont requisitioned some of the riding horses as pack animals, forcing Milligan, Oliver Fuller, and two other men to walk. They were only four days away from William Bent's trading houses at Big Timbers, where they hoped to obtain fresh mules. Milligan's boots "gave out" after two days on foot. He borrowed a pair from Carvalho, but they did not fit well. By the time he reached camp that night he was "foot sore and weary." His feet were covered with blisters "from heel to toe." They were so sore that he could barely hobble when he reached Big Timbers. His last eight miles of walking had seemed like a hundred. He was in no condition, nor mood, to continue with Frémont to the Rockies.

The incident between Frémont and Milligan over journal-keeping permanently clouded their relationship. Frémont apparently decided to avoid using force to obtain Milligan's journal. An effective and less confrontational alternative was to drop the volatile Irishman from the expedition at the earliest opportunity. That opportunity came when Frémont's party stopped at Bent's trading houses to purchase needed supplies and to obtain fresh mules.

Big Timbers was the name given to a forest of immense cottonwood trees which extended for several miles along the Arkansas River in what is now Bent County in southeastern Colorado. Big Timbers provided sheltered winter camping grounds for the Southern Cheyenne and

Arapaho people, and was a logical site for a trading post. When Frémont's party arrived at Big Timbers in mid-November, 1853, they found William Bent and his men operating a trading post in a compound of log cabins. Although he had not yet begun construction, Bent was completing plans to build a new stone fort on a nearby bluff. This post would become known as Bent's New Fort.

After a candid discussion in which both men aired their differences, Frémont in effect cashiered Milligan by placing him in charge of the expedition's lame mules. The Irishman was to care for the mules at the post until the following May, when Frémont was expected to pick them up on his return journey from California. He also left Dr. Ebers behind at the post, not wishing to take the portly doctor over the mountains.

Frémont never returned to Big Timbers. With twenty-one men and fifty-four horses and mules, he left the Big Timbers post on November 25.[18] His party headed up the Arkansas past the ruins of Bent's Old Fort toward the Spanish Peaks which loomed on the horizon to the southwest. Frémont now faced the most important and most challenging segment of the journey. On the horizon he could see the jagged peaks of the front range of the Rockies. Beyond lay the elusive Cochetopa Pass over the continental divide, the gateway to California. In Frémont's mind Cochetopa Pass had become the paramount landmark of the central route and the key to public acceptance of that route as the best possible all-weather road to the Pacific.

Frémont had the advantage of being able to follow Gunnison's wagon tracks along much of the route from Bent's New Fort to the crossing of the Green River in Utah. Gunnison's route was even visible beneath mountain snows, for in many places he had felled trees to open a road

[18] Frémont's letter from Big Timbers is contained in a letter from Thomas Hart Benton to the editor, Wash., D.C. *National Intelligencer,* Mar. 18, 1854.

for his wagons. Frémont undoubtedly noted where Gunnison's wagon tracks left the Arkansas at the mouth of the Apishapa River. Gunnison had mistaken the Apishapa for the Huerfano, an error which resulted in a needless detour to the southwest.

Avoiding Gunnison's blunder, Frémont continued up the Arkansas to the mouth of the Huerfano, and up that stream to its headwaters in search of more northerly passes across the lofty ridges of the Sangre de Cristo Range. He found two passes through the range: Robidoux Pass (now called Mosca Pass); and Sand Hill or Williams Pass (present-day Medano Pass). He had crossed over Robidoux Pass in 1848, and now took time to escort Carvalho to its summit to make a daguerreotype view. Selecting Sand Hill Pass for his 1853 crossing, he and his men entered the broad San Luis Valley on December 5. They arrived on the valley floor on the edge of what is now Great Sand Dunes National Monument. Frémont must have been relieved to find the valley free of snow and the way clear to passes in the majestic San Juans, which form the western rim of the valley. By traveling north up the valley to Creston Creek, he was on an almost direct line to Cochetopa Pass, which lay nestled in the San Juans over fifty miles to the northwest. Today there are two passes which carry the name Cochetopa. The highest is North Cochetopa Pass, with an elevation of 10,149 feet. This pass is the Cochetopa Pass of Frémont's day. Ten miles to the south is present-day Cochetopa Pass with an elevation of 10,032. In 1853 this lower pass was called Carnero Pass. Modern scholarship suggests that Carnero Pass was the elusive object of Frémont's quest during the winter of 1848-49.[19]

---

[19] Recent scholarship concerning Frémont's route across the San Luis Valley and into the San Juans is based upon Patricia Joy Richmond's fieldwork. *See* Weber, *Richard H. Kern,* 38-50; and Jackson and Spence, eds., *The Expeditions of John Charles Frémont,* III, xxviii-xxx.

Frémont was correct in his assessment of North Cochetopa Pass. Whether approached from the east or the west, North Cochetopa Pass offers the traveler a gently sloping, easy route across the continental divide. Approaching the continental divide across the San Luis Valley up Saguache Creek, Frémont's party once again struck Gunnison's wagon tracks. Although Saguache Creek narrows toward its headwaters, and at intervals is enclosed by bold rocky bluffs, the creek bottoms are characterized by level meadowland which offers no serious obstacles to overland travel. The pass itself forms a broad saddle with gentle approaches which belie its elevation. Frémont reached the summit on December 14. He was elated! The mere four inches of snow in the pass seemed to justify his contention that the pass could be crossed easily in winter.[20]

In light of the undoing of his fourth expedition in the San Juans in 1849, Frémont's preoccupation with the Cochetopa Pass is understandable, but it obscures the fact that he and his men still faced hundreds of miles of mountainous terrain through a virtually trackless wilderness in the midst of winter without the services of a knowledgeable guide.

On the western slope Frémont and his men dropped down to the Gunnison River via West Pass and Tomichi creeks. Although more turbulent than Saguache Creek and restricted by occasional narrows, their canyons did not pose serious obstacles.

Frémont's party followed Gunnison's route down the Gunnison River. They avoided the Black Canyon of the Gunnison by skirting to the south of the canyon until they struck the Uncompahgre River. They traveled down the Uncompahgre to its confluence with the Gunnison at

[20] *See* Frémont's letter to Benton, Feb. 9, 1854, Wash., D.C. *National Intelligencer*, Mar. 18, 1854.

modern Delta, Colorado. Since they were now below Black Canyon, they were able to resume their journey down the Gunnison, which they followed to its confluence with the Colorado at Grand Junction. By Christmas they were on restricted provisions, but in good spirits. Crossing the Colorado River at Grand Junction, they headed west down the Colorado along the base of the Book Cliffs. They left the river near the Utah-Colorado border, heading west over the wedge of arid tableland separating the Colorado from Green River. According to Carvalho, they were still following Gunnison's wagon tracks. Continuing westward along a route which took them to the north of present-day Arches National Park, they soon struck traces of the Old Spanish Trail.

The Old Spanish Trail was a commercial trading route connecting Santa Fé to Los Angeles. Indian slaving expeditions, trappers, horse traders and horse thieves used the trail extensively in the 1830s and 1840s. It was strictly a pack route until the late 1840s when emigrants opened up the section from the Wasatch Front to Los Angeles to wagon travel. When viewed on a map the trail resembles an enormous oxbow which extends north from Santa Fé to an apex in the Wasatch Mountains of central Utah before dipping to the southwest toward Los Angeles. Reflecting the wisdom of an old, well-worn trail, it followed the path of least resistance through the labyrinth of canyons, mountains and tablelands of the Colorado Plateau, and therefore was an anathema to railroad surveyors attempting to chart an east-west line along a parallel of latitude.[21]

After discovering its traces in the arid tablelands north of present-day Arches National Park, Gunnison followed the trail to the Green River crossing near the modern community of Green River and then across the Wasatch

---

[21] An excellent study of the Old Spanish Trail in Utah is Crampton, "Utah's Spanish Trail," 361-83.

Mountains to the Mormon settlements in the Great Basin. Logic suggests that Frémont too followed the trail as far as the Green River ford, although his map indicates a crossing some twenty miles to the south opposite the mouth of the San Rafael River.[22]

Having crossed the Green near 39° north latitude, Frémont was eager to set a course which would correspond more closely to his much touted 38th parallel central route. Leaving the Old Spanish Trail, the pathfinder veered to the southwest, hoping to find a mountain pass along the headwaters of the San Rafael River. After heading up that stream for several miles, he found his route blocked where the San Rafael cuts through the upthrust ramparts of the San Rafael Reef. That great stone wall marks the eastern rim of the San Rafael Swell, an enormous, deeply eroded anticline which extends on a north-south axis for over fifty miles. The route up the San Rafael River was impassable. Frémont had no choice. He turned south, traveling over the desert floor parallel to that imposing hogback for some seventy miles until he reached the turbid waters of the Frémont River. His party headed up the Frémont in a west-northwesterly direction into the high mountain country northwest of Thousand Lake Mountain. It was here in the Wasatch Mountains that cold weather and deep snows shattered Frémont's dreams of an easy winter passage through the Rockies. In subsequent newspaper accounts Frémont laconically admitted that his party had "encountered a good deal of difficulty . . . passing through this bed of mountains," but putting his best face forward,

[22] Frémont's route from the mouth of the Huerfano River to Sacramento is plotted by intermittent dotted lines on a map entitled "Map showing Country Explored by John Charles Frémont from 1841 to 1854 Inclusive" which was bound in Frémont's *Memoirs of My Life*. That map indicates a crossing of the Green opposite the mouth of the San Rafael. However, distortions concerning the location of the Book Cliffs suggest that Frémont may have used the Old Spanish Trail Green River ford. For conflicting views concerning his route, *see* Spence, "The Frémonts and Utah," 298; Crampton, *Standing Up Country*, 56; and Jackson and Spence, eds., *Expeditions of Frémont*, III: 489 n. 6.

downplayed his men's suffering by reporting that "the deepest snow we here encountered being about up to the saddle-skirts, or four feet."[23]

Frémont's men faced the Wasatch Mountains on reduced rations. Game had been scarce in Colorado and Utah, and with the provisions laid in at Bent's New Fort running low, his men were reduced to a diet of porcupine, as well as tough sinewy mule and horse flesh garnished with occasional cactus stems. During the 45 days they subsisted on this fare, they grew accustomed to gnawing on mule bones and drinking horse soup seasoned with tough giblets of boiled hide. J.C.L. Smith, who met the starving explorers shortly after they staggered into the Mormon settlement at Parowan, wrote the following graphic description of their diet:

> They reported that they had eaten twenty-seven broken-down animals; that when a horse or mule could go no farther, it was killed and divided out, giving one-half to the Delaware, and the other to the Colonel and his men; the hide was cut in pieces and cast lots for. After the bones had been made into soup, they were burned, and carried along by the men for luncheon. The entrails were shaken, and then made into soup, together with the feet and eyes, thus using up the whole mule. They stated they had travelled forty five days living on this kind of fare.[24]

Frémont's men spent almost two weeks (January 24 to February 7) working their way over the Wasatch Mountains into the Sevier River Valley. To reach the Sevier, they crossed over the frigid Awapa Plateau striking the Fish Lake Branch of the Old Spanish Trail where it heads south through Grass Valley and down Otter Creek. Caching excess baggage in Grass Valley, they continued down this variant of the Old Spanish Trail to the confluence with the Sevier at modern Junction, Utah.

---

[23] Wash., D.C. *National Intelligencer,* June 14, 1854.

[24] John C.L. Smith to editor, Salt Lake City *Deseret News,* Mar. 16, 1854.

Upon reaching the Sevier, Frémont and his suffering men were once again on the main branch of the Old Spanish Trail, the trail they had left near the Green River Crossing in hopes of finding a short cut through the mountains.

Tottering on the verge of starvation reminiscent of the fourth expedition, they followed the trail south up the Sevier River. Since the trail was obscured beneath the snow, they were probably unaware that they were once again on the Old Spanish Trail. Upon reaching Circle Valley, Frémont and Carvalho made crucial astronomical observations while standing in waist-deep snow. Having regained their bearings, the pathfinder and his men continued along the Old Spanish Trail route through Circleville Canyon. Leaving the river near Bear Valley Junction, they headed up Bear Valley, over the Hurricane Cliffs and on into Parowan. Oliver Fuller, suffering from frostbite and exposure, died within a day's ride of the little Mormon village. The Mormons, after first mistaking them for Indians, welcomed them into their homes.

The expedition was in shambles. Although the *Daily Alta California* reported that Frémont and his men were "worn and much reduced in flesh," J.C.L. Smith who saw them at Parowan more accurately described their condition as "a state of starvation."[25] One man was dead. Solomon Carvalho and Baron von Egloffstein, the principal members of his "scientific corps," were too weak to continue. Frémont's remaining men were on foot without provisions, pack animals, or the money to purchase them. Fortunately, Frémont's credit was good, enabling him to purchase fresh animals and new supplies.

Despite his discouraging situation, he presented the

[25] San Fran. *Daily Alta California,* Apr. 21, 1854; and Salt Lake City *Deseret News,* Mar. 16, 1854.

results of his expedition in the best possible light in a report to Senator Benton.[26] Downplaying the hardships he and his men had encountered in Utah, he justified the practicality of the central route by stressing the ease with which they had crossed the continental divide at Cochetopa Pass.

Frémont and his men recuperated less than two weeks in Parowan. With single-minded determination and "dauntless energy," Frémont proceeded with plans for his reconnaissance across the Great Basin toward San Francisco.[27] He pressed Max Strobel into service to replace von Egloffstein as topographer, and with the aid of a Mormon guide, set out with the remnant of his party on February 21, to trace a railroad route across the basins and ranges of southern Nevada. He considered, but rejected, the Old Spanish Trail to San Bernardino, since it dropped too far to the southwest. In hopes of discovering a more direct route to San Francisco, he charted a course which took him "a little south of West" from Parowan. Upon reaching the Mormon settlement at Cedar City, he headed "directly westward" toward the rim of the Great Basin, and into "a high tableland, bristling with mountains," which appeared so wild and grotesque that he characterized it as an "unfinished country."[28]

Although Frémont later promised to redact his notes and calculations, published accounts of this journey are disappointingly vague.[29] Since he had been forced to cache most of his baggage and scientific instruments in the

[26] Frémont to Benton, Feb. 9, 1854, Wash., D.C. *National Intelligencer,* Apr. 12, 1854.

[27] San Fran. *Daily Alta California,* Apr. 21, 1854.

[28] Wash., D.C. *National Intelligencer,* June 14, 1854.

[29] Our account of Frémont's route from Parowan to California is based primarily upon Frémont's map cited above, and upon the field work of Todd Berens, who assisted Mary Lee Spence in working out Frémont's route on this segment of the expedition. *See* Jackson and Spence, eds., *Expeditions of Frémont,* III: 106-107; 475-77.

mountains of Utah, it seems unlikely that he was equipped to make careful astronomical observations, relying instead upon his compass and dead reckoning. Since he made his crossing from the Wasatch to the Sierra Nevada in less than thirty days, it seems evident that he had become less occupied with carrying out a careful railroad reconnaissance, and more concerned with making a rapid passage to San Francisco.

The Basin and Range province is characterized by a series of parallel mountain ranges separated by broad open valleys which extend along a north-south axis. It was neccessary for Frémont to chart a course across each broad valley in order to reach a suitable pass or enable him to skirt intervening ranges. In picking his way through this "unfinished country," he was forced to make substantial detours from his desired east-west axis. The *Daily Alta California* characterized this route as "indirect and unsuitable for a railroad."[30] His party struck the present Utah-Nevada line southwest of Modena, Utah. Temporarily leaving the Great Basin, he headed down Clover Creek to its confluence with Meadow Valley Wash, a tributary of the Virgin River. Continuing to the northwest, he crossed intersecting basins and ranges before reaching White River, an intermittent stream which drains to the southeast toward the Virgin. Frémont headed up the White to a point just north of the thirty-eighth parallel. He left the White but, unable to maintain his east-west axis, he dropped to the west-southwest down Coal Valley, and over the Worthington Range. Passing through the northern edge of present-day Nellis Air Force Range and Nuclear Testing Site, he crossed over the Kawich Range, across Cactus Flat and the adjoining Cactus Range, and southwest along Stonewall

[30] San Fran. *Daily Alta California*, Apr. 21, 1854.

Flat to the Palmetto and Magruder mountains. He crossed into California via Lida Pass, probably reaching the floor of Owens Valley near modern Big Pine.[31]

Finding passes through the high Sierra blocked by snow, he headed south toward Walker Pass. He missed Walker Pass, and instead crossed over into the Kern River drainage and to the San Joaquin Valley via Bird Spring Pass, situated some ten miles to the south. He reached San Francisco on April 16, reporting that his transcontinental odyssey had clearly established "the practicability of the route at all seasons."[32]

Frémont had succeeded in "forcing a passage" of the continent in mid-winter, but in so doing had also demonstrated the impracticability of the proposed 38th parallel route. Frémont's failures, combined with Gunnison's murder at the hands of vengeful Pavant Indians in Utah, marked the death knell of the Benton-Frémont route.

After resting for only a few days in San Francisco, he booked passage for New York on a Panama-bound steamer. His decision to return to New York by sea was a tacit admission that the mountains had triumphed.

MILLIGAN'S LIFE AT BENT'S NEW FORT

Milligan spent the winter tending Frémont's animals, presumably awaiting the pathfinder's return from California. Milligan's life at Big Timbers bore out James Larkin's observations written at Bent's New Fort in 1856 that "the manner of living among the Squaws is rather looser than civilized people generally permit."[33] Milligan stayed at Big

[31] Walt Wheelock, who made a careful study of Frémont's route across Nevada and Calfornia, reached a diffierent conclusion. *See* Wheelock, "Following Frémont's Fifth Expedition," 194-200.

[32] San Fran. *Daily Alta California*, Apr. 21, 1854.

[33] James Larkin Memorandum Book, 1856, journal entry for Oct. 13, 1856 (MS, Bent's Old Fort Nat. Historic Site).

Timbers for a little over three months; about half of his journal is devoted to describing life at Bent's New Fort and provides the only known intimate account of life at that post. The young Irishman fit easily into the pace, "married" a Cheyenne woman, and spent much of his free time in the Cheyenne lodges. He also tried his hand as a bufffalo robe trader, an experience which he thoroughly enjoyed. His earthy journal provides insight into the interaction between Bent's traders and the Cheyenne people.

Milligan chronicled the activities of a number of mountain men and travelers, including Francois Lajeunesse, Joseph Chatillon, John S. Smith, Lucas Murray, and the enigmatic English nobleman, Charles William Wentworth Fitzwilliam. En route from Taos to Missouri, Fitzwilliam stopped at Big Timbers the very day Frémont started for the mountains. He was on his way back to England at the conclusion of two years of hunting and adventure in the plains and the Rockies. He and Milligan became good friends during his brief visit at Bent's Fort.

Milligan's journal is the only contemporary first-hand account of the initial phase of construction of Bent's New Fort, clearing up much confusion concerning the early chronology of that post. He not only provides the exact date when construction began but also gives the reasons which compelled William Bent to build his new stone post on a nearby bluff. Bent's trading houses consisted of three log buildings arranged in the shape of a U with a log palisade across the front. This structure was located on bottomlands beneath the stone bluff, about three-fourths of a mile west of the site he selected for his new fort. By 1853 his trading houses were overrun with rats. They were eating his supplies and destroying his profits. By moving to a higher location on a barren sandstone bluff he hoped to evade the rats and save his business.

Most secondary accounts of Bent's New Fort rely on a chronology published in Henry Inman's *The Old Santa Fé Trail* in 1897. According to this account, Bent employed ten stone cutters during the winter of 1852-1853 to quarry building stone for the new post, while Bent and his traders traveled two hundred miles to the southwest on a winter trading foray with the Kiowas and Comanches. According to Inman, after Bent returned to Big Timbers in the spring of 1853, "construction of the new post was begun, and the work continued until completed in the summer of 1854."[34]

Milligan's journal states that Bent began construction of his New Fort on February 2, 1854, and that it was substantially completed by the end of the month. The post which he helped to construct was a log structure. Since Milligan makes no mention of masonry work, it seems probable that construction of the massive stone perimeter did not begin until Bent's return to Big Timbers in the fall of 1854. The masonry work was probably not completed until 1855.[35]

In the spring of 1854 Bent traveled east over the Santa Fé Trail to Missouri with several wagonloads of buffalo robes. These he traded for supplies and trade goods in preparation for a return journey to his new fort. Milligan traveled to Missouri with Bent's party. He left Bent's caravan near Uniontown, and after attending to business concerning Frémont's mules, he booked passage on a

---

[34] Inman, *The Old Santa Fe Trail*, 391-92.

[35] Health seeker James Larkin wrote the best early description of Bent's New Fort in 1856: "Bent's Fort is situated on the north side of the Arkansas River on a bold bluff — being very accessible however from the North Side. It is built of brown sandstone — being about 170 feet long [and] 380 feet wide. The walls are about 14 feet high, & the houses range around the inside next to the walls — bearing a large open space in [the] center. There are 15 rooms, being used for sleeping rooms, store rooms, dining room & [the] entrance is surmounted with a large pair of Antlers." *See* James Larkin Memorandum Book, 1856, journal entry for Oct. 13, 1856 (MS, Bent's Old Fort Natl. Historic Site).

Missouri River steamer for St. Louis. He reached St. Louis about two weeks after Frémont set sail from California, ending his association with what he considered "a man totally devoid of gratitude." There is no indication that he and Frémont ever communicated with one another again.

Milligan continued to make occasional entries in his journal after his return from Bent's New Fort. From time to time he pasted newspaper clippings on blank pages in the back of his diary; many related to John C. Frémont. With the exception of an excerpt published in the Norfolk *Southern Argus* during Frémont's 1856 presidential campaign, Milligan appears to have made no effort to publish his journal.[36]

[36] Norfolk *Southern Argus,* Aug. 26 and 27, 1856.

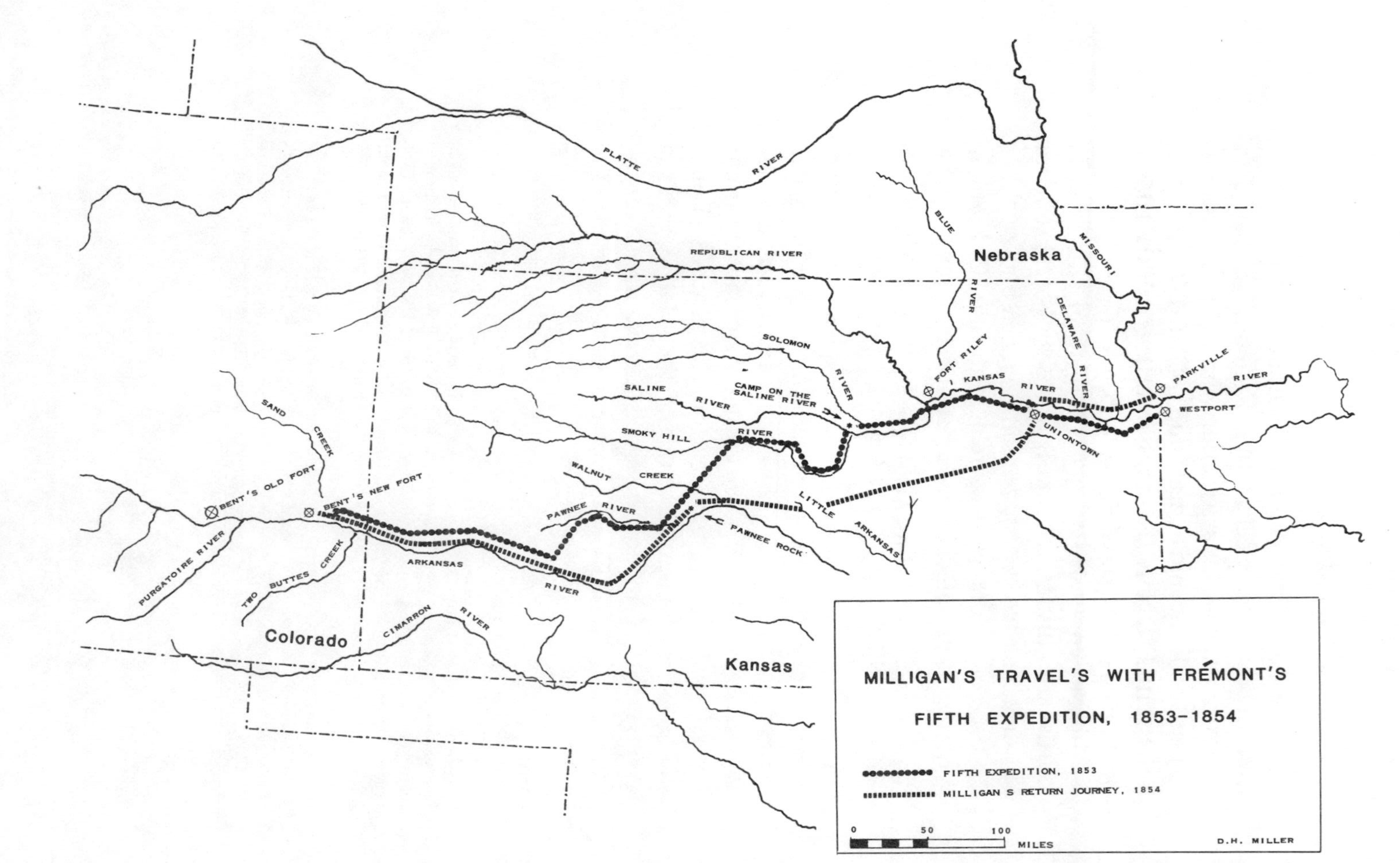

PLATTE RIVER
REPUBLICAN RIVER
BLUE RIVER
Nebraska
MISSOURI
DELAWARE RIVER
SOLOMON RIVER
FORT RILEY
KANSAS RIVER
PARKVILLE
RIVER
WESTPORT
UNIONTOWN
SALINE RIVER
CAMP ON THE SALINE RIVER
SMOKY HILL RIVER
WALNUT CREEK
LITTLE ARKANSAS
PAWNEE RIVER
PAWNEE ROCK
SAND CREEK
BENT'S OLD FORT
BENT'S NEW FORT
PURGATOIRE RIVER
TWO BUTTES CREEK
ARKANSAS RIVER
CIMARRON RIVER
Colorado
Kansas
MILLIGAN'S TRAVEL'S WITH FRÉMONT'S
FIFTH EXPEDITION, 1853-1854
FIFTH EXPEDITION, 1853
MILLIGAN S RETURN JOURNEY, 1854
0
50
100
MILES
D.H. MILLER

5

Journal of Frémont's Fifth Expedition and life at Bent's New Fort by James F. Milligan

September 6th 1853. Left St. Louis on board steamer "Polar Star"[1] in company with Wm. H. Palmer[2] and Alexander Lee,[3] a servant of Col. Fremont's, for Kansas.[4] Col. Fremont was detained in consequence of the non-arrival of his Daguerreotype artist and some important instructions connected with the expedition in which I am *volunteered* to endure viz. the testing of a practicable route for a railroad to San Francisco from this place (St. Louis) during the winter and also, to find the relative depth of snow and other important objects in favour of a central route to the Pacific Ocean. Feel exceedingly depressed in spirits in consequence of several little circumstances which have transpired during the last week emanating entirely from my want of discretion and hasty temperament.

---

[1] The *Polar Star* was considered "one of the finest and most popular boats" to sail on the Missouri. Constructed in 1852 by Captain Tom Brierly of St. Joseph, she broke a speed record in 1863 by making the 600 mile run from St. Louis to St. Joseph in 68 hours. She served as a flagship during the siege of Vicksburg, and later burned on the Tennessee River. *See* Chappell, "A History of the Missouri River," 293 and 308.

[2] *See* Appendix, pp. 265 for a sketch of Palmer.

[3] Alexander Lee = Albert Lea. *See* Appendix, pp. 265-66, for a sketch of Lea.

[4] Milligan is referring to Kansas City, which had its origin with Francis G. Chouteau's trading post, established in 1821 on the Missouri's right bank about three miles below the mouth of the Kansas River. Kansas City was platted in 1838, but the town did not begin to grow until the mid-1840s. It was incorporated in 1853. *See* Brown, *Frontier Community,* 13-81.

Sincerely hope that the hardships and privation which I am about to endure may have a salutary influence over my future course.

September 13th 1853. After several days delay Col. Fremont and suite consisting of Egloffstein,[5] Topog. Engineer, and Carvalho,[6] Daguerreotype artist, arrived here, (Kansas)[7] on board the Steamer F.X. Aubry,[8] procured waggons and move camp equipage out to "Vogels" pasture[9] where we struck camp until we prepared for a final start for California Ho! The Scientific Corps not being inured to camp life took lodgings at the "Harris" House[10] in Westport. Found Fuller[11] and myself stowed all things safe under cover and prepared for rain. During my short intercourse with Mr. Fuller, his inestimable virtues with which he is so much endowed has endeared him to me more as a brother than a boon companion and I feel proud

---

[5] *See* Appendix, pp. 266-67, for a sketch of von Egloffstein.

[6] *See* Appendix, pp. 267-68, for a sketch of Carvalho.

[7] Frémont's party left St. Louis on Sept. 8. The *Missouri Republican* reported that five of Frémont's eight companions were residents of St. Louis. The other three were "friends of Col. Frémont who came on from the East, accompanying him as fellow voyageurs." Frémont's baggage included "sixty riding and packing saddles." St. Louis *Daily Missouri Republican,* Sept. 9, 1853; and St. Louis *Daily Evening News,* Sept. 9, 1853.

[8] The steamer *F.X. Aubry* was constructed in Pittsburgh in 1853 and was operating on the Missouri between St. Louis and St. Joseph as early as May of that year. Named for Francois X. Aubry, the famous Santa Fé trader, explorer and frontiersman, it was considered one of the "finest and most popular" steamers on the Middle Missouri. It remained in service until 1860. *See* Chaput, *Francois X. Aubry,* 174; Barry, *The Beginning of the West,* 1148; Chappell, "Missouri River," 293; and St. Louis *Daily Missouri Democrat,* June 2, 1853.

[9] "Vogel's pasture" was part of a large farm owned by Prussian immigrant and land speculator Louis Vogel. It was located on the southwestern edge of Westport astride the Oregon Trail. *See* Slavens, "Historical Atlas Map of Jackson County, Missouri"; Honig, "Map of the Town of Westport in 1855"; Goff, *Old Westport*; Christopher, "The Old Vogel Saloon," 10-12; and Brown, *Frontier Community,* 27-29.

[10] The Harris House was a spacious three-story brick hotel which John Harris constructed in 1852 on the corner of Pennsylvania and Main Street in Westport. It was on the main road connecting Westport to Independence, and as such did a brisk business with travelers bound for Oregon and California.

[11] *See* Appendix, pp. 268, for a sketch of Fuller.

in knowing that the regard I entertain for him is returned. We have become sworn friends only parted with death and I sincerely hope we may both live for to shed a lustre upon our names not easily sullied.

September 14th 1853. Went to Independence[12] this morning to buy mules, hire hands & other business connected with the expedition. Visited Col. Gilpin[13] at his farm some few miles north of Independence. Had the extreme felicity of hearing from Home through him. He accompanied me to town from thence to the camp of Col. Fremont. Purchased several mules at prices ranging from $60 to $75 considered exceedingly low.

September 15th 1853. During the day employed arranging packs and attending to other business incidental to our Expedition. Hired the only Mexican which would trust himself to such a hazardous journey at such a late season of the year. His named Americanized is Frank Dickson, a native of New Leon, Old Mexico. Found him to be quite

---

[12] Now a part of greater Kansas City, Independence was laid out in 1827. It was among a number of competing towns which served as outfitting points for the Santa Fé trade and for Oregon and California-bound emigration. Most travelers regarded Independence as the eastern terminus of both the Santa Fé and Oregon Trails. Guide books measured distances on both trails from the corner of the Independence court house square. Independence remained a major "jumping-off" point throughout the 1840s. In the early 1850s it began to yield much emigrant traffic to neighboring Westport and to upriver towns such as Weston and St. Joseph. *See* Mattes, *The Great Platte River Road,* 106-108; and Haines, *Historic Sites Along the Oregon Trail,* 11.

[13] William Gilpin (1815-1894) was reared in Philadelphia in a politically prominent family. He settled in St. Louis in 1838, where he practiced law, specializing in land claim litigation. He was active in state politics as a Benton Democrat. In 1841 he settled in Independence, a move which reflected his interests in the westward movement. He joined Frémont's second expedition to Oregon in 1843, and the following year returned to Independence via the Oregon Trail, Fort Bridger, Bent's Fort and the Santa Fé Trail. He fought with the Missouri Volunteers during the Mexican War, and patrolled the Santa Fé Trail from 1847-1850. When Milligan met him in 1853, Gilpin was active in Independence as a publicist and town builder. He was a strong advocate of the transcontinental railroad and of the South Pass, rather than the Frémont-Benton route along the Arkansas. In 1861-62 he served as Governor of Colorado. *See* Karnes, *William Gilpin.*

useful. Nothing of any importance transpired from the above date until the 19th inst. when "all hands" were called at an early hour to break up camp prior to start for the "*Western Ocean.*" As usual on all such occasions everything is confusion, the "Scientific Corps" making arrangements for their general comfort in procuring everything which is useless for the trip and being particularly supplied with nothing that they want. Mr. Bomer[14] makes particular enquiry through the aid of Mr. Egloffstein, his interpreter, that it is necessary to make arrangements to have a "dark room" to enable him to carry out his Scientific project of taking Daguerreotypes upon chemical-prepared paper, but in consequence (ironically speaking) of not being able to get a portable house prepared for his especial benefit and to the promotion [of] the branch of Science he advocates, I am very much afraid he will be exceedingly disappointed.

---

[14] Frémont had attempted unsuccessfully to take daguerreotypes of Oregon Trail landmarks during his 1842 expedition, but that same year Edward Anthony of the Northern Boundary Survey made successful daguerreotypes along the United States Canadian border.

In 1853 while in London en route from France to the United States, Frémont read a copy of Alexander von Humboldt's just-published *Cosmos.* The eminent German geographer expressed the hope that photography might prove to be the best means of securing "Truth in Nature." When Frémont decided to make a photographic record of the central route, he purchased daguerreotype equipment in New York and employed artist Carvalho.

Frémont apparently met Bomer in St. Louis. Although Milligan uses the term "Daguerreotype" in the generic sense in reference to Bomer, the German photographer employed a process far different from that invented by Louis Daguerre in the 1830s. The daguerre process utilized a light-sensitive silver plate (or silver-coated copper plate), which was exposed in the camera and then developed in mercury fumes, producing a positive image. By contrast, Bomer made his photographs on sensitized paper utilizing a process invented by W.H. Fox Talbŏt in England about 1835. The Talbotype or Calotype as it was generally known, produced a negative, which in turn could be used to make paper prints. The daguerreotype produced no negative, and was thus a one-of-a-kind picture. Daguerreotypes made sharper images which showed more detail.

See Carvalho, *Incidents of Travel,* 22; Jessie Benton Frémont, "Some Account of the Plates," xv-xvi; Jackson and Spence, eds., *Expeditions of Frémont,* I:xxxiii; Newhall, *Daguerreotype in America,* 88-89; and Taft, *Photography and the American Scene,* 102-108.

September 19th 1853. Everything being packed and all hands mounted, we made our final start, the Expedition consisting of the following persons: Col. J.C. Fremont, W.H. Palmer, S.N. Carvalho, ______ Egloffstein, ______ Bomer, Oliver Fuller, J.F. Milligan, Frank Dickson, Jos Carter (Wyandott Indian), Nick Carter do, Jno Brown do, ______ Lee servant of the Col's, Wolf, James Harrison, Wahalope, Smith, Solomon, Jacob Enis, Wahone, and three other Deleware Indians,[15] names not now recollected.[16] Camped at the Baptist Mission,[17] about 4 miles from the state line. Several amusing little accidents happened after we got to camp which was exceedingly edifying to those that were not the victims. Fuller and myself tried our Carbines at long shot at a "Genus Canni" which sneaked into our camp and when discovered was some distance from it with a piece of our Evening meal in his mouth which glutton-like he was making off with. A shot from our Guns made him drop the "provision" and accelerate his speed as well as to convince us that we were provided with tools good at a long range.

The tent blowed down during the night. When the Scientific Corps rebeled, stood on their dignity and refused

[15] *See* Appendix, pp. 268-69, for a sketch of the Delawares.

[16] Milligan provides us with the most complete list of expedition personnel. His roster agrees with Carvalho's shorter list with the exception of the Delaware Hunter Wahalope, whom Carvalho calls Welluchas. Milligan also dispells the notion that Alexis Godey was a member of the fifth expedition. Jessie Benton Frémont initiated the idea in her manuscript entitled "Great Events," which is the unpublished second volume of Frémont's *Memoirs of My Life* (1887). The error is repeated by Ferol Egan, Frémont's most recent biographer. *See* Jessie Benton Frémont, "Great Events During the Life of Major General John C. Frémont," (MS, Bancroft Liby., Univ. of Calif. at Berkeley), 180; and Egan, *Frémont,* 494.

[17] In the summer of 1831, Dr. Johnston Lykins and family arrived at the Shawnee Reserve to establish a Baptist mission among the Shawnees. In 1831 Lykins constructed a house for his family on the tract of land east of the Missouri-Kansas border and began mission activities, although construction of mission buildings was delayed until the following year. The mission was constructed in present Johnson Co. KS, and continued its operation until mid-1855. *See* Barry, *Beginning of the West,* 205; and Schultz, *An Indian Canaan: Isaac McCoy,* 156-57.

to assist in putting up, Fuller and I with the independence evacuated and took the praire for it much to the discomfiture of the Worthy Corps who remained under the wreck of the tent Sleepless until morning.

September 20th 1853. Col. Fremont returned to Kansas to telegraph on business connected with the expedition. During his absence Mr. Bomer tried to take a view of the camp and after several unsuccessful efforts gave up in despair that his new project was no go without the aforesaid "darkened chamber." Quite a discussion between the Corps as [to] the practicability of taking Daguerreotype upon Bomer's principle in the open air which resulted in Mr. Bomer's resignation from the expedition and return to Westport, where no doubt his theory may be more successful.[18]

September 21st 1853. Struck camp at an early hour. Packed the animals, and after several little accidents peculiar to packers proceed again on our long journey. The animals doing much better than yesterday but occasionally a restive mule made us industrious by securing him and readjusting their packs. After proceeding several miles at a pace which averaged several miles in as many hours, we encamped at the Methodist Mission[19] for the night, where

[18] According to Carvalho, Frémont was uncertain whether Carvalho's or Bomer's process would produce a better photograph. Once the expedition reached Westport, Frémont ordered a contest under field conditions. Carvalho completed his daguerreotype within half an hour. Bomer's photograph required development overnight. This unacceptable delay cost Bomer his job. *See* Carvalho, *Incidents of Travel,* 24; Rudisill, *Mirror Image,* 102-103; and Newhall, *Daguerreotype in America,* 88-89.

[19] Reverend Thomas Johnson established the Shawnee Methodist Mission and Indian Manual Labor School in Oct. 1839 on a two-thousand-acre site in present Johnson County, KS. By 1851 the mission school trained Indian children as well as a considerable number of settlers' children. Kansas Territory's first governer established his offices at the mission in 1854, and it housed the first territorial legislature. The school was closed in 1862. *See* Caldwell, *Annals of Shawnee Methodist Mission;* and Ross, "The Old Shawnee Mission," 417-35.

we enjoyed luxuries which as many a weary day will come before we have the pleasure of again doing so. Mr. Strobel,[20] late of Gov. Stevens' expedition, camped with us, and after making all secure for the night I retired quite fatigued from the labours of the day. Tender to Mr. Strobel the hospitality of our camp by inviting him to our tent for the night. Col. Fremont complaining of indisposition, which forbodes at least delay for the Expedition, and at this late Season delays may prove more dangerous than at present anticipated.

September 22nd 1853. My anticipations last night are certainly verified this morning by Col. Fremont informing the camp in consequence of his increased indisposition he is compelled to return to Westport and perhaps to St. Louis for Medical advice.[21] This unlooked for delay forbodes no good to the success of the expedition and I feel exceedingly depressed in consequence of it. He appoints Smith's old mission[22] near Union Town[23] as the place of

[20] *See* Appendix, pp. 269-70, for a sketch of Strobel.

[21] Max Strobel accompanied Frémont to Westport but returned shortly thereafter. Frémont's health had not improved when he reached Independence on Sept. 23. Unable to find adequate medical help, he booked passage the following day for St. Louis on the steamer *Clara.* He arrived in St. Louis on Sept. 27. The *Missouri Republican* reported that his return had been "forced upon him by ill health." St. Louis *Daily Evening News,* Sept. 9, 1853; St. Louis *Daily Missouri Republican,* Sept. 9 and 28, 1853; and Carvalho, *Incidents of Travel,* 29.

[22] Dr. Johnston Lykins established the Potawatomi Baptist Mission in Mar. 1848 under the auspices of the American Indian Mission Association. The mission, located in present Shawnee Co. KS, was situated on Mission Creek near its confluence with the Kansas River, about nine miles downstream from Uniontown (about six miles west of modern Topeka). Reverend B.W. Sanders and his wife opened the mission in Sept. 1849, and soon thereafter Lykins opened an Indian boarding school known as the Potawatomi Manual Labor School. There is no record of a Reverend Smith having served at the mission. However, Sidney W. Smith moved to Uniontown in 1848, and in 1852 homesteaded immediately northwest of the Potawatomi Baptist Mission Farm. Smith opened a ferry across the Kansas that same year, which he operated for several years. Smith's proximity to the Potawatomi Mission explains why Milligan associated Smith's name with the mission. *See* Barry, *Beginning of the West,* 741, 800, 889-90, 1062 and 1088; and Haines, *Historic Sites,* 40.

[23] Indian agents R.W. Cummins and A.J. Vaughn established Uniontown in Mar.

Rendezvous and there await his coming or further orders. Packed up and started. We had not proceeded far before we missed one of our most valuable mules and pack and after several hours search without finding the lost animal we fortunately had her brought to us by two Indian boys who had overtaken her upon the road and returned pack and all safe. Remunerated them for their trouble by giving them a $. It is my opinion these young Denizens of the prairie knew exactly how she came to leave the Cavayard[24] but on this occasion we were very glad to receive the animal without further search, which would cause more delay than desirable in reaching the place of rendezvous where we were to be joined by our 10 Deleware Indians employed as Hunters for the Party. Camped on Kill Creek[25] for the night. A drunken Indian who came into camp caused us a great deal of diversion by his antics and also caused some uneasiness for the loose things which were laying about, which no doubt the Gentleman would be particularly desirous to obtain, not being less conscientious by having the advantage of an established mission in his Country and listening every Sunday to a lesson of ignorance from the pulpit of the aforesaid mission. When the gentleman stayed as long as courtesy of the Plains would admit, I gave him a gentle invite to retire as it was now getting too late for any company but that of the camp. Grass at this camp exceedingly poor. Fed the animals with corn we procured

---

1848, as the official Potawatomi trading post. It was situated in present western Shawneee Co., KS, on the south bank of the Kansas River. Uniontown functioned as a trading post as well as a supply depot for California and Oregon-bound emigrants through 1853. Carvalho noted that "two or three stores with no assortment of goods, and about thirty shanties make up the town." *See Barry, Beginning of the West,* 737-38, 949; Mattes, *Great Platte River Road,* 139; and Carvalho, *Incidents of Travel,* 31.

[24] Cavayard = remuda. Milligan used the term to include the saddle horses and mules as well as the pack mules.

[25] Kill Creek heads north of Gardner, KS. It flows through Johnson Co. joining Spoon Creek, which in turn enters the Kansas immediately east of DeSoto, KS.

at an Indian House close by. Wood plenty but not so handy as might be desired.

September 23d 1853. Up and under weigh early in consequence of being compelled to make the next desirable camp where we can procure those things most essential to a traveller of the Prairies, viz. wood and water with good pasturage for the Animals. Mr. Palmer after proceeding some distance discovered that he had lost his small arms, viz. Revolver and Bowie Knife. He retraced his steps and found them where he had very carelessly layed them at our deserted camp on Kill Creek. Animals doing well after we arrived in Camp late in consequence of long drive. Several of the animals which were packed with the hampers were found to be severely chafed. It will be essential on our arrival at the rendezvous to dispense with these ponderous articles and substitute something which can be carried upon a mule with more ease to the animal. The success of our trip in a manner depends upon saving our animals as much as possible. During the day passed two waggons on their way to Union Town with goods for the traders of that Post situated on Caw River 90 miles from its mouth, in the midst of a well-wooded and fertile country and destined ere long to become sought by those who will add more to its improvement by settling and cultivating it.

September 24th 1853. In consequence of our long drive yesterday and our animals being and the animals appearing a little stiff, we made a short drive and camped on a well wooded creek called Chunge Nunge.[26] We here learned that our Deleware Hunters had been several days awaiting

[26] Shunganunga Creek heads in central Shawnee Co., KS, flows toward the northeast through Topeka, entering the Kansas northwest of Tecumseh. Mrs. Julia Ann Stinson, who lived on the Shunganunga in 1853, remembered meeting Frémont, and recalled that his men camped in the vicinity. *See* Statement of Mrs. Julia Ann Stinson, Apr. 15, 1914 (MS, Stinson Coll., Kansas State Hist. Soc., Topeka).

us at Smith's Mission. Procured from an Indian some corn for our mules which was quite a treat for our poor jaded beasts. Found that several of the mules were badly galled in consequence of the carelessness of the packers in not properly adjusting the blankets under the saddles. Camped near my old camp of 1850 when with the Salt Lake mail.

September 25th 1853. Met our Indian Hunters at the appointed place, who accompanied us to our camp at the Big Spring.[27] Before arriving at camp I was taken with a violent fever and was compelled to dismount. Was taken into camp and well provided for as the circumstances of our situation would admit. Mr. Carvalho gave me some pills which broke the fever upon me. Attribute the fever to overexertion and excitement attendant upon our starting with raw hands and unbroken mules.

September 26th 1853. Feel exceedingly relieved this morning, so well indeed that I am again at my post much to the dissatisfaction of my estimable friend Fuller, who with his Kind attentions has endeared him to me more than ever. Took the mules which were bought after leaving Westport to the Mission Shop at Union Town to get shod. Was unable to get them shod in consequence of not being able to procure an order from the Agent. Majors' train[28]

---

[27] Big Springs (Coon Hollow) is situated in Douglas Co., KS, near the community of Big Springs. The springs were located on a fork in the Oregon Trail, one branch leading up the Kansas to the Uniontown Ferry, the other branch turning directly north to Papin's Ferry at the lower crossing near modern Topeka. John W. Gunnison, who camped at Big Springs in the summer of 1853, noted that the springs were located in a hollow about two hundred yards from the main road. The springs consisted of "several small jets from the bank." *See* Haines, *Historic Sites,* 37-38; and *Reports of Explorations and Surveys,* II:14.

[28] Alexander Majors (1814-1900) entered the Santa Fe Trade in 1848 with six wagons. Headquartered in Westport, he ran a successful freighting operation as an independent contractor until 1855, when he joined the partnership of William H. Russell and William B. Waddell. The famous firm of Russell, Majors, and Waddell specialized in military freighting, and dominated plains' freighting during the 1850s.

Majors was not traveling with the freight train which Milligan saw returning from

from Santa Fe by the new Fort Reilly[29] camped near us. Wrote a few lines by them.

September 27th 1853. Mr. Strobel arrived this morning from the Colonel with dispatches to proceed out as far as Buffalo and there await his arrival from St. Louis, to which place he returned for medical advice. Made preparations for a start to the Hunting Grounds.

September 28th 1853. Substituted Small Boxes (quilted on the Sides to prevent chafing) in lieu of the large Basket Hampers.[30] Covered the girths also with robes to prevent chafing their bellys. Had a relapse of the fever and while confined to my tent a sudden squall of wind blew it down and the pole fell across my nose and cut considerably. John Campbell's train, from Fort Laramie on their return to the states consisting of 21 waggons, 14 of which were loaded with Buffalo robes for R. & W. Campbell of St. Louis Mo.[31] Wrote by Mr. Campbell to Father and the Editor of the "Missouri Democrat."[32]

Santa Fé. On Sept. 15 he was at Fort Leavenworth, signing a contract to transport army freight to Fort Union, NM, at the rate of $16 per one hundred pounds. *See* Majors, *Seventy Years on the Frontier,* 140; Barry, *Beginning of the West,* 1178; and Lass, *From the Missouri to the Great Salt Lake,* 45-48.

[29] Fort Riley had been in existence a little over four months when Milligan passed by. Situated on the north side of the Kansas River opposite the junction of the Republican and Smoky Hill rivers on a site selected by Bvt. Major Edmund A. Ogden in Oct. 1852, it was the first named Camp Center since it was near the geographical center of the United States. In late June 1853, the post was renamed in honor of the late Major General Bennett Riley. Although Milligan noted limestone buildings, major construction did not begin until 1855. For a chronology of events at the post in 1853, *see* Barry, *Beginning of the West,* 1154-55; Frazer, *Forts of the West,* 57; and Hart, *Old Forts of the Southwest,* 113-15.

[30] The boxes were used to carry Carvalho's daguerreotype camera and equipment. Carvalho was convinced that the muleteers had sabotaged the baskets originally used to pack his camera equipment because it was bulky and difficult to load onto mules. Carvalho broke up some old dry-goods boxes for lumber and headed for a blacksmith's shop near Uniontown. Since the smith was not home, he fashioned the camera boxes himself, using a borrowed saw and hatchet. *See* Carvalho, *Incidents of Travel,*, 32.

[31] Robert Campbell (1804-1879) was a prominent St. Louis businessman and financier

September 29th 1853. Made a start in the direction of Smoking Hill fork[33] where we purpose camping and should the Buffalo be plenty as expected we will cure enough meat to last us to the Mountains. Solomon acted as guide having accompanied Col. Fremont over the same route before. Suffered exceedingly in consequence of having the fever still upon me. Fuller attended to my duty. Mules and packs becoming steady. Camped [on] Stony creek[34] above the Pottawatomi village. Mr. Palmer went to the village in order to procure a chicken for me. Rained all night incessantly.

September 30th 1853. Rained all day without intermission which with my fever added much to my uncomfortable situation. Fuller in constant attendance upon me. Did not of course move camp and made everything as comfortable as possible. Towards night felt much worse.

October 1st 1853. Made another start. Had the first sight of Antelope today. The Indians found it impossible to approach within shot as they were too shy. Made 22 mile

---

whose business interests were concentrated in the western fur trade. He and William Campbell were partners in the firm of R. & W. Campbell, which specialized in the buffalo robe trade on the Upper Missouri and the Great Plains. The company also supplied Indian trade goods and operated freighting outfits. Robert Campbell entered the Rocky Mountain fur trade in 1824 and spent most of the following decade in the mountains in association with Jed Smith, Thomas Fitzpatrick, Jim Bridger, and the Sublette brothers, before settling down in St. Louis. President Fillmore appointed him commissioner of the Fort Laramie Treaty Council of 1851. John G. Campbell was his nephew and a native of Philadelphia. *See Barry, Beginning of the West,* 708, 875, 881, 948, 1087, and 1113; and Carter, "Robert Campbell," in Hafen ed., *The Mountain Men and the Fur Trade of the Far West,* VIII:49-60.

[32] A search of the *Daily Missouri Democrat* and several other St. Louis newspapers failed to reveal this letter. *See* note 47 below.

[33] Smoking Hill Fork = Smoky Hill River.

[34] This was probably Mill Creek, which heads in Wabaunsee Co. and flows to the northeast, entering the Kansas about three miles upstream from Willard. It is likely that the explorers followed up this stream for several miles as they traveled west toward Fort Riley.

and camped at the junction of Ash and Rock creek.[35] Heard the drum at fort Reilly. Fever still upon me. The hunters killed several deer.

October 2d 1853. Passed Fort Reilly on our right. Found it situated at the junction of Solomon's[36] and Republican fork of Kansas river. The buildings are of limestone and there is a fine saw mill above it on the Republican. Camped at an old Indian Camp on Crow creek[37] and found plenty of Timber which was quite desirable.

October 3d 1853. Called camp at an early hour and started. Crossed Solomon's fork. Several of the mules mired after unpacking and larieting them. Succeeded in getting them out. Wet some of our provision. After crossing the stream, ascended it for a few miles and camped upon its bank. Feel much better from the effects of the fever and I think much stronger. The Surrounding Country rough and only the bottoms adapted to Cultivation.

October 4th 1853. Lee, the Colonel's servant, with one of the Delewares for a guide returned to Smith's Mission agreeable to the Colonel's instructions to conduct him to our designated Camp on Salt creek,[38] where we are to

---

[35] Ash and Rock creek = Humboldt and Clark creeks, which flow northward to the Kansas River through Morris and Geary counties. Their confluence is about three miles southeast of Fort Riley and about four miles south of the point where Clark Creek enters the Kansas. John W. Gunnison, who crossed Clark Creek on July 3, 1853, noted: "It is rightly named Big Stone, for at the ford we found its bed covered with boulders." *See Reports of Explorations and Surveys,* II:16.

[36] Solomon's Fork = Smoky Hill River. The Solomon River flows into the Smoky Hill River immediately south of the town of Solomon on the Dickinson-Saline Co. line. The Smoky Hill joins the Republican River near Junction City to form the Kansas River.

[37] Crow Creek = Lyon Creek, which flows northeastward through Dickinson and Geary counties. It enters the Smoky Hill River about one mile north of Wreford, KS. This was a logical point to cross the Smoky Hill to its left bank. Immediately upstream from the confluence, the bluffs on the right bank encroach to the river, restricting travel on that side.

[38] Salt Creek = Saline River. The Saline flows into the Smoky Hill River from the northwest. It enters the Smoky Hill about five miles east of Salina, KS.

remain until his arrival. Mr. Strobel lost the Col's riding horse through negligence in not securing him with the Cavayard. Had the first sight of Buffalo today in the shape of an old Bull. The Hunters, followed by the whole party, out for a chase. In the excitement the whole Cavayard were left. The poor old Bull fell pierced within 20 miles after the exciting chase of upwards of an hour. Camped on the Saline fork of the Kansas river. Buffalo in sight during the day. Our hunters returned abundantly supplied with Bull meat, no cows being seen. All hands busily engaged cooking to their own taste. The Scientific Corps in ecstasy at the prospect of such a sumptuous repast. Came very near losing my life by being too familiar with one of our Indians. I drew my butcher Knife across his head pretending to scalp him and in so doing came near losing my own. Dangerous fun. Had I not been a general favourite among them, I should certainly have fallen a victim to my own incredulity.

October 5th 1853. All hands with the exception of the hunters busily engaged cutting and drying meat for our journey through the mountains at places [in] which game may be scarce. Strobel returned with Indian guide to Solomon's fork to look for the Horse lost yesterday. The Indians preparing for a Big Hunt tomorrow. Strobel returned at night having been unsuccessful in his search for the lost Horse. Kept watch for the first time since my recovery. Now in good Health. A great number of wolf around camp all night coming within a few yards of the fire. Dare not fire upon them for fear of alarming the camp.

October 6th 1853. The Delewares started on a big hunt about 20 miles up the Smoky Hill fork where cows are plenty. Around camp nothing but Bulls. Sent the Mexican Frank with them in charge of a pack mule to bring in meat.

Had a fight with the fire, the Prairie have caught near our camp. Came near burning the Indian's tent up. The Hunters returned loaded with choice meat. Enjoyed a Hump rib feast. Cut & dried what was not used. Indian Summer which is very pleasant. Had quite a sumptuous repast of Hump rib and pumpkins. Enjoyed it far better than the less wholesome repast of a city life. Here luxurys are procured which a King may well envy. With but thanks to an all bountiful providence and a steady hand to aim at the Game. All night the monotony of the Camp was broken in upon by a general chorus of the Howl of the wolf and the owl's screetch with an occasional higher note from some mule scared by the appearance of some wolf more daring than his fellows within the bounds of our corral.

October 7th 1853. This morning our Camp presents the appearance of a Game Depot on a large scale, having everything in the game line from a teal duck to a Buffalo. Quite at a loss what species of Game to make our repast of. Commenced shoeing the mules, but in consequence of my late attack of fever I found myself too weak and consequently was compelled to desist. During my watch pleasant & clear.

October 8th 1853. Commences clear & pleasant. Part of the Indians on a hunt and part looking for their horses, three of which strayed from the Gang last night. Let (Fremont) my pony run loose today for the first time. Shoed two mules and Capt Wolf's (Deleware Capt) horse. Abundance of small game in camp. Commenced drying some KinnaKinic.[39] Two of the Indians taken with the fever. Our party all well and exceedingly hearty. The

[39] Kinnikinnick is a term of Algonquian origin with many variant spellings. It is a mixture of dried leaves and bark such as sumac leaves and the inner bark of dogwood. It was often mixed in tobacco. It was commonly smoked on the frontier when tobacco was in short supply.

Hunters returned loaded with meat & Game. They brought in some fat cow, the first we have yet had. The Scientific Corps had an opportunity to judge between Bull and fat cow meat. Saddled my pony and took a hunt for the mules. Drove them in and picketed them for the night.

October 9th 1853. Commences clear & chilly. The Thermometer stands this morning at 50°. Yesterday it stood 85°, quite a sudden change. Employed cutting up and drying meat. Felt a touch of the Rheumatism in my knees. Mr. Palmer and myself had a little misunderstanding, but it was soon settled. I notice a general dissatisfaction among the Indians and all the cause I can attribute it to is the protracted absence of the colonel. We expect him daily.

October 10th 1853. Commences clear and pleasant with wind from the E[d]. The Hunters started out after Buffalo. No cows to be had near camp. Our presence here has caused them to be quite shy. Made a narrow escape today in shoeing a wild mule. We were compelled to throw him with a lariat and tie his legs so that he could not stir. I commenced trimming his feet to fit the shoe and while so engaged by some means he got loose and I became entangled in the rope. The rope was immediately cut and I narrowly escaped being kicked to death. Employed drying meat. Two Indians sick with the fever. Getting tired of the monotony of the Camp. Wish to be on the trail. Colonel anxiously looked for. Had a mess of granola or Indian Hominy. A stampede took place among our mules. Did not lose any. Indian sign in the neighborhood.

October 11th 1853. Commences hazy with drizzling rain. Five of our mules missed this morning. Sent Carter (Wyandott Indian) to look for them. Cut some more forks and poles to dry meat upon. The Sick Indians better this morning. Rearranged the packs with rawhide lashings in place of rope. Feel stiff today from the effects of my accident with the mule yesterday. Four of the Hunters started out on a Hunt, the Buffalo being high up the river. They are not expected back tonight. Done some washing today. Took a hunt for two stray mules. Brown (Wyandott Indian) down with the fever.

October 12th 1853. Commences hazy but pleasant. All the Camp more or less down with the dysentery. Three of the Indians horses took the back track for home. Sent a party in search of them. The Hunters returned with plenty of cow meat. Moved our Camp higher up the creek. The prairie caught fire and came near burning everything up. The fire originated from our old Camp. Quite a busy time to extinguish it before it got a good start. All the blankets about Camp in requisition. After the excitement of the fire I took a cool bath in the creek and feel quite refreshed from it.

October 13th 1853. Commences clear & pleasant. The Indians which went in search of the runaway animals returned not having seen any sign of them. Brown the Wyandott very sick. Pack saddles all in order. Appearances of rain. Picketed the mules in fresh Grass.

October 14th 1853. Commences cloudy but pleasant. Sent two Indians to Fort Reilly in hopes that the missing animals might have been taken up as they passed that place. Also sent an order for some salt & other provision to the Commissary at the fort. Caught the 2 American mules, threw them down and washed the sores caused by the chafing of the pack saddles. Feel exceedingly depressed in spirits at the prolonged absence of the Colonel. Commenced a long letter to my club the "Earthquake Rangers."[40]

[40] Milligan's volunteer fire company in St. Louis called itself the Earthquake Rangers. It was a unit in the Missouri Fire Co. and served as a social club. The name probably celebrates the earthquakes of 1811 and 1812 which centered in New Madrid, MO.

Shod a horse for Capt. Wolf (Deleware chief). Heard firing to the W^{d}. Supposed to be Caw Indians on a hunt. Up to this date our party have killed 30 Buffalo, 2 only of which were Cow. A large Gang of Elk passed near the Camp.

October 15th 1853. Commences rainy. One of our Hunters killed an Antelope, the first we have had in the Camp. Washed all the mules' sores and herded them on the opposite side of the creek in taller Grass. Got a good supply of wood in Camp. Preparing for rain. Brown a little better. Troubled myself with a nervous Headache.

October 16th 1853. Commenced raining during the morning watch. Camp entirely out of sugar & salt. The latter we miss exceedingly in consequence of having nothing but fresh meat. Some of the Indians out on a hunt, others engaged shoeing their ponys. Brown very sick during the night. He will be compelled to return in consequence of being so debilitated by the fever to attempt the trip. Expect our express today which went to Fort Reilly. The wolfs came into camp last night and destroyed the better part of our meat which we were drying. All hands out of patience waiting on Colonel Fremont. The Indians getting exceedingly dissatisfied, having great fear of cold weather. The prairie on fire all around us. Rained during the night.

October 17th 1853. Commences pleasant. Our express arrived from Fort Reilly with salt and other provision. The Camp in better spirits at the prospect of a feast. The news from the fort in regard to the Colonel is that he returned to St. Louis for medical advice which will delay the expedition at least two weeks longer. Capt. Wild Cat[41] and party on a trapping expedition, visited the camp who has been out about one month and has secured 25 fine large Beaver Skins. Fires are around us.

October 18th 1853. Commences foggy. All hands out looking for a valuable mule which has been gone two days. The Indians out on a Deer Hunt. Did not find the mule. Had Slap Jacks for supper which went fine with buffalo meat. I expect if the Colonel does not arrive soon all the Indians will return very much dissatisfied at the long delay which unfortunately has taken place beyond the power of the most zealous in the prosperity of the expedition. Had not the Colonel been compelled to return we would have ere this encountered the snows of the Sierra Nevada and our trip would have been completed in the time proposed, viz. 60 days. Our Camp is not as yet regularly organized and consequently some little contention prevails among the white portion of it. The Colonel's presence would add much to the general Harmony of it and future prospects. Mr. W.H. Palmer, the person Colonel Fremont gave up charge to, is inexperienced in the management of a Camp and further more does not possess courage or resolution to carry out order and discipline, for the welfare of the expedition depends entirely on these first principles which if properly carried out cannot fail to be crowned with success.

October 19th 1853. Commences cloudy with prospect of rain. All but the Camp guard turned out for a last and general Hunt for the missing mules but without success. In consequence of our present camp becoming unpleasant from the smell of spoiled meat, we up sticks and made a General move of bag & baggage to a more desirable location one mile to the E[d] where pasturage and other requisites for a good Camp are handy. Washington &

[41] Not to be confused with the Seminole Chief Wild Cat, whom Milligan mentioned in his entry of Mar. 18, 1854. Wild Cat, the Delaware, is listed in the 1862 Delaware Census as well as the Delaware Allotment Treaty of May 1860. Wild Cat was 25 in 1853. *See* Delaware Census for Feb. 15, 1862; and Delaware Allotment Treaty Allottees, May, 1860 (MSS, Witcher Coll., Oklahoma Hist. Soc.).

Caperessis (Delawares) went about 20 mile to the N^d^ in order to get among some good fat cows. No flour in Camp.

October 20th 1853. Commences with thick fog and rain. Went in company with Capt. Wolf to hunt mules. Found one of the long lost strays shortly after parting with Capt. Wolf. She was fast by her lariat to the root of a tree were no doubt she had been for several days. Several large wolfs were near at hand ready to pounce upon her. Shot one of the largest of the gang which I venture to say in regard to size had but few equals. One of the Wild Cat's trappers came into Camp and informed us that he had seen a large Black mule on the East side of Salt creek. During the night a heavy storm of rain with thunder and lightning.

October 21st 1853. Commences cloudy with prospects of rain. General appearance of the weather dark and gloomy. Feelings in accordance with the weather. Mr. Palmer & John Johnny Cake (Delaware) went to Fort Reilly after provision. Wrote by them to Father and my friends. Expressed my opinions freely in regard to the future success and operations of the expedition. The Delawares, in order to dispel the gloom and monotony of the time, started on a hunt to be gone three or four days. They took with them several pack animals to bring in the meat. They go out after cow and may have to go some distance as the Buffalo are making to the S^d^ [southward] a sure sign of a hard winter. Branded the remainder of the mules with the Colonel's Mark. My faithful steed affected with the distemper which has brought him down considerable. Went on the East Side of Salt creek for the Black mule seen a day since by Wild Cat's man. The Black mule proved to be a large Buck Elk. Seen a fox and gave him chase to try the Heels of my pony. Find that they are good. During the night very cold with a heavy black frost. The water froze ½ inch thick in our buckets.

October 22d 1853. Commences clear and cold with the wind from the N^{d} & E^{d}. Frank the Mexican and Carter (Wyandott) started over on Caw river to take a final hunt for the Black mule which so far has not been found. Out of fresh meat until the Hunters arrive from the chase. One month today since the Colonel left us. Our Hunters returned loaded with meat of the fattest cows. Report Buffalo plenty to the N^{d} & W^{d}. During the Hunt one of the Indians shot a wild horse from among a Band of Buffalo.

October 23d 1853. Commences clear & very cold. During the night the water in the buckets froze tight. Thermometer at daylight 15°, at sunrise 18°. Cold weather now regularly set in. Our camp at present is well protected from the northerly winds by a wide strip of Timber. Found thick underclothes exceedingly comfortable. The wolfs made a descent last night again on our dried meat but with the loss of one of their number. Mr. Fuller succeeded in shooting one more bold than the rest, which came rather closer to him than was desired.

October 24th 1853. Commences clear & cold with heavy black frost flying. The Hunters started out on a Deer Hunt up Caw river. Had a little excitement in Camp at breakfast between Mr. Strobel and Frank the Mexican. The former individual, whose gluttonous propensities were predominant, drank all the Coffee, leaving the Mexican short of ration but eager for a fight. Let the mules loose to graze. Find my pony improving and recovering from the distemper which he had had for some time. Had a feast of Hump rib Soup & Coon. Trouble today with the d-d rheumatism. A party of trappers were seen today on Kaw river by the Hunters.

October 25th 1853. Commences cloudy with wind from

N^{d} & W^{d} & cold with prospect of Snow. Drove the Cavayard in the timber to protect them from the Storm. Found an increase in our Cavayard by Strobel's mare having a colt. It froze during the night. All Hand[s] still impatient at the long delay and, not hearing from the Colonel, have no doubt but the expedition is broken up and look soon for our recall. This to me will be exceedingly unfortunate and extremely unfortunate as many of my future prospects depend on the success of the expedition.

Since writing the above, Mr. Palmer has returned from Fort Reilly bringing papers containing news calculated to raise our much depressed spirits. The papers state that the Colonel "has recovered and will proceed on the trip at all hazards."[42] We all are on the Qui Vive and exceedingly anxious for his arrival. Hailed very hard during the storm. The tent blew down. The Scientific Corps had to raise and secure it. Our side all tight.

October 26th 1853. Commences with wind from the N^{d} & E^{d} and snowing. Drove the Ponys to the timber for shelter from the snow. Found one of our best mules with his neck broken, having become entangled in his lariat during the night. Caught a wild buck. A fair foot race. Divided blankets with my Pony.

October 27th 1853. Commences clear & cool with wind from the N^{d} & E^{d}. The Hunters started on a Deer Hunt with one pack mule. Employed at Target Shooting. Won Egloffstein's share of pancakes. Shot 2x with Carvalho. Cleaned my arms and got them in order. The Hunters returned with plenty of doe's meat. The "Aurora Borealis" visible in the N^{d} & E^{d}.

---

[42] The St. Louis *Daily Evening News* reported that Frémont left St. Louis on Oct. 15 aboard the steamer *Clara*. *See* the St. Louis *Daily Evening News*, Oct. 17, 1853; and the St. Louis *Weekly Tribune*, Oct. 21, 1853.

October 28th 1853. Commences clear and pleasant. Light frost during the night. Employed Target Shooting. Won a pan cake at pistol shooting and lost it with the carbine. Met with a serious misfortune. Burnt my boots, the only pair I had. As necessity is the mother of invention, I managed to mend them, but I expect to suffer *some.* All hand[s] living with boots and Caps with Skins of various animals to protect their extremities from the cold we most certainly will encounter. The Hunters returned without any meat, reporting the Buffalo all making to the S^{d} which among mountain men indicates the sure sign of a hard winter.

October 29th 1853. Commences clear and pleasant with light frost and wind from the N^{d} & E^{d}. Fuller out for small game. Being a good sportsman, he always returns with a full pouch. Egloffstein being in particular want of a wolf's skin, he is watching the Carcass of the mule which broke its neck a few nights since. So infatuated is he with the sport that he has been for the past 15 hours exposed to the cold and enjoying the luxuries of being seated on a limb of a tree. His watchfulness has at last been rewarded by killing one after firing at least 20 shots at them.[43] Mr. Strobel, in

[43] Carvalho was amused at von Egloffstein's persistence, and wrote the following account of the wolf hunt: "Our engineer, who wanted a wolfskin for a saddle-cloth, determined to remain to kill one of them. I assisted him to ascend a high tree immediately over the body of the mule, untied the lariat, and attaching his rifle to one end of it, pulled it up to him. The rest of the party returned to camp. About four o'clock in the afternoon, he being still out, I roasted some buffalo meat and went to seek him. I found him still on the tree, quietly awaiting an opportunity to kill his wolf. A heroic example of perseverance on an eminence smiling at disappointment.

Mr. Egloffstein declined to come down; I told him of the dangers to which he was exposed, and entreated him to return to camp. Finding him determined to remain, I sent him up his supper, and returned to camp, expecting him to return at sundown.

About this time the prairie was on fire just beyond the belt of woods through which Col. Fremont had to pass. Becoming alarmed for Mr. Egloffstein, several of us went to bring him in. We found him half-way to camp dragging by the lariat the dead body of an immense wolf which he had shot. We assisted him on with his booty as well as we could." Carvalho, *Incidents of Travel,* 57-58.

going to assist his friend to bring in his wolf, was attacked by these ferocious beasts and but for his presence of mind would have been devoured. His revolver and shot gun marked several of them. The circumspect young Corps rebelled in consequence of Mr. Strobel being ordered to keep watch by Mr. Palmer. They proposed to take horses and go into Fort Reilly, but, as I had charge of the Cavayard, I showed *my authority* and prevented their so doing. And to bring them under submission they were forbidden the tent, and, as it was exceedingly cold, their temperament was affected with the air and they came down.

October 30th 1853. Commences clear and pleasant. Egloffstein after being up all night still infatuated with the sport of Wolf killing and has repaired with his gun to the old spot and resumed the sport. John Johnny Cake (Deleware) and Amos (Wyandott Boy) returned to the States in consequence of being *afraid* to proceed, they giving as an excuse the lateness of the Season and not having the proper outfit to proceed. Wrote to Father about the general condition of the Camp and presented the future prospects of the expedition.[44]

October 31st 1853. Commences clear & pleasant and exceedingly windy. Endeavored to drive the mules over Salt creek where there was better pasturage. Succeeded by getting part of them over but in consequence of the ford becoming too mirey recrossed higher up the creek and herded them near Camp. Fuller after small game returned with a good supply. Suffering exceedingly with cramps and dysentery. Darned my socks which needed repair.

Strangers in sight appear to be whites. Feel quite overjoyed at the Strangers' near approach. Prove to be Col. Fremont, Doct. Ebers,[45] Lee, & Solomon with a waggon from the Catholic Mission loaded with corn &c for the use

Frémont's Arrival

Woodcut of Frémont's arrival at camp on the Saline River in Kansas Oct. 31, 1853. From left: Dr. Ebers, Albert Lea, Frémont, and Solomon Everett.

From Bigelow's *Life of Frémont*

Prairie Fire

Engraving from an oil painting by James Hamilton entitled "Buffalos Escaping from Prairie Fire." Painted by Hamilton under Frémont's supervision using a Carvalho daguerreotype taken in western Kansas, Oct. 1853.

Published in Frémont's *Memoirs*.

of the expedition.[46] Made every preparation for the continuation of the expedition after our long and much regretted and as I fear unfortunate [delay], for at least some of us which are not endowed with the power of endurance. Camp roused out by the prairie being [on] fire near us. Drove the mules into the creek for preservation, and

[44] Excerpts from this letter were published in the *Daily Missouri Democrat* on Nov. 19 under the heading "Fremont's Expedition."

"A gentleman of this city has placed in our hands a letter written to him by a member of Col. Fremont's party, and dated 'Saline, Fork of the Kansas River, October 30th.' The party had been camping at this place for several weeks, anxiously waiting for Col. Fremont to join them, but he had not arrived at the date of the letter, although he left Independence on the 22d ult. The distance between that point and the camp is about three hundred and fifty miles.

"There was a great desire in the camp to get forward. The Indians of the party, particularly, manifested impatience at the delay. The weather was very cold, the thermometer standing at fifteen degrees, and there had been several hail and snow storms. The Indians predict a long and very severe winter, with much falling weather, and the reasons they assign for it are the appearance of the 'fire light,' as they call the aurora borealis, and the migration of the buffalo southward; the latter, they say, is an unfailing indication.

"The company are well armed, and have been employing their leisure time in acquiring a skillful use of their rifles. It is confidently asserted, that there is not a man in the party who cannot bring down a 'red skin,' at a distance of two hundred yards, with the greatest ease, should occasion require it.

"The health of the party was generally good, though some of them had experienced the ill effects of partaking too plentifully of buffalo meat before becoming accustomed to it.

"Mr. Egloffstein, the topographical engineer of the expedition, had made a thorough survey of the country lying around the encampment. The soil is rich and fertile, well timbered and watered, and is admirably adapted for settlement and cultivation. There are large quantities of stone in the bluffs suitable either for building or fencing."

[45] *See* Appendix, pp. 270-71 for a sketch of Ebers.

[46] Frémont arrived at Westport on Oct. 22 and was at Uniontown by Oct. 25. He crossed the Kansas and reached St. Mary's Potawatomi Catholic Mission the following day. The mission was established in Sept. 1848, by Father Felix L. Verreydt at the site of present St. Mary's, KS.

On Oct. 27th, Frémont enjoyed a breakfast of "good coffee and excellent bread" at the mission. He purchased from Father Duerinck "twenty-five dollars worth of provisions in corn, flour, sugar and beef, which he paid for in cash on the same day." With the borrowed wagon, he headed up the north side of the Kansas over a new military road which connected Fort Leavenworth to Fort Riley. Frémont's entries for Oct. 27-28 are the only extant segment of his 1853 journal. *See* Frémont, *Memoirs,* 27-28; Father Duerinck's diary in Garraghan, *The Jesuits,* II:656; and Barry, *Beginning of the West.* 773-74, 1007.

prepared to burn around our camp. Wind strong and variable which may preserve our Camp.

November 1st 1853. Commences clear & cold, wind from the N^{d} & E^{d}. Fire all around us. Called camp at 4 o'clock and made preparations for a start. Brown the Wyandott returned with the waggon. Wrote by this opportunity.[47] Got started at 11½ A.M. Diverged from our proposed line in consequence of not being able to cross the river. Packs worked well. Compelled to ride through the fire at full speed. Made about 10 mile and camped at a place with plenty of wood and water. Took charge of the Culinary Department of a newly formed mess. Frank the Mexican received a severe kick from his pony.

Col. Fremont at supper informed us that during his illness in St. Louis that he had seen communications from some gentleman in the Camp to the newspapers. I informed him that I was that individual. He requested me not to again do it as it was never customary in any of his former expeditions for any person but him, and also to give up all journals, that he would not *allow* one being kept by any person of the expedition. Mr. Fuller complyed with this exceedingly modest request but I did not.[48] The sequel of

---

[47] On Dec. 9 the *Daily Missouri Democrat* published the following article based upon Milligan's letter:

"FREMONT'S EXPEDITION

By a letter from the Saline Fork of the Kansas River, we learn that Col. Fremont arrived there and joined his company on the 31st of October, and would proceed on his expedition on the next day. The unexpected delay and the anticipation of an unusually cold winter, will make his journey toilsome and difficult, and probably subject him and his companions to many severe hardships. But he and they will go bravely through them. And these vigorous labors are undertaken at his own expense, that his government may be informed where the best route exists for building a great highway to the Pacific."

[48] A search of the *Daily Missouri Democrat* and other St. Louis newspapers failed to reveal this letter. Since Frémont did not know the identity of its author, we can presume that Milligan signed it with his nickname "Bricks," a name he signed to several letters published in the Wash., D.C. *States* between 1859-1861. Frémont, or his wife Jessie — who had hurried to his side after learning of his illness — probably saw the letter in the

this selfish demand of the Col. remains to be seen. Selfishness, the predominant feature with which he appears to be endowed, has been to me fully illustrated, and I look upon his success so far to the silence of those whom he has had brief power over, much to their discredit and want of that degree of Independence which all men ought to be endowed with but policy prohibits. How many men have fell by this the victims of a designing & intriguing man's ambition, backed by political intrigue and poor infatuated, incredulous would use smart men who have been but the tools for a greater one's designs.[49] My impressions *may* be wrong and I sincerely hope that I may be never led to explain:

> "Oh, my prophetic soul"[50] I knew it.
> Great men have greater ways
> Than poorer men with Smaller
> Says.

November 2nd 1853. Commences clear & cool. Came to Buffalo in Large Herds, but shy. The Hunters out among them. Had some trouble with the packs and preventing the mules stampeding in consequence of the Buffalo. Our route today lay through a beautiful and open country occasionally rough & broken. Stone mostly sand stone and on some creeks where we crossed noticed lime stone. Made

---

offices of the *Daily Missouri Democrat* and had it suppressed. It is significant that Frémont mentioned communications "to" the newspapers, not "in" the newspapers. It seems likely that the letter Frémont saw was never published.

The fact that few journals exist for previous Frémont expeditions indicates that Frémont's prohibition may have been a long-standing policy. Isaac Cooper, who kept a secret journal on his third expedition, noted that Frémont brought up the subject of journal-keeping early by announcing "his intention to have no journals kept in his camp," explaining that he would do his "own writing." *See* Montaignes, *The Plains,* 22.

[49] Milligan rewrote this sentence in a letter published in the Norfolk *Southern Argus* on Aug. 25, 1856. Milligan's corrected version read "How many men have fallen by this great want of independence, the victims of a designing and intriguing man's ambition, backed by strong political patronage."

[50] The quotation is from *Hamlet,* Act I.

24 mile and camped on Smoky Hill fork of Kansas river. Wood scarce mostly large Cotton Woods. Country surrounding rough appearance.

November 3d 1853. Commences clear & frosty. The Hunters which started out yesterday were led so far away by the excitement of the chase that they did not return last night. Indian sign about. Heard a gun fired to the W^{d}. Soon after discovered an Indian Camp on the river which proved to be Caws.[51] Buffalo thick. The Hunters all out. Frank (the Mexican) and myself took a Buffalo chase on our own hook. Found that my pony was a fine and fleet hunter. Killed three fat cows. All the Hunters returned to Camp. The country over which we travelled today is rough and broken with gravelly soil. Camped on Smoky Hill fork. Made 20 mile [to]day.

November 4th 1853. Commences clear and pleasant. Wind from the S^{d}. Crossed the Caw river and travelled S^{d} & W^{d}. Country broken and Sandy Soil. One of our mules gave out and we were compelled to leave him a prey for ravenous wolfs. Made 20 mile and camped. Wood plenty but grass bad in consequence of the immense Herds of Buffalo being over it lately.

November 5th 1853. Commences with wind from the N^{d} and cold. Travelling on the divide between two thickly timbered creeks. Country of a gently rolling character with a rich black soil. Passed several strata of hard rock similar to granite. Buffalo thick. A large Herd passed near us. Hunters out but the cows proved too fast for their horses. Camped on Walnut creek.[52] Made 25 mile.

---

[51] The Caw or Kansa Indians are Siouan speaking people, who in 1853 lived on a reservation situated on the north side of the Kansas River. The Kansa people migrated to Kansas from original homelands east of the Mississippi beginning in the mid-sixteenth century. Before 1800 they inhabited lands from the mouth of the Kansas River to its junction with the Republican. *See* Unrau, *The Kansa Indians.*

November 6th 1853. Commences cloudy with drizzling rain & sleet. Made about 15 mile and camped, it being too foggy and disagreeable to proceed. Cleared off toward evening. Daguerreotyped the surrounding country which is exceedingly beautiful and well adapted to cultivation with rich Sandy Soil. Some fine cows near on the divide between Cow[53] & Walnut creeks. Wolf out with Washington, our brave hunter. Timber thick of various kinds.

November 7th 1853. Commences cloudly with drizzling rain and sleet. Made a later start than usual. Saw a large band of Buffalo. Our Hunters killed a fine fat cow. Saw a wild pony among a Band of Buffalo, tryed to catch him but did not get even near enough to shoot him. Crossed Pawnee fork.[54] Country rough & broken, timber scarce. Travelled up the stream. Made about 20 mile and camped. Tryed to Daguerreotype but it proved too windy.

November 8th 1853. Commences clear & cold. Stopped and got out the Daguerreotype apparatus and sent out the Hunters after a Herd of Buffalo in sight to take a picture of the Hunt and surrounding country, which is level and good soil.

Washington run an old Bull out of the Herd within 10 yards of the Camera. Seignor Carvalho the artist beat a

[52] Walnut Creek heads in Lane and Ness counties and flows easterly through Ness, Rush, and Barton counties of KS. It enter the Arkansas from the north immediately east of Great Bend, Ks.

[53] Cow Creek heads in Barton Co., KS. It flows north of the Arkansas River in a southeasterly direction through Barton and Rice counties, entering the Arkansas at Hutchinson.

[54] The Pawnee River heads northwest of Dodge City. It flows toward the east, entering the Arkansas at Larned, Ks. Frémont's party struck the Pawnee River a few miles west of Larned. By traveling up the Pawnee instead of continuing to the Arkansas, the route along the Pawnee River was one of the several variants of the Santa Fé Trail which avoided the Great Bend. The route Frémont followed most closely approximated Heth's Cutoff, which left the Arkansas near Larned, followed up the Pawnee River, and struck the Arkansas again west of Ingalls. *See* A.B. Hulbert, "The Santa Fé Trail," map no. 25 (MS, Kansas State Hist. Soc.).

retreat and we met Mr. Bull with a shower of balls or he certainly would have run over some one of us.[55] Saw three ponys with a Band of Buffalo. A large Gang of Elk in sight but the Hunters could not approach near enough for a Shot. Made about 35 mile and camped near Pawnee fork.

Knocked the Mexican down for calling me a liar. Col. Fremont gave me a lecture about "contention in camp" and exercised his power "by suspending me from duty until I became better tempered."

November 9th 1853. Commences clear and moderately cool. Took a Daguerreotype view of the country. Saw immense Herds of Buffalo, Elk, and antelope. The plain literally covered with the former. Recrossed Pawnee fork. Saw Indian Sign in the creek and as this is the general crossing of war partys, I fear we are in a dangerous position from one tribe or another. The Sign indicated either Cheyanne or Arrapahoe. Camped on Pawnee fork. Timber and grass scarce.

November 10th 1853. Commences clear and pleasant. Missed three mules and two ponys. All hands out in Search. Capt. Wolf and myself struck a trail which satisfied us they were stolen. It must have been in the morning watch, for Egloffstein being on the watch this morning was caught asleep by his partner the Deleware. Replaced our pack animals by taking 4 of the Deleware Ponys. Made a start on the trail of the Indians. After travelling about 14 mile found one of the mules which the Indians had abandoned, it being give out, and they, no doubt learning by their scouts that we were upon their trail, left it in their hurry to escape being overtaken. Camped in order to rest the recovered mule. Was again restored to duty at my request

[55] Carvalho described his efforts to photograph bison. "I essayed, at different times, to daguerreotype them while in motion, but was not successful, although I made several pictures of distant herds." *See* Carvalho, *Incidents of Travel,* 64.

and went on the morning watch, having exclusive charge of the mules from four in the morning until eight at night. The morning watch is considered the most dangerous as the Indians generally chose a few hours before day to steal animals or attack a Camp as the case may be.

November 11th 1853. Commences hazy and thick. Left Pawnee fork & crossed the plateau between that stream and the Arkansas. Struck the Arkansas near Pawnee Fort.[56] Discovered a war party of Cheyannes. Our Delewares started to have a talk with which is done by Sign. Some of them came into Camp. They showed us 5 scalps which no doubt were Pawnees taken the same day our horses were stolen, which no doubt these gentle[men] have cached about here now and would take advantage of an opportunity to steal a few more, but we will from *experience* be more Careful and vigilant for the future. Hard work to collect enough wood to cook a scanty supper. Could not even find a tent pole and had to lay all night under wet Blankets. I particularly notice that the Col. is all right and snug in his little tent. Indians around all night crossing and recrossing the river all night.

November 12th 1853. Commences clear & pleasant. A War party of 17 Cheyannes travelling in company with us and every one "looking if we dare we would." Made about 15 mile and camped on an Island. Used dry willows for our fire. Found good grass. Took a view of the river country, generally rolling and level towards the river. Our Indian

[56] Lewis Garrard described Pawnee Fort in 1846 as "a grove of timber in which a war party of Pawnees, some years before, fortified themselves when besieged by a hostile tribe. Nothing now remains but a few crumbling logs to mark the site of this Indian bulwark." In 1839 Matt Field described the fort as "a ghostly looking place... enclosed on three sides by rude walls, composed of trunks and fallen limbs of old rotten trees." The "fort" was situated on the Arkansas in Gray Co. about five miles upstream from Ingalls. *See* Garrard, *Wah-to-yah and the Taos Trail* (Hafen, ed., *Southwest Historical Series*), VI:82; and Sunder, ed., *Matt Field on The Santa Fé Trail,* 107.

travelling companions left us and proceeded up the river.

November 13th 1853. Commences clear & pleasant. Left a mule which had given out. Saw a great number of Rattlesnakes and killed several during the day. Saw immense herds of Buffalo & Antelope. Camped on an Island. Wood scarce, grass tolerable.

November 14th 1853. Commences clear & pleasant. Left a mule, the same which was recovered after being stolen by the Indians on Pawnee Fork. Met a large war Party of Cheyanne Indians. Our mules travelling slowly in consequence of their feet being worn out. Took a view of the Country. Generally level and sandy, entirely destitute of timber.

November 15th 1853. Commences clear and pleasant. Took the west side of the river, for the purpose of getting better pasturage. Mules becoming worn down for want of sustenance. Several of us on foot in consequence of having no animals to ride. Gave up my pony for the packs. Fuller, the Wyandott and myself were compelled to wade the river about ¾ of a mile wide. Not so pleasant this late in the season. Found our party camped on the East side of the river. Shod two horses for the Delewares.

November 16th 1853. Commences clear and pleasant. My boots gave out. Borrowed a pair from Carvalho. Four of us afoot driving the broken down mules. A war party of Cheyannes in Company with us. Some of the Delewares traded ponys with them. Made about 13 mile and camped. The Cheyanne camped with us. Got our eyes open as experience has taught us to do so.

November 17th 1853. Commences cloudy. Four on foot and all hands likely to be so if we do not soon procure more animals. Can strictly say in the language of some eminent writer "foot sore and weary." My feet are now blistered from heel to toe and indeed so painful I can scarce stand upon them. Stopped behind to rest my feet and bring in a broken down mule. Arrived in camp late.

November 18th 1853. Commences cloudy with drizzling rain & sleet. The Col. with Doct. Eber and two Delewares went ahead and left the main body to follow. My feet very painful. Made about 8 mile which to me was 100, and camped near Bent's fort[57] and close to a large village of Cheyannes & Arrapahoes. On duty until 8 o'clock. Feet painful. Got some "*Pan Dulce*" from some Mexicans who were trading with the Indians. Camp full of Indians. Towards evening rained very hard.

November 19th 1853. Commences cloudy with drizzling rain. Preparing for continuing our journey. A Blacksmith from the Fort shoeing the best of the mules. Col. Fremont at the Fort buying mules, provisions, and other articles

---

[57] Milligan is referring to Bent's trading houses at Big Timbers. These log houses were situated in the bottomlands beneath Apache Stone Bluff on the north bank of the Arkansas, about 37 miles downriver from Bent's Old Fort and about a mile upstream from the site of Bent's New Fort. They were located opposite the town of Prowers, and about a mile downstream from the mouth of Graveyard Creek in Bent Co., CO. Old Fort Lyon (known as Fort Wise until 1862) was built on the site of Bent's trading houses in 1860.

According to W. M. Boggs, William Bent built log trading houses at this site "some years" prior to 1844. Boggs, who worked with Bent as a trader, noted that Bent lived at the trading houses with his family during the winter of 1844, where he carried on a successful buffalo robe trade with nearby Cheyenne and Arapaho villages. Boggs described the houses as "double log cabins."

Bent's New Fort had not yet been constructed when Frémont's party reached Big Timbers. Neither Gwinn Harris Heap nor John W. Gunnison's men mentioned Bent's New Fort in 1853. Heap passed the site in May. Gunnison and his men were in the vicinity in late July. Gunnison's German botanist, Frederick Kreutzfeldt, referred to "Bent's New Houses," while Gunnison noted "two or three log-houses occupied as a trading station by Mr. Wm. Bent during the past winter." *See* Hafen ed., "The W. M. Boggs Manuscript About Bent's Fort, Kit Carson, the Far West and Life among the Indians," 48-49; *Reports of Explorations and Surveys,* II:28; and Frederick Kreutzfeldt Journal, entry for July 27, 1853 (MS, Smithsonian Institution Archives, Wash.).

BIG TIMBERS ON THE ARKANSAS

A lithograph based on a Carvalho daguerreotype near the site of Bent's New Fort in Nov. 1853.

Published in Frémont's *Memoirs*.

necessary for our comfort. Sent two shirts to the Indian village to trade for mocassins having no boots and being near bare footed. Could not keep guard today in consequence of my feet being sore. Expect to increase our Camp by the addition of two more men, Mexicans and good Packers.

November 20th 1853. Commences clear and pleasant. Camp variously employed. Went to the Cheyanne Village and traded for two pair of moccasins. Carvalho at the village taking Indians' Daguerreotypes.[58] Blacksmith from the fort employed Shoeing the Delewares' ponys. Had a talk with Col. Fremont in regard to his domineering and selfish manners. Made up my mind to proceed no farther with him as circumstances have occurred which are exceedingly trying upon my feelings, and all I require is an opportunity to express them. My position at present requires me to be silent.

November 21st 1853. Commences clear and pleasant. The Col. informed me this morning that he intended making other arrangements for me. As yet I am entirely ignorant of what they are but anything is better than serving an ungrateful man. Went on duty. Palmer, the Telegraph of the Camp, went to the fort. Carvalho at the

[58] Carvalho's view of the Cheyenne village may be the only surviving daguerreotype dating from this expedition. It is a damaged plate showing tipis in a wooded area. The photograph is part of the Mathew Brady Coll. in the Lib. of Cong. This photograph's association with Carvalho is circumstantial. During the winter of 1855-56 Frémont employed Mathew Brady to make negatives and photographs of Carvalho's daguerreo types. Apparently through oversight, this daguerreotype remained in Brady's possession.

Carvalho was proud of the portrait he made of a Cheyenne "princess," and described her and her dress in considerable detail in his *Incidents of Travel and Adventure*. The portrait has survived as a woodcut entitled "Cheyenne Belle," in Frémont's *Memoirs*. She may have been Am-eer-tsche, the Fast Walker, the daughter of Chief Old Bark. James Abert, who sketched her portrait in 1845, called her "the belle of the nation." *See* Frémont, *Memoirs*, xvi and 40; Carvalho, *Incidents of Travel*, 67-68; Rudisill, *Mirror Image*, 105-107, and 228; Wheelock, "Frémont's Lost Plates," 51; and Abert, *Through the Country of the Comanche Indians*, 3, 41.

village taking Daguerreotypes. A Grand Scalp Dance will come off tonight at the Indian village in honour of their recent victory over the Pawnees.[59] It strikes me very forcibly that those admirers of the "Indian Drum" as sung by Mrs. Howard[60] would not appreciate as well were they to hear it in the true Cheyanne style. Their cries of "*Perfection would be Horrible*" [-] *bah*!

November 22d 1853. Commences clear & frosty. Moved camp about 1 mile NW of Bent's fort. Recd. 14 Mules and Horses from the Post, also 2 Indian lodges and a quantity of stores — robes, moccasins, and other articles for the Comfort of the expedition. Left a packed mule in our old camp through oversight. Sent the Mexican back and recovered her. Left two animals at fort in consequence of their being entirely useless. Took a Daguerreotype of Bent's Fort.

November 23d 1853. Commences clear & cool. Recd.

---

[59] The Cheyenne-Pawnee enmity dated back several decades and had been extremely intense after 1830, the year that Pawnees managed to seize the Cheyenne's sacred medicine arrows on the battlefield. The Cheyenne were probably the first to break the general peace established at the 1851 Fort Laramie Treaty Council when they sent a raiding party against Pawnee villages within a month of the treaty's signing. In the summer of 1853 John W. Gunnison reported that the Cheyenne had gone to "wipe out the Pawnees." That raid ended in disaster when the Pawnees and their allies routed the Cheyenne warriors. When Cheyenne warriors returned to the Arkansas in Nov. with "twelve or fifteen" Pawnee scalps, the Cheyennes had good reason to celebrate. Carvalho provides a vivid description of the scalp dance and Egloffstein tried to write down the music of their songs. *See* George Bird Grinnell, *The Fighting Cheyennes,* 72-96; Paul Wilhelm, Duke of Württemberg, Journal entry for Oct. 26, 1851 (MS, Univ. of So. IL. at Edwardsville); *Reports of Exploration and Surveys,* II:16, 19, 25, 28; Berthrong, *The Southern Cheyennes,* 127; and Carvalho, *Incidents of Travel,* 69.

[60] Rosina Shaw and her sister Mary were well-known in the New York theatre when she married Charles Howard in Albany, NY in June 1845. She was an accomplished actress and singer. Milligan, who was an avid theatregoer and stagehand at the St. Louis Varieties Theatre, had ample opportunity to see her perform during her appearances at the St. Louis People's Theatre in 1852 and 1853. The St. Louis *Daily Missouri Democrat* reported that "she possesses a charm which wins the admiration of all who see her." *See* the St. Louis *Daily Missouri Democrat,* June 1, 2, 13, 25, and 28, 1853; and Brown, *A History of the New York Stage,* I:74, 180, 259-60, 312, and 356.

two more animals from the fort. The Indians brought two of the five animals to Camp that were stolen from us on Pawnee fork but the Col. would not receive them in consequence of being poor and entirely worn out.[61] I was informed by the Col. that Doct. Eber and myself were to remain at the fort until his return. I was to be in charge of the animals left and on business otherwise connected with the expedition. Feet exceedingly sore and painful. Could not have proceeded farther in consequence of my feet, had not other circumstances caused me to stay. Branded all the animals bought of Bent with Fremont's Brand.

November 24th 1853. Commences cloudy and cool. The Camp making preparations for a start. Returned my arms, ammunition, and Horse to the Col., reserving only my Blankets. Packed the mules and struck the Lodges. Made up the packs for an early start in the morning. Camped again. Went to the Fort and made preparations for my stay until the return of the party in May as informed by Col. Fremont.

November 25th 1853. Commences cloudy. Camp up early for a fair start. The expedition now consists of 21 men and 54 shod animals. The men have facilitys of firing 70 shots without loading, with two Comfortable lodges and everything in fact for the general comfort of the expedition at this advanced season. Bid all hands good bye. Hated exceedingly to part with Fuller. His noble traits of character won the friendship of all in the camp and with all contention that others had, I venture to say that there was not a man of

[61] Milligan reported that Cheyenne Indians had stolen three mules and two ponies from the explorers' camp on Pawnee Fork sometime during the early morning hours of Nov. 10, the same day that von Egloffstein was found asleep on guard duty. Carvalho wrote that the Cheyennes told Frémont they had taken the animals when "one man left his watch, and went to warm himself at the camp fire," and that if they had had an additional hour, they would have taken more animals. Carvalho, *Incidents of Travel,* 63-64.

the expedition who had the slightest feeling of animosity against him. That Magnanimity of Soul and general conduct won him friends in every circle and may the bright prospects he has open before him never be darkened by clouds of misfortunes. When I took his hand to bid him adieu, my feelings were so overcome that I shed tears. With tenderest regards he desired to be remembered to his friends in St. Louis. Oh that the sequel of this expedition were known. Nothing good surely can be the consequence for where ambitions and selfishness predominate, many noble and refined followers fall victims to designing leaders.

Took up my lodging at the fort in the mess with Bent's Hands. Doct. Eber quartered with Mr. Murry,[62] Bent's trader. Some Arrapahoes arrived at the fort. They report having had a Battle at the foot of the mountain with the Utahs and lost 100 head of Horses. In regard to the loss of their own heads they're silent and I expect (to use the Language of the immortal trapper Bill Williams),[63] "some few were 'sent under' without their *har.*"

---

[62] Lucas Murray was an irascible Irishman who came to New Mexico in 1828. He was associated with Bent's Fort at least as early as the mid-1830s. By the 1850s he was Bent's chief trader, and took charge of the post in Bent's absence. According to George Bird Grinnell, Murray was "one of the most important men" at Bent's Fort. He "was a good hunter and trapper and a brave man." The Cheyenne called him "Flat Nose." According to David Lavender, the Indians also called him "Goddamn," since that oath was such an integral part of his vocabulary. In 1854 "Uncle" Dick Wootton shot Murray in the arm after a squabble over money. *See* Grinnell, "Bent's Old Fort and its Builders," 56-57; Lavender, *Bent's Fort,* 151-52 and 181; Hammond, *The Adventures of Alexander Barclay, Mountain Man,* 197-98, 72n; and Tyler, *Sources for New Mexican History, 1821-1848,* 58.

[63] William Sherley Williams (1787-1849) was one of the best-known mountain men in the Southwest. Born on the North Carolina frontier, but reared on a farm near St. Louis, he spent most of the 1820s and 1830s in the Rocky Mountain fur trade. He gravitated toward Taos in the mid-1820s, and by the 1830s had established an intermittent residence there. He trapped beaver on the Upper Gila, explored the Colorado Plateau, and conducted horse raids into California. He and Kit Carson signed on to guide Frémont's third expedition, but Williams left the expedition after an unresolved dispute. He served as guide on Frémont's disastrous fourth expedition of 1848-49. He and Benjamin Kern were killed in 1849 while attempting to recover property Kern had cached that winter. *See* Voelker, "William Sherley (Old Bill) Williams," in Hafen, ed., *Mountain Men and Fur Trade,* VIII:365-94.

November 26th 1853. Commences clear and pleasant. The Indians preparing for a Buffalo Hunt. Went down to Bark's Village[64] for the purpose of seeing Normus,[65] a Cheyanne chief, in regard to some Horses and mules which were left there by Col. F. Found that they were dead. Lord Fitzwilliam and party arrived from Taos N.M. on their way to the states. Lord F. has been for the last two years travelling in Oregon and California with no other motive but love of adventure.[66]

November 27th 1853. Commences clear and pleasant. Took advantage of having soap and took a wash, the first I have had since I left Salt creek. *Water wet.*

---

[64] Old Bark was also known as Ugly Face. According to Grinnell, his real name was Feathered Bear. Lieutenant James W. Abert, who met him at Bent's Fort in 1845, called him "'Nah-co-men-si,' or The Winged Bear, more generally known as Old Bark." Abert added that the old chief was second in rank to Yellow Wolf and that he was "remarkable for perseverance, enterprise, and bravery, although now very old." Old Bark was an accomplished orator. Abert recorded part of the old chief's eloquent speech in a council held between the Cheyennes and Delawares at Bent's Fort on Aug. 9, 1845. Jim Beckwourth called him "the patriarch of the Cheyennes." He was one of the four Cheyenne chiefs who signed the Fort Laramie Treaty of 1851. *See* Grinnell, *Fighting Cheyennes,* 102, 11n; Abert, *Through the Country of the Comanche Indians,* 18-20; Garrard, *Wah-to-Yah,* 86; Hoig, *The Peace Chiefs of the Cheyenne,* 50-52, 168; and Bonner, *James P. Beckwourth,* 428.

[65] Normus' (also Nah-Mouste, Nah-Moose or Namos) name meant "Big Left Hand." Lieut. James Abert, who sketched him in the summer of 1846, described him as "one of the largest Indians of the tribe, measuring 6 feet 2½ inches in height, and . . . very stout and broad shouldered. He has grown so large that he has been obliged to give up hunting, of which he was fond in his more youthful days, for few Indian horses could sustain his weight through a buffalo chase. He is extremely ingenious, and handles his knife with great skill, and is considered the best arrow-maker in the village." Normus was one of six Cheyenne chiefs who signed the Fort Wise Treaty of 1861. He is sometimes confused with the Arapaho chief Left Hand. *See* Abert, *Report . . . of his Examination of New Mexico, in the Years 1846-47,* 423. Abert's watercolor portrait of Big Left Hand is reproduced in Abert, *Western America in 1846-47,* opposite 18. *See* also Kappler, ed., *Indians Affairs,* II:810.

[66] Charles William Wentworth Fitzwilliam (1826-1883), a young English nobleman described by a St. Louis newspaper correspondent as "a modest, unassuming young man of fair intelligence and attainments," set out in 1850 at the age of 24 for a tour of the Western Hemisphere. He became enamored with the American West, and between 1851

Normus or Left Hand
A Southern Cheyenne chief described by James Abert as "one of the largest Indians of the tribe, measuring 6 feet 2½ inches in height and . . . very stout and broad shouldered."
From a watercolor by Abert published in *Western America in 1846-1847.*

November 28th 1853. Com. clear & pleasant. Had a feast today which consisted of duff[67] & cost $5. Eat the duff half raw, it not being done through. Feel unwell & lonesome. Caught a severe cold. Boys about the fort practising shooting at a mark.

November 29th 1853. Com. clear & pleasant. All hands hauling wood for the winter.

November 30th 1853. Com. clear & pleasant. Had a wash of part of my dirty clothes. Doctored the wounded Mare left in my charge by Col. Fremont. Lord Fitzwilliam's & our mess had a candy pulling. Suffer with a severe dysentery.

December 1st 1853. Com. as before. Finished washing. Fitz presented me with a pair of "Leather Breeches." A war party of Cheyannes from the Pawnee country with 11 scalps & 12 Pawnee Horses arrived at the fort. They lost one of their party. Lord Fitz's horses among the things that

---

and 1854 spent much time touring the plains and Rockies on well-financed hunting expeditions. He traveled with one or more personal servants, and usually in the company of other "gentlemen." At New Orleans in the summer of 1851, he joined a party of George Wilkins Kendall, editor of the New Orleans *Picayune,* who planned to attend the Fort Laramie Treaty Council. Their journey from Kansas City to Fort Kearny proved so difficult and time-consuming that Kendall and his friends gave up and returned to New Orleans. Fitzwilliam and two friends continued to Fort Laramie but arrived too late to attend the treaty council. From Laramie Fitzwilliam visited the Black Hills, the Badlands of South Dakota, and forts Union and Pierre. In 1852 he traveled the length of the Oregon Trail to Fort Vancouver. In 1853 he spent considerable time at Bent's Fort and Taos before returning to England in 1854. Fitzwilliam wrote a series of letters to his father detailing his western experiences, including a letter written from Fort Laramie on Sept. 14, 1853, indicating that he planned to return to Missouri via the Arkansas River and the Santa Fé Trail. Henry Chatillon, whose father had served as Fitzwilliam's guide, remembered talking with him in 1854 when the Englishman stopped in St. Louis en route to England. *See* Charles William Wentworth Fitzwilliam letters (MSS, Northamptonshire Record Office, Northampton, and in the Sheffield City Libraries, Sheffield, England); and Henry Chatillon to Denver *Evening Post,* Aug. 20, 1897 (MS, State Hist. Soc. of CO). Newspaper reports of Fitzwilliam's movement between 1851 and 1854 are noted in Barry, *Beginning of the West,* 1033-34, 1105-1106, and 1194.

[67] Duff is a flour pudding which usually contains raisins or currants and is cooked by boiling in a bag.

were yesterday, [and] are not to be found this morning. The general opinion is that they are "Cashed"[68] by some of the knowing red men of the tribe for the purpose of a reward. Suffering with a Dysentery from the effect of the Molasses Candy.

December 2d 1853. Com. clear & pleasant. A war party of Cheyannes started for the Utahs. Mr. Lajeunesse,[69] a trader for Mr. Bent, arrived from Taos.

December 3d 1853. Com. clear & pleasant. The Cheyannes started going towards the Utahs. Had a grand scalp & Gift dance in the Plaza of the fort in honor of the Cheyannes' victory over the late fight with the Pawnees. Bent, in accordance with the custom of the Traders gave them a feast and received a fine Horse in return to reciprocate the obligation. A party of Mexican traders passed from Taos. They report that they were robbed by the Cheyannes. Employed making a Hunting shirt.

December 4th 1853. Com. clear & pleasant. Got the lame mule up. Operated on him by applying hot ashes to the

[68] Cashed = cached.

[69] Francois Lajeunesse was a voyageur who, along with his brother Basil, was active in the Rocky Mountain fur trade. He worked as a hunter for William Drummond Stewart on the Scotsman's famous journey to the rendezvous of 1837, and appears as the subject of one of Alfred Jacob Miller's beautiful water colors. He worked for Frémont in 1843-44. Frémont characterized him as "an experienced mountaineer," but was disappointed when Lajeunesse lost his way while leading a party from the mouth of Bear River to Fort Hall. By 1846 he was living in Taos. Lewis Garrard met him near Bent's Fort in early 1847 and provided a lively description of the old voyageur: "By the expiring embers of the campfire sat Lajeunesse, without hat, which he never wore, or possessed, puffing the dear pipe thoughtfully. A queer genius was the same Lajeunesse. For years a voyageur, undergoing between the Platte and Arkansas even more than the usual hardships, he now was settled in the quiet vale of Taos, with a wife; but, like his brother Canadians, no better off in property than when a young man, he first came to the Far West. True to the mountaineer's characteristic, he was kindhearted; for, of seemingly unsociable dispositions, they are generous, even to a fault." *See* DeVoto, *Across the Wide Missouri,* 310; Jackson and Spence, eds., *Expeditions of Fremont,* I:150n; Ross, *The West of Alfred Jacob Miller,* 36; and Garrard, *Wah-to-yah,* 189.

wound & burning it. Employed on my hunting shirt. Chatteon[70] went out with the Beaver traps.

December 5th 1853. Com. clear & pleasant. Chatteon returned having found a desirable place for his traps. Played Euchre[71] & won 31 games.

December 6th 1853. Com. clear & pleasant. Mr. Lajuenesse & Davidson[72] started over to Dry Creek with one waggon to trade for meat with Yellow Bear's band of Arapahoes.[73] Lord Fitzwilliam accompanied them. Charley the Blacksmith started for Fountain Que Boit[74] to erect shop preparatory to the spring emigration. A lot of Arapahoes visited the fort. Bent gave them a feast.

December 7th 1853. Com. clear & pleasant. Quite a feast

---

[70] Joseph Chatillon was employed as Fitzwilliam's guide. According to Joseph's son Henry, Fitzwilliam engaged Chatillon at Fort Bridger. Joseph's brother, Henry Chatillon, was Francis Parkman's guide in 1846, and became famous upon publication of Parkman's *The Oregon Trail.* According to Barry, both brothers served as guides on Sir George Gore's extravagant 1854 hunting excursion. *See* Henry Chatillon to Denver *Evening Post,* Aug. 20, 1897 (MS, State Hist. Soc. of Co); and Barry *Beginning of the West,* 1220.

[71] Euchre or Trumps was one of the most popular nineteeth century card games. It is believed to have originated from the Spanish game of Triomphe, and was probably introduced into the United States via French Louisiana. *See* Scarne, *Encyclopedia of Games,* 234-37.

[72] Charley Davidson was Bent's wagon master. He is probably the same man whom Grinnell identifies as "Charles Davis," one of Bent's traders from Missouri whom the Cheyenne Indians called "Wolf." *See* Milligan's entry for Dec. 29, 1853; and Grinnell, "Bent's Old Fort," 57.

[73] Yellow Bear was an Arapaho Dog Soldier and chief of one of eleven Arapaho bands. He pursued a policy of accommodation with the United States Government during the reservation period, and greatly impressed George Armstrong Custer. Yellow Bear was one of the four principal Arapaho chiefs who signed the Medicine Lodge Creek Treaty of 1867 which removed the Cheyenne and Arapaho people to a reservation in western Oklahoma. George Bird Grinnell noted that Yellow Bear was the second chief of the Arapahoes in 1868. *See* Trenholm, *The Arapahoes, Our People,* 228-29, 239, 242-43; Kappler, ed., *Indian Affairs,* II:984-89; Grinnell, *Fighting Cheyennes,* 87, 307; and Coel, *Chief Left Hand, Southern Arapaho,* 313-14.

[74] Fountain Que Boit = Fountain Creek. Fountain Creek, called Boiling River by the Cheyennes, heads in the Rockies northeast of Colorado Springs. It flows southeast, entering the Arkansas at Pueblo, CO.

for supper, viz. roasted beaver & Tea. Visited the Arapahoe village. The Mexican Traders started for Mexico, having made but a poor trade.

December 8th 1853. Com. clear & pleasant. Working on my hunting shirt. Boys hauling wood.

December 9th 1853. Com. clear & cold. Discovered Ice in the river. Winter has no doubt set in. The oxen which hauled the waggon to Dry creek[75] returned having eluded the watch. Bent sent them back with two Mexicans. Fringed my Hunting Shirt.

December 10th 1853. Com. clear & cool. The oxen which were sent out yesterday returned again in consequence of the Carelessness of the Mexicans, which were sent to guard them. Bent exercised them in his usual manner with a yard stick.

December 11th 1853. Com. clear & pleasant. Ice thick in the river (Arkansas). Sent the Cattle back again with Pelow (a Mexican but adopted by the Cheyannes) and a Shawnee. Caught several foxes in our traps.

December 12th 1853. Com. clear & pleasantly cool. Finished fringe on my hunting shirt. Got an Arapahoe mad and refused to smoke with me. Played cards to see if I should fight or make peace with him. Beat him two games of moccasin,[76] a favourite game among Indians introduced

[75] Dry Creek = Sand Creek. Sand Creek enters the Arkansas from the north about fifteen miles downstream from Bent's New Fort in Prowers Co., CO. According to Grinnell, the Cheyenne called the stream Dry Creek because its mouth "was a mere dry bed of sand without any timber." *See* Grinnell, "Bent's Old Fort," 91.

[76] Moccasin was a variant of a well-known Plains Indian gambling game called "hands," which was usually played by two groups who sat in a line or half circle opposite each other. The game is still popular among Plains Indians. One of the players manipulated two small sticks or bones in his hands, one of which was specially marked. The object of the opposing team was to determine in which hand the man was hiding the marked bone. According to Grinnell, the players used two sticks in the Cheyenne

no doubt by some of the Canadian French Traders for their own designs.

December 13th 1853. Com. cloudy & cool with prospects of stormy weather. Caught two Big Injin lice[77] on me & a fair chance to have any number on me before I get from this Hell Hole. The fact is our quarters are continually crowded with Arrapahoes Indians and we are bound to put up with it or lose trade, as a big opposition is looked for on this river when trade commences. Their continual presence adds much to our filthy condition.

December 14th 1853. Com. cloudy with occasional rain. Cooked my turn, fixed our latch and cleared our room of the Indians, being determined to suffer no longer, having done until "forebearance has become a Sin."

December 15th 1853. Com. dark & stormy with rain, hail, sleet & snow. Hauled 5 loads of wood from opposite side of the river. From 15th to 20th nothing of importance transpired at the fort.

December 20th 1853. Bent's Fort, N.T.[78]

Pelow arrived from Dry creek. Reports that the waggon

---

version of moccasin, each having a different mark. These sticks might be hidden in a pair of moccasins or in the hand. Milligan's reference to cards is perplexing, since moccasin was not a card game. *See* Grinnell, *The Cheyenne Indians,* I:326-29.

[77] Lewis Garrard noted in 1846 that one of "the pleasures of an Indian village is that the inhabitants are troubled with a persecuting little animal — a roamer through the unbroken forests of hair on children's heads — now ascending the mountain of self-esteem, or reposing in the secluded vales around about combativeness. These creatures (the bugs), here, are white, and nearly the size of wheat grains. They do not confine their penetrating researches to the caput alone, but traverse the immense surface of the whole body." James Larkin, who visited Bent's New Fort in 1856 noted: "The Indians are not very neat in their toilet. When I was sitting there on their blanket, the old squaw commenced making researches in the cranium of one of the children for some hidden object. I know not if she was successful." *See* Garrard, *Wah-to-yah,* 147-48; and James Larkin Memorandum Book, Oct. 19, 1856 (MS, Bent's Old Fort Natl. Historic Site, CO).

[78] The area beyond Iowa and Missouri had been known as Nebraska since the early

will be here in a few days. One of the horses which he brought in with him was severely wounded in the flank by being gored by a Buffalo Bull during a chase. Opposition expected soon from the Platte to trade against Bent.[79]

December 21st 1853. Com. clear and cold. Lord Fitzwilliams and Lajuenesse, trader for Mr. Bent, arrived from Dry creek, also their waggon loaded with meat and robes. Traded my revolver for a Horse to Lord Fitzwilliams. Gave a Blanket and four $ for a Saddle & Bridle. Traded a white Blanket for a Navahoe serape. Went to the Arrapahoe village at night to see the squaws.

December 22d 1853. Com. as before. Fixed my breeches with Buckskin. Hauled wood during the day.

December 23d 1853. Com. as before. Sold my gauntlets to Smith[80] for four $ to be taken out in the Store. Bought a

---

1840s. There were bills to organize Nebraska Territory as early as 1844. An 1853 bill was passed in the House before failing in the Senate. Apparently the term Nebraska Territory was in common usage at Bent's Fort in 1853, although the Kansas-Nebraska Act did not become law until 1854. *See* Ray, *The Repeal of the Missouri Compromise,* 95-100; and Robert W. Johannsen, *Stephen A. Douglas,* 390-400.

[79] The three major trading posts on the South Platte — Fort Platte, Fort Lupton, and Fort St. Vrain — had been abandoned by the mid-1840s. In 1853 there was no organized trading on the South Platte. Bent's opposition came from a number of traders who had trading posts on the North Platte in the vicinity of Fort Laramie. These included Elbridge Gerry, who carried on an extensive trade on the South Platte and the Arkansas in the 1850s. Gerry's account books indicated that John Simpson Smith was trading buffalo robes for him in 1853. Other traders from the Fort Laramie region who occasionally traded on the Arkansas were William Guerrier and Seth E. Ward, James Bordeaux, Jean Baptiste Moncravie, and Jean Baptiste Richard. Richard was notorious for bootlegging liquor from Taos to the Platte and using it liberally to gain an edge on his competition. *See* Ann Hafen, "Elbridge Gerry," in Hafen ed., *Mountain Men and Fur Trade,* VI:153-60; John Dishon McDermott, "James Bordeaux," *Ibid.,* V:65-80; Charles E. Hanson, Jr., "J. B. Moncravie," *Ibid.,* IX:289-98; McDermott, "John Baptiste Richard," *Ibid.,* II, 289-303; and Hoig, *John Simpson Smith,* 105.

[80] John Simpson Smith (1810-1871) entered the Rocky Mountain fur trade in the early 1830s. His nickname, "Blackfoot," commemorates his early association with the Blackfeet and his mastery of their language. The Southern Cheyenne, among whom he spent most of his life, called him Gray Blanket. Smith moved to Bent's Fort about 1840, married a Cheyenne woman, and worked as a trader for Bent for several years thereafter.

CHEYENNE BELLE
A lithograph probably based on Carvalho's daguerreotype made at the Cheyenne village at Big Timbers on Nov. 20, 1953.
Published in Frémont's *Memoirs.*

Spanish Bridle for 4$. Volunteered to go with Murry to the Cheyanne Village as clerk for Mr. Bent. Took a list of the trading outfit and prices to be demanded. Fitz and I went down to Bark's village to see Smith. On our return had to give way for a war party of Cheyannes on their return from an incursion against the Apaches. They had 4 Scalps.

December 24th 1853. Com. clear and very cold. The Arkansas entirely closed with Ice. Started with 2 waggons with Murry in charge for the Cheyanne Village to trade. Camped about 10 mile from the fort on the Arkansas with a war party of Arapahoes.

December 25th 1853. Com. as before. Last night our oxen ran back to the fort. Sent the Herder in pursuit. He returned with all but 2 yoke. Traded my Knife with an Arapahoe for a Hair Lariet. Sent the Spaniard back after the lost two yoke of Cattle. Went on with the waggon and camped at thousand Islands,[81] 15 mile from the village. The Spaniard returned to Camp after dark with one more yoke of Cattle. He reported that a party of 4 Arapahoes stopped him and demanded a piece of meat he had but would not give it up, so they contented themselves by taking his Knife away, which he could not help under the Circumstances, as he was exceedingly fortunate to retain his hair. Apache, a Cheyanne Indian who was going down to the village, a Semi Arapahoe himself, informed Mr. Murry that they followed us from the fort on purpose to rob the waggons but was prevented by him informing

In the late 1840s and early 1850s he served as Indian agent Thomas Fitzpatrick's interpreter. He was official government interpreter for the Cheyenne at the 1851 Fort Laramie and 1867 Medicine Lodge Creek treaty councils. He conducted Indian delegations to Washington, and in his later years concerned himself increasingly with the welfare of the Cheyenne people. He moved with the Cheyenne people to their reservation in Western Oklahoma, where he died in 1871. *See Ibid.;* and Grinnell, "Bent's Old Fort," 57.

[81] Thousand Islands cannot be located precisely.

them [of] the consequences. Crossed the Arkansas on the Ice. Hobbled the oxen to prevent them from running off.

December 26th 1853. Com. clear & pleasant. Camped at "Campo Bonito."[82] Made a drive of 27 miles. This with oxen is considered Extra travelling but we shoved them in order to tire them down so that they would not feel so much like returning to the fort. Apache left us and went to the village which is some six miles below.

December 27th 1853. Com. clear & pleasant. Arrived at the village at [and] stored our things on "Oakum Muctavas"[83] Lodge. Commenced trading for meat & tongues. Traded in the course of an hour 110 pieces of meat varying from 10 to 20 lbs., 60 tongues & 3 Robes. Had a grand dance at night by all the exewons[84] and young squaws of the village in honour of our arrival. A false alarm in Camp in consequence of a report that the Pawnees are about. On the "Qui vive" all night. Visited Normus' lodge (or the Left Hand) on business connected with some animals left by Col. Fremont, which Normus was to negotiate their recovery.

December 28th 1853. Com. as before. Roused out before daylight by the ever-going infernal Indian Drum beating

---

[82] Lewis Garrard characterized Campo Bonito or Pretty Encampment as "the loveliest on the river . . . The pleasant position and grouping of trees render this spot picturesque, and it is well known to travelers as the 'Pretty Encampment.'" *See* Garrard, *Wah-to-Yah,* 88, 326; and Hafen, ed., *Ruxton of the Rockies,* 273-74.

[83] Oakum Muctavas = Black Coyote. According to linguist Wayne Leman, the proper pronunciation is o?kohomoh-mo?kohtavaestse. We have been unable to identify this Cheyenne Indian. We are indebted to linguists Danny Alford and Wayne Leman for help with these Cheyenne words. *See* Danny Alford to Stegmaier, Oct. 5, 1981; and Wayne Leman to Alford, Oct. 8, 1981, letters in possession of the editors.

[84] Exewon = medicine bundle. In the context of Milligan's journal, the term means "young men." The proper Cheyenne pronunciation is *esevone*. Milligan's use here appears to be a mistaken use of metonymy. Apparently Milligan heard the term for medicine bundles and associated it with young warriors. We are indebted to Wayne Leman for the correct pronunciation.

time for a war Dance. Loaded the waggon with the meat traded yesterday. Feasted the Big Dogs of the tribe in order to get their influence to promote trade. Druming up recruits all day & making medicine for a Big War Party to go out against the Pawnees. Went to Bob Tail Bear's[85] Lodge to drink my own Coffee with the Squaws. Mrs. Bear offered to trade me her niece but [I] declined having one squaw already to support and all her family. I find married life among the Cheyannes quite expensive enough with *one* wife.

December 29th 1853. Com. as before. Sent the waggon loaded with meat to the fort in charge of Charly Davidson, Bent's waggon Master. Wrote to Bent all the items of trade. Gave the village a Grand Blow out. The lodge was well crowded and Bald Face Bull[86] opened the ceremonys with a speech in favour of fur Trade and Bent particularly.

Sudden change of weather with every prospect of a heavy Snow storm. A Cheyanne Indian, who was wounded some time since and is now dying, sent to Murry for a Cup of Sugar to "sweeten his last moments." The Drum going all day for volunteers. Dancing all night accompanied with a moderate amount of yelling.

December 30th 1853. Com. clear & *very* cold. The Squaws, who were up all night exercising themselves as votaries of the God Terpsicore,[87] pulled me out of bed to have a look at me. Caught the nearest one to me and made

---

[85] According to George Bent, Bobtail Bear led the warriors who surrounded and killed Major Joel Elliott and his detachment at the Battle of the Washita on Nov. 29, 1868. *See* Hyde, *Life of George Bent,* 320.

[86] According to Grinnell, Bald Faced Bull was born in 1835. He lived to an old age, although he was wounded in Gen. Ranald S. Mackenzie's attack on Dull Knife's village in 1876. He was one of Grinnell's informants concerning Cheyenne life, and dictated an account of how as a young boy he had joined a war party against the Pawnees. *See* Grinnell, *Cheyenne Indians,* II:5-6; and Grinnell, *Fighting Cheyenne,* 380-81.

[87] In Greek mythology, Terpsichore was the muse of dancing.

myself pretty familiar, considering the short aquaintance. The Lodge was filled by Indians who commenced singing & dancing for a gift. Murry knuckled under at last and gave them stuff enough for a feast, when they left though reluctantly. Old "Twist"[88] tryed to scare me last night but I gave him the soft end of my Pistol butt over the head for his pains. The Day very windy and Buffalo plenty in close to the river. Took advantage when the Lodge was clear and got a nap to repay me for the loss of Sleep last night.

December 31st 1853. Commences cold. Rested more tonight than last night. *Spent the night* at the other end of the village with the Lady I made free with yesterday at the particular request of *her Mother*. In the Morning I was informed that I now had to clothe my *esposo*.[89] Gave her a Blanket and played Quits.[90] Boarders and old squaws pretty thick in the lodge all day.

January 1st 1854. Com. clear & pleasant. After mature consideration & reflection, I have come to the conclusion to settle myself down to some permanent employment, be it what it may. I now enter my 24th year. For the last 9 I have been wandering to & fro, and I find the old addage particularly applicable to myself and fully verified, viz."a rolling stone gathers no moss." Went to Hunt. Repose at

---

[88] Old Twist has not been identified. He may have been the old man whom Abert called Isse-wo-ne-mox-ist. Abert painted his portrait in 1845 and described him as "a very old man who wore his hair twisted into an immense horn projecting from his forehead." In 1856 James Larkin met an old Indian at Bent's New Fort who may have been Old Twist. His arm had been broken four times in the same place and had failed to heal properly. Larkin noted that "it is now hanging by the skin & flesh and turns at will. He can twist and work it about almost as he pleases. It is almost unpleasant to see him work it about, especially as it causes him no pain. Quite a curiosity." *See* Abert, *Through the Country of the Comanche Indians*, 3; and James Larkin Memorandum Book, Oct. 28, 1856 (MS, Bent's Fort Natl. Historic Site).

[89] Esposo = esposa. Spanish for wife.

[90] Quits is a version of the card game Monte Carlo. *See* Scarne, *Encyclopedia of Games*, 390.

Bob Tail Bear's Lodge. Took coffee & sugar along with me for a feast. Let our waggon & team haul wood today for the Squaws.

January 2d 1854. Com. clear & cold. Our teams employed all day long hauling wood for the squaws. Gave my Lady permission to accompany the waggon for exercise. She reported Manuel the Mexican for taking libertys with her not becoming Mrs. M. (temporarily). Broke his head with the whip stock much to the satisfaction of her connections, and for defence of her virtue presented her with 4 yds of domestic.

January 3d 1854. Com. clear & pleasant. All the Indians started on a Big hunt accompanied with the Squaws to Butcher the meat killed. My Squaw went with her Brother. Wrote to Bent by an Indian who belonged to the Upper Village of old Bark.

January 4th 1854. Com. cloudy & Stormy. Lord Fitzwilliams arrived in Camp on his way to the U.S. Sent Manuel with Lord Fitz's horse to his Camp with orders for them to come on & camp below the village on the river. Fitz and I slept together, much to the regret of Mrs. M., who refused to cook hump ribs for me. Borrowed her brother's Lariat and warmed her back to make her heart more tender to the want of strangers & my guests.

January 5th 1854. Com. cloudy, Stormy and very cold. Invited to a feast in Twist's Lodge which consisted of the young unborn Calf of the Bufflalo. I found it quite a treat. Returned the Compliment to Twist by having a feast on the Sly in order to steal or play "Oakum" on our Setters which fill the Lodge all day.

January 6th 1854. Com. cold & cloudy. Kept in the lodge all day and employed doing nothing but eating. Fitzwilliam's Camp went below the village and [I] came too. Visited the Boys and found them all well. Bought Doctor Eber's[91] revolver for $20. Fitz and I bought a squaw for the night. Gave Bob Tail Bear some Coffee for finding her. Indians Dancing all night.

January 7th 1854. Com. clear & cold. Snowed during the night. Got up late as usual and missed my rib. Wrote to Buck and the Boys at Home. Gave Doctor Eber an order for $20 for his Pistol. Lord Fitzwilliams had a fine mare stolen last night by Little Bear's[92] Gang. They offered a Lame in restitution but Fitz refused when they informed him that he was Masone,[93] [and] he'd get nothing. Every prospect of a row with the Indians. They appear to [be] disposed for a fight and with *our* small force against a body of 2 Thousand Cheyannes and 100 others of different tribes, we stand a fair chance ironically speaking. Murry succeded in getting the Indians to offer a robe on the Horse as the difference, which Fitz accepted by the advice of Murry to avoid further difficulty.

January 8th 1854. Com. clear & excessively cold. Started with the express for the Fort. About 12 o'clock at night when near the fort & mistaking the trail and it being very dark, my mule fell over the Bluff and fortunately I only sprained my ankle from the fall. Gave Mr. Bent all the

[91] Dr. Ebers was returning to St. Louis with Fitzwilliam's party.

[92] Little Bear survived the Sand Creek Massacre and related a vivid account of that unfortunate event to George Bent. He was one of fourteen Cheyenne chiefs who signed the Medicine Lodge Creek Treaty of 1867 which established a Cheyenne reservation in Western Oklahoma. He was killed in a battle on Sappa Creek in 1875. *See* Hyde, *George Bent,* 144, 153-54, 368-69; and Kappler, ed., *Indian Affairs,* II:989.

[93] Masone = foolish or crazy. Lewis Garrard noted at Bent's Fort in 1846 that the Cheyennes considered him "mah-son-ne" or "a fool" when he began making a glossary of Cheyenne terms. Linguist Wayne Leman suggests that Milligan was attempting to write the Cheyenne word *masaha* which means "crazy male." *See* Garrard, *Wah-to-Yah,* 110; and Leman to Danny Alford, Oct. 8, 1981, letter in possession of the editors.

news of trade and &c. Visited Mrs. Murry and gave her the admonition that her husband sent her, and also informed José that Murry said that he would have his hair when he came up from the village. The Lady endeavored to depict to me the Horrors of married life and said that it was hard to confine her charms to a man she detested. She invited me to share her couch that night if I was not afraid of Murry. The ironical manner which she expressed appeared as if she was casting reflections upon my Courage. I accepted her offer and had not long been in her arms when Jose came to the door. I politely informed him I was about for the night at least.

January 9th 1854. Com. clear & pleasant. Started back to Murry's village. Hove to at Dry creek and stayed all night with Lajuenesse in Consequence of my mule giving out.

January 10th 1854. Com. cloudy & cold. Hurried to reach pretty Encampment before it commenced snowing. After exercising my spurs considerable, I reached Camp about 1 o'clock having rode in two days and on the Same Mule *160* Miles. Delivered Bent's orders to Murry, also his wife's letter written by me and dictated by her in Spanish. Gave Murry my candid opinion of his wife and informed him what I knew of her virtue. He thanked me. I would have never divulged the affair had not she *insisted* upon me if I was *not afraid* to inform Murry of our *liaison*, for her object is plain to be seen. She does not want to live with Murry and never will be *true* to *any* man.

January 11th 1854. Com. clear & pleasant. Old Murry despite Bent's letter went to the Fort as he said to wreak vengeance upon José's Head and his unfaithful spouse. His threat in regard to José was too truly kept. Sent a waggon load of meat to the Fort with Murry. Took an a/c [account] of goods as directed by Mr. Bent. Gave the Indians some coffee. Charles Davidson, Bent's waggon master, remained here to act as trader in connection with me. Done my first trading with Indians. Traded 14 Robes during the day, more than Murry traded during the whole time he was down here. I attribute it to my wife's (Pro tem) influence.

January 12th 1854. Com. clear & pleasant. Made a large Camp Kettle full of Coffee for the Indians, and made an entire change in the management practiced by Murry, much to the Satisfaction of the Indians. Davidson & I had a small snack after our Setters left us. The oxen strayed away this morning. Sent the Spaniard in pursuit. He overtook them and drove them back.

January 13th 1854. Com. clear & pleasant. Packed up to start for the fort but the Indians would not let us go. They said if we stayed they would trade faster. Traded 9 robes, 40 Ropes and 25 tongues. Sent an Indian with an express to the fort, for more goods.

January 14th 1854. Com. clear & pleasant. Part of the village moved below to the Sueti Band.[94] Trade getting brisk. Traded 1 Pack of robes during the day, a lot of meat, Tongue &c. Hauled wood with our teams for the Squaws. Wood getting scarce. The Squaws have to go 9 mile for it. A report brought in Camp by an Indian just returned as the remains of a war Party [says] that Fremont's Party has been cut off by the Utahs near Fort Massachusetts and the Col. and 2 Delewares killed. For my part I do not credit

[94] The Sutai (Suhtai) Band formed one of the eleven Cheyenne tribal divisions in the Cheyenne camp circle. According to Peter J. Powell, the Cheyenne called them the Buffalo People. Lewis and Clark in 1804 mentioned them as a separate tribe, although they spoke a Cheyenne dialect and were related to the Cheyenne. By 1853 they had lost their separate tribal identity and were recognized as one of the component divisions of the Southern Cheyenne Tribe. *See* Powell, *Sweet Medicine,* 24n; Hodge, ed., *Handbook of American Indians North of Mexico, I:252-55; and Berthrong, Southern Cheyennes,* 9-10.

it.[95] The same Indian informs me that 5 Arapahoes were killed by the Utahs near the same ground where the Col. is reported to have been killed. My squaw made me two pair of moccasins. During the night a violent Hurricane blew down our lodge. Layed snug in our blankets while the Squaws got up and cleared away the wreck and made all fast again.

January 15th 1854. Com. very cold & trade dull. Set in the Lodge all day and killed time by Smoking.

January 16th 1854. Com. clear & pleasantly cool. The whole village moved down the river. We of course followed, not having received order[s] from the Fort to the Contrary. Our waggon heavily loaded with Robes, goods, and Murry['s] traps. Twist's daughter and my Squaw had a fight. Normus intimated to me that the Green-eyed Monster had a hand in it. My squaw well *voleped.*[96]

January 17th 1854. Com. clear & pleasant. The *Indians* started to move again but we would not go any farther until we heard from the fort. They struck Camp and dusted, leaving us alone in our Glory. Traded some few robes, which they could not carry. Tied my Squaw to the waggon to keep her from following the other Indians off.

January 18th 1854. Com. clear & cold. Up Camp and followed the village which moved yesterday. Sent the Squaw ahead to tell them I was coming. Arrived at the Village, unloaded the goods and put them in the Lodge. Mr. Lajuenesse arrived from the Fort with orders to

[95] The report was erroneous. Fort Massachusetts was a frontier military post established in 1852 near the site of Fort Garland, CO. It was relocated in 1858 and renamed Fort Garland. *See* Hart, *Old Forts,* 103-105.

[96] Voleped = walloped. Milligan is using a German pronunciation, probably in jest of Dr. Ebers' accent.

relieve me. Delivered over all the Equipment to him as directed preparatory to starting for the fort Tomorrow.

January 19th 1854. Com. Snowy and consequently did not start for the Fort on a/c of the weather. Went to Medicine Arrow's[97] lodge and read the Treaty made by Major FitzPatrick in 1850[98] and saw some trophies taken from the Utahs by the Cheyannes. Among them was a large Silver Medal as big as a Plate belonging to some Big Chief of the Utes. Lent my wife to Medicine Arrow's Son and in return he lent me an Arapahoe squaw (to take to the fort where her people were now camped) until he returned Manawa my Squaw. Both appeared to be pleased with the trade at least for a change. Slept in Arrow's lodge with my borrowed Lady.

January 20th 1854. Com. clear & excessively cold, in fact the coldest day I have experienced in the course of my existence. Started for the Fort with one Pack animal and a Mexican Herder. Camped after travelling about 10 miles in consequence of the Squaw being cold & no way to warm her. Came to at "Campo Bonito." Two Indians came into

[97] Medicine Arrow, also known as Medicine Arrows, was an important chief and leader of the Cheyenne soldier societies. According to Grinnell, his Cheyenne name meant Rock Forehead. He rejected reservation life and refused to participate in the Medicine Lodge Creek Treaty negotiations of 1867. In the early 1870s he and his band fought intermittent battles with the United States Army. George Armstrong Custer considered him a major adversary. *See* Grinnell, *Fighting Cheyennes,* 307n; Berthrong, *Southern Cheyennes,* 258, 293-99, 336-37, 353-400; and Custer, *My Life on the Plains,* 354-60.

[98] Milligan is in error. Indian Agent Thomas Fitzpatrick (1799-1854) did not negotiate a treaty with the Cheyenne people in 1850. Most likely, the treaty which Milligan saw was the Fort Laramie Treaty of 1851, although it could have been the amended Fort Laramie Treaty which Cheyenne and Arapaho leaders signed on the South Platte on Aug. 31, 1853. Fitzpatrick's role in negotiating the Fort Laramie and Amended Fort Laramie treaties is found in Hafen, *Broken Hand: The Life of Thomas Fitzpatrick,* 267-314. *See* also "Documents Relating to Negotiations of Ratified and Unratified Treaties, 1801-69," T494, reel 4, frames 796-97, RG 75 — Records of the Bureau of Indian Affairs, NARS; and Kappler, ed., *Indian Affairs,* II:594-96.

camp and camped with us. Actually felt cold with 8 blankets and 3 robes over me and a squaw along side.

January 21st 1854. Com. clear & cold but far more pleasant than yesterday. Started at daylight for the Fort. Saw numbers of Buffalo on the river. Arrived at the Fort about midnight and had a good hot supper. Let my squaw go to the Arapahoe village about a mile above the Fort with strict orders to be on hand in the morning. Woke up about daylight and found her along side of me, she having paid her visit and returned. Gave her a Cup of Sugar for her Kindred for her punctuality.

January 22d 1854. Com. clear & pleasant. Had Fremont's Cavayard up and found them improved very much. Set my Squaw to washing my clothes.

January 23d 1854. Com. clear & pleasant. Pressed some robes and overhauled the waggon sheets and made other repairs upon them to fit. Buffalo near the fort. Weather cloudy and every appearance of a Snow storm.

January 24th 1854. Com. clear & pleasant. Bent sent another equipment to the Lower village in charge of Ed Foster[99] to deliver to Lajuenesse. Painted an American flag for Ed Foster. Suffering from 3 large bites upon my thigh much to the regret of my borrowed squaw who does all *she can* to relieve me. Set her at mending & washing my clothes.

January 25th 1854. Com. clear & pleasant. Cleaned up the Corridor & Plaza of the Fort.[100] Teamsters employed trying out grease for the waggons. Commenced making me an overcoat out of white Skin.

---

[99] Ed Foster has not been identified.

[100] Bent's log trading houses consisted of three buildings which formed three sides of a square. The open side or plaza faced the river and was enclosed by pickets. *See* Mumey, *Old Forts and Trading Post of the West,* 125.

January 26th 1854. Com. cloudy with snow. Myself and Squaw employed on my Coat. Clearing up. Prospect of good weather again.

January 27th 1854. Com. clear & pleasant. Employed on overcoat. Bites troublesome despite the Care of my Squaw.

January 28th 1854. Com. clear & pleasant. Employed lining my overcoat. A number of Arapahoes visited the fort. Bent feasted them. A young Arapahoe made a dash at my Squaw with a Tomahawk and was saved by Henry Dougherty,[101] a Shawnee Indian, from being killed. Told Mr. Arapahoe that she did not belong to me, that I only swapped for her for a little while. When he found out who she belonged to, he did not appear so rampant. It appears before Arrow traded for her, that he himself had made proposals, but not coming down heavy enough he failed to get [her] & thus the Cause of enmity.

January 29th 1854. Com. clear & pleasant. Employed on my coat. Shawnees hauling wood. My Squaw stuck pretty close to the house all day, being afraid of her disappointed *Lover*.

January 30th 1854. Com. clear & pleasant. Finished binding my coat. The Arapahoes exceedingly troublesome and was compelled to throw four or five out of doors.

January 31st 1854. Com. Clear & exceedingly pleasant weather. A Number of Cheyannes arrived from the Lower Village on a war Party against the Utahs. My old Squaw accompanied them from below. She informed me that it was the only opportunity she had to come to the fort and, during the trip up, the young men made a matter of

[101] Henry Dougherty has not been identified. A search of the Indian Archives Division of the Oklahoma Hist. Soc. failed to reveal Dougherty's name on Shawnee census schedules.

convenience of her which was exceedingly pleasant for me to hear, and, as she appeared to be disposed to go to war with them despite the manner she had been treated, I gave her a outfit and let her rip. So my horse, the price I paid for her, is gone with but little for him, as I did not care about keeping squaws for the convenience of War Partys. I sent Arrow's squaw away, determined to hire for the future, which is said to be less expensive. The waggon arrived from the village with Robes, meat & Tongues.

February 1st 1854. Com. clear & pleasant. Pressed 5 pack of Robes. My thigh much better this morning.

February 2d 1854. Com. clear & pleasant. Commences hauling logs to build a new Fort, the rats having entirely ran away with this one. The new Fort is to be placed in a more commanding position & on the site chosen by Col. Sumner of the U.S.A., but Mr. Bent refused to dispose of the Land at the price offered.[102] Two of the Mexicans attached [to] the Fort had a fight. Cooked for the Boys, they all being at work.

February 3d 1854. Com. clear & pleasant. Employed hauling logs.

February 4th 1854. Com. clear & pleasant. Employed hauling logs. Bent made up an Equipment to go to Dry

---

[102] In the summer of 1851 Colonel Edwin Vose Sumner (1797-1863), new commander of the Ninth Military District of New Mexico, led a command of several hundred recruits over the Santa Fé Trail from Fort Leavenworth. Sumner established Fort Union shortly after arriving in Santa Fé, and soon thereafter moved the headquarters of the Ninth Military District to that post. In Aug. he sent Capt. John Pope of the Topographical Engineers to survey a new route from Fort Union to Fort Leavenworth which would avoid the arid plains. Pope's new route intersected the Arkansas at Big Timbers, thus making the site of Bent's New Fort an ideal location for a military post. By 1855 the government was using the fort to store supplies, and in 1856 Bent began efforts to sell his post to the government. *See* Barry, *Beginning of the West,* 1003-4; and Mumey, *Old Forts,* 124-27, 137.

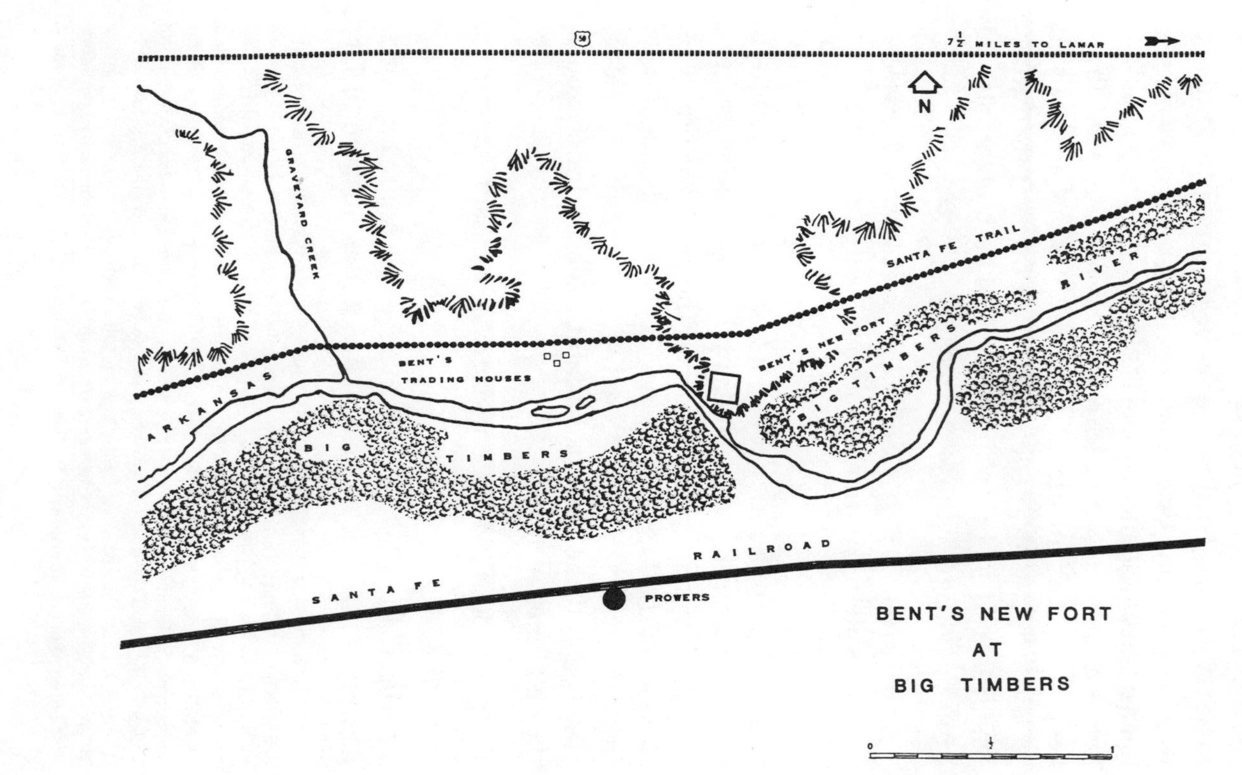

50
7 1/2 MILES TO LAMAR
N
GRAVEYARD CREEK
SANTA FE TRAIL
ARKANSAS
RIVER
BENT'S TRADING HOUSES
BENT'S NEW FORT
BIG TIMBERS
BIG TIMBERS
SANTA FE RAILROAD
PROWERS
BENT'S NEW FORT AT BIG TIMBERS
0
1/2
1

creek and trade against the Platte opposition. Trade getting brisk. Went up to Coho's (an Arapahoe chief)[103] Lodge to fix a handle in an axe for him, for which service he gave me one of his Squaws to *use* when I felt so *disposed.*

February 5th 1854. Com. clear & windy. Bent started for the village accompanied by his squaw and family.[104] Boys Employed raising the fort. Tim Goodwell[105] in charge of the Fort in Bent's absence. Found the Lariat I lost a few days since.

February 6th 1854. Com. clear & pleasant. Painted two guns, one for my old friend Coho, for which I received the

[103] Coho "The Lame" was an influential Arapaho chief who had a reputation for being on bad terms with the whites. John S. Smith warned Lewis Garrard in 1846 that Coho was "the most infernal and mean of the tribe — the leader of the worst band in the mountains." Englishman George Ruxton met Coho and his warriors when they returned to the Bent's Fort vicinity after an unsuccessful raid against the Utes. Although the warriors were tired and hungry, Ruxton was impressed. He noted that Coho and his men could serve as models for Apollo. *See* Garrard, *Wah-to-Yah,* 136; Hafen, ed., *Ruxton of the Rockies,* 239-40; and Trenholm, *Arapahoes,* 124-31.

[104] William Bent's second wife was Yellow Woman. She was the daughter of Cheyenne chief Gray Thunder, and the sister of Bent's first wife, Owl Woman. Bent had followed Cheyenne custom and married her after Owl Woman died in childbirth. According to George Bent, Yellow Woman bore William Bent one child, a boy named Charles. Bent's children by his first wife were Mary, Robert, George, and Julia. *See* George Bent to George Hyde, Mar. 9, 1905 (MS, Bent Papers, Denver Public Lib.).

[105] Timothy Goodale (variant spellings include Goodwell, Goodall and Goodell) was a free trapper in the Colorado Rockies and in Northern New Mexico in the 1840s and 1850s. He came to the mountains about 1839. In the 1840s he lived in the Upper Arkansas villages of Pueblo and Hardscrabble. He also worked from time to time at Bent's Old Fort. In 1850 he helped Kit Carson drive horses from New Mexico to Fort Laramie to sell to passing emigrants. He participated in Carson's sheep drive to California in 1853 and had just returned from California when Milligan met him. He worked as a guide for the army in the late 1850s. Percival G. Lowe characterized him as a "celebrated mountaineer" and noted that "Goodale belonged to a class of mountaineers who ranked with Sublette, Fitzpatrick, Bridger, etc., with Carson as the recognized head — reliable characters, unmixed with false heroism, intelligent and trustworthy." The Cleveland *Daily Plain Dealer* proposed the slate of Carson and Goodale in the 1856 presidential election as a means of ridiculing Republican candidate John C. Frémont. *See* Carter, "Tim Goodale," in Hafen, ed., *Mountain Men and Fur Trade,* VII:147-53; Grinnell, "Bent's Old Fort" 65; Lowe, *Five Years a Dragoon,* 216; and Cleveland *Daily Plain Dealer,* July 26, 1856.

usual price — a dash at his squaw. Heard from Mr. Bent. He wants two waggons to go down the river where the Indians purpose going. Had a fight with an Arapahoe who, finding my door locked, got in at the window and, when I offered to put him out, drew his Tomahawk upon me. So I knocked the gentleman down with a King Bolt[106] to one of the waggons. Boys at work on the fort.

February 7th 1854. Com. clear & pleasant. Hauling logs to finish the fort. Pressed 7 Pack of Robes. Made buttons out of raw hide for my new Skin coat. Gave old Coho his Gun and slept all night at his lodge with his wife.

Febraury 8th 1854. Com. clear & pleasant. *Woke up* this morning and found I had another bed fellow. It proved to be a Utah Squaw, a prisoner of Cohoe's. The first Lady I turned in with I found lying along side of Coho. All hands about the fort employ[ed] on the hill raising heavy logs for to cap off the fort with preparatory to covering.

February 9th 1854. Com. clear & pleasant. Spring-like weather which is said to be unusual here for this Season. Hauled more logs for the fort. Traded 11 Robes. Had a Calf Feast at "Big Mouth's"[107] Lodge.

February 10th 1854. Com. clear & pleasant. Boys employed on the new fort. Helped Tim Goodwell to trade and keep Squaws from stealing.

February 11th 1854. Com. clear & pleasant. Took two waggons down to the village where Bent is trading and brought back 33 Pack of robes.

---

[106] A king bolt is the large vertical bolt which connects the running gear on a wagon to the front axle and serves as a pivot when the wagon turns.

[107] Big Mouth was an influential Arapaho Chief whose name appears frequently as a signatory on Indian treaties. He signed the Fort Wise Treaty of 1861 and was one of seven Arapaho headmen to sign the Little Arkansas Treaty of 1865. During the 1860s

February 12th 1854. Com. cloudy & very windy. Pressed 25 pack of robes. Feel low spirited today. Went and consoled myself with Coho's Utah Squaw. The Arapahoes had a big dance in the Plaza of the fort during the night, but we did not get up so they went away after having sung the song. They got no supper. Pelow & Billy Bent Jr.[108] came from the village.

February 13th 1854. Com. cloudy & windy. Got up 3 hours before day and started for the lower village with 2 waggons to move Lajuenesse to the Fort. Camped at Beaver Island[109] 20 miles from the fort. Bothered along the road during the day by the bow Keys[110] coming out. Lost my revolver on the road but went back and found it.

February 14th 1854. Com. clear & windy. Passed a

Big Mouth conducted raids along the Santa Fé Trail and in 1868 participated in the destruction of Major Joel Elliott's troops during the Battle of the Washita. Characterized in 1864 by General S.R. Curtis as a "rascal," Big Mouth became a leader in helping his people adjust to reservation life during the 1870s. In hopes of encouraging his people to follow the "corn road," he personally fenced, plowed and planted an eighty-acre farm, an action unheard of for an Arapaho chief. In return, Indian agent John D. Miles provided him with a new two-story house. The house was considered the finest at the agency. Big Mouth refused to live in the house, preferring his tipi. Agency employee John Seger reported that the chief used the house as a dog kennel and as a warehouse for his buffalo hides. *See* Kappler, ed., *Indian Affairs,* II:807-11 and 887-91; Trenholm, *Arapahoes,* 183, 189, 212, 242, 264-65; and Seger, *Early Days Among the Cheyenne and Arapahoe Indians,* 16-19.

[108] According to Charles Bent, William Bent had two sons by his first wife, Owl Woman. These were Robert (b. 1841) and George (b. 1843). Yellow Woman, Bent's second wife, bore their half brother Charles, ca. 1847. Milligan's "Billy Bent Junior" was either Robert or Charles. Both boys were traveling with their father to Missouri where they would attend school. In 1915 there was a Bill Bent living in Montana who claimed to be the son of William Bent and Sarah Sullivan. Bill Bent stated that he was born in St. Louis in 1846. His relationship to William Bent has not been verified. There is no evidence that he ever lived with his father at Bent's New Fort. *See* Bent to Hyde, Mar. 9, 1905 (MS, Bent Papers, Denver Public Lib.); Carter, "Kit Carson," in Hafen ed., *Mountain Men and Fur Trade,* VI:130; Meriwether, *My Life in the Mountains and on the Plains,* 232-33; and Luebers, "William Bent's Family and the Indians of the Plains," 21-22.

[109] Beaver Island was situated about twenty miles down the Arkansas from Bent's New Fort in Prowers Co., CO.

[110] Bow keys were the bowpins used to fasten the oxbows to the ox yoke.

miserable night. Waked at dawn & started. Arrived at the Site of the late village and found old Lajuenesse on the "Siesta". Mr. Ed Foster undertook to exercise me at something I should have said, but fortunately for him he did not make good his threat of striking me or I should have shot him. Caught several wolfs in a snare.

February 15th 1854. Com. clear & windy. Loaded the waggon and made a start on the back trail for the fort. Traded six ropes. Camped at Pretty Encampment.

February 16th 1854. Com. clear & pleasant. Started at sunrise and nooned in the Middle of Salt Bottom.[111] Watered the Cattle & started. Camped for the night at the head of Salt bottom. Two Exewons in Company.

February 17th 1854. Com. clear & pleasant. Off at Sun-up. Our Indian friends killed a Buffalo close to Camp Deserted. Nooned at "Rue Mantaka".[112] Camped at night within 8 miles of the fort. Lige[113] & a Spaniard went ahead to get into the fort that night.

February 18th 1854. Com. clear & pleasant. Arrived at the fort & pressed the robes. Found they fell short 9 pack. Had a feast. Went to Coho's Lodge to see my women. Remained all night. Bent bought young Pawnee Prisoner.

February 19th 1854. Com. clear & pleasant. All hands at work covering the new fort and hauling wood. Made a pistol Scabbard and repaired the Seat of my Saddle. Bent

[111] Big Salt Bottom was situated on the Arkansas just above the mouth of Wild Horse Creek in Prowers Co., CO. According to Grinnell, the Cheyennes called it Red Willow Bottoms because of the red willows which grew profusely there. *See* Grinnell, "Bent's Old Fort," 91.

[112] Rue Mantaka was a camping place on the Arkansas in Prowers Co., CO. The editors have been unable to identify the meaning of this term, although it is definitely not a Cheyenne word.

[113] Lige = Francois Lajeunesse.

trading fast. Having run the opposition out of goods he has it all his own way.

February 20th 1854. Com. clear & pleasant. All hands working at the new fort. Old Lajuenesse preparing to start for Taos. Trying to buy a young Spaniard taken prisoner by the Kioways near Chihuahua. Offered a horse for the poor little fellow but do not know if the avarice of the Indians will allow him to accept it. He says he has two hearts on it. I've made my mind up to have the boy at all hazards. Old Murry's Mozo[114] came from the Fountain Que Boit with two horses after his Makite.[115] Bent traded 8 pack of robes.

February 21st 1854. Com. clear & pleasant. Old Lige started for Taos and Murry's boy for the Biszoni.[116] Bent's Squaw traded her horse "Pigeon Toe" for two fine mules. Bent trading robes fast, it being the close of the season. Boys dubing & chinking the new fort. Charley got home from the Pickitway[117] with 12 pack of robes.

February 22d 1854. Com. clear & pleasant. Had a Sight at and perusal of a St. Louis News Paper, the first for several months. Tim Goodwell brought the news down from the Fountain Que Boit that the Utahs were on the divide on their way against the Cheyannes and Arapahoes, accompanied by 300 Mexicans. He says Hatcher,[118] Joe

---

[114] Lucas Murray's male servant was named José. We do not know his last name. *See* entry for Jan. 8, 1854.

[115] Makite = Ma'kaeta, a Cheyenne word for money. The editors are indebted to linguists Danny Alford and Wayne Leman for this information.

[116] Biszoni = bisonte, a Spanish word for bison.

[117] Pickitway = Purgatory River. The Spanish name for the river was Rio de las Animas Perdidas. The French version was Purgatoire. Americans called it the "Picketway" or "Picketwire." The Purgatory heads in South-central Colorado. It flows northwest through Las Animas, Otero, and Bent counties before entering the Arkansas downstream from the town of Las Animas. *See* Lecompte, *Pueblo, Hardscrabble, Greenhorn,* 34.

[118] John L. Hatcher (ca. 1812-1879) was a native of Virginia who came west in the

Play[119] & St. Vrain[120] are on their way from Taos to the U. States. Boys at work on the new fort which is very nearly completed. Bent intends moving in it as soon as done. The rats are eating up all his goods here. Gave Carvalho's Box of Paints[121] away to Charley Davidson, they being of no use to me. A Mexican made me a hair girt which completes my outfit for the U.S.

February 23d 1854. Com. clear & pleasant. Tore down and hauled the Indian house to the new fort to be reerected. Pressed 27 Pack of robes. Unshipped the press.[122] Loaded

---

mid-1830s and found employment at Bent's Old Fort. According to Mumey, the Cheyennes called him "Freckled Hand." Lewis Garrard described him as the "beau ideal of a Rocky Mountain man" and immortalized Hatcher's tale of how he met the devil near the Spanish Peaks while in a drunken stupor. Lieutenant J.W. Abert employed Hatcher to guide his expedition into the Comanche country in 1845. In 1853 Hatcher joined Kit Carson, Lucien Maxwell, and other mountain men in driving herds of sheep to California. He was impressed with the Golden State, and settled in Sonoma in 1859. He moved to Oregon in 1867, where he remained until his death. *See* Carter, "John L. Hatcher," Hafen, ed., *Mountain Men and Fur Trade,* IV:125-36; Mumey, *Old Forts,* I:43; and Garrard, *Wah-to-Yah,* 219.

[119] José Pley was a merchant and trader who operated a store and mill in Mora, NM. He also ran a distillery which provided bootleg liquor for the soldiers at Fort Union. *See* Hammond, *Alexander Barclay,* 206; and Hafen, ed., *Mountain Men and Fur Trade,* III:187.

[120] Ceran St. Vrain (1802-1870) was a leading citizen of New Mexico and a successful Santa Fé trader, merchant, land speculator, and politician. Reared in the St. Louis vicinity, St. Vrain entered the Santa Fé trade in the mid-1820s. He became a naturalized citizen of Mexico and in 1830 formed with Charles Bent the well-known partnership of Bent, St. Vrain & Co. He and Bent established Bent's Fort in 1834. St. Vrain was associated with the Bent family until about 1850. From the end of the Mexican War through the 1860s, he was active in both public and private affairs. In 1855 he moved to Mora, NM, where he lived until his death. *See* Dunham, "Ceran St. Vrain," in Hafen, ed., *Mountain Men and Fur Trade,* V:297-316.

[121] Solomon Carvalho noted that he left his paints behind at Bent's Fort in Dr. Ebers' care since the cold weather made it "inconvenient" to use them. This helps explain why there are no existing Carvalho sketches of Frémont's journey through the mountains of Colorado and Utah in 1853-54, and why he began making sketches and painting in Utah when artists' supplies once again became available. *See* Carvalho, *Incidents of Travel, 72.*

[122] *Unship* is a nautical term meaning to remove gear or equipment from its usual place. Milligan's meaning is to unload and dismantle the press. There were two types of fur presses which Milligan might have been using at Bent's New Fort. One was the fulcrum-and-lever type which was relatively inexpensive and crude. The other was the

ROBE PRESS

Woodcut of a press of the type Milligan may have used at Bent's New Fort in 1854.

From *Harper's New Monthly Magazine* (January 1869).

5 waggons with robes. Put the sheets on & commenced to prepare for a start. Mended a few sheets for the waggons. Trade about closed for the season. Indians all leaving for the Pickitway.

February 24th 1854. Com. clear & pleasant. Bent commenced preparing his Equipment for the Comanche, Kioway & Apache trade. Put up the house tore down yesterday and prepared it to live in. All the teamsters busy preparing their bows and yokes and of course the usual excitement attendant on such occasions prevails. Every body swearing the best yokes belong to them. The Poor Greasers of course get Paddy's choice, viz. those which are left. Our evil genius the Arapahoes are preparing to move over to Dry creek where they intend leaving their women and children, and march to meet their deadly foe the Utahs. For the good of the Spring Emigration, I sincerely hope that the Utahs may give them a lesson not so easily got over. Their presumptuous and overbearing conduct this winter deserves something of a decisive character to be taken in regard to that. Moral suasion is lost upon them and I fear they premeditate something serious. Our government is thought quite insignificant by her with drawal of the troops from the lower Arkansas, which eventually they will be compelled to order back, or I have no idea of Indian character. The agent is not at all feared and they do with him as they like. They pay no respect to the Treaty of 50[123] but treat it with impunity. For this at least they ought to be severely punished, that it might

large rotary screw press which Bent used at Bent's Old Fort. The press was more than eleven feet long. Its use indicates the ascendancy of bison robes over beaver pelts in the 1840s and 1850s. Bison robes were usually pressed ten to a pack with each pack weighing from eighty to a hundred pounds. *See* Moore, *Bent's Old Fort,* 15, 36; Hanson, "Robe and Fur Presses," 3-6; and State Historical Society of Colorado, *Bent's Old Fort,* 166.

[123] There was no treaty of 1850. Milligan is referring to the Fort Laramie Treaty of 1851. *See* note 98 supra.

enable them for the future to pay more regard to Treatys and strictly adhere unto them. It is my opinion before one year there will be a general Indian war, for the insolence and barbarity of the Indians of the plains is no longer endurable and has become to be serious.

February 25th 1854. Com. clear & pleasant. Employed loading up the rest of Bent's waggons with meat, corn and other provisions. Squared yards[124] with all I owed. Bought a robe and pair of pants. Wrote to my father and informed him that in Consequence of Mr Bent's start I would be home much sooner than at first expected. Also requested him to make arrangements upon my arrival in Westport, to have money for me to come home with.

February 26th 1854. Com. clear & pleasant. Loaded up more robe waggons. Greased all the waggons & Bent's Carriage. Move the goods left to the new fort. Put up the corn mill and ground meal for our trip in. All the Arapahoes left for dry creek. My friend Coho came to get his last payment for the use of his women but was too busy to listen to him. When she came I gave her what she most desired and she departed in quite a good humour. A wounded Mexican came into the fort & reported that the Cheyannes had attacked a party of five of them while in their village trading, and killed four of them and he only escaped death by running. This has caused quite a sensation among our Dagos at the fort. Some of them sleep at the new fort to watch the Mexicans do not steal anything in case they are disposed to desert.

February 27th 1854. Com. Stormy with Snow. Covered the empty waggons and prepared to start tomorrow. Counted the oxen. Had a last blow out at the old fort which

[124] "Squared yards" = settled accounts.

consisted of Doughnuts. Bent fixed his bed in the Carriage for the trip.

February 28th 1854. Com. clear & pleasant. Hitched up and made a start. The train consisted of 14 waggon[s], ten of which are loaded with robes. Camped about 5 mile below the fort. Hatcher, Play & St. Vrain camped with us. Their train consisted of 29 waggons and 60 mules.

March 1st 1854. Com. clear & pleasant with high winds. Mr. Bent bought an Indian Lodge. Started with St. Vrain's train in company. Camped at Dry creek. Hatcher and the Hunters killed several antelope.

March 2d 1854. Com. cloudy & cold. It being to[o] cold to ride I let my mule go, and went ahead of the trains afoot. Overtook and had a long talk with Jno Radford[125] of St. Louis, who was just on his return from California flatbroke and had to beg his passage into the Mexican settlements with Kit Carson and Maxwell, who had taken a drove of sheep to California.[126] Found Bent camped at the head of Salt Bottom. Had the first Drink of Whiskey for *8 months.*

---

[125] John Desborough Radford was born in Maysville, Kentucky, in 1816 to Dr. John Radford and Harriet Kennerly. After his father's death, his mother moved to St. Louis and married William Clark, the famed explorer. John and his half-brother, William Preston Clark, joined Sir William Stewart's fourth western expedition to the Rendezvous of 1838. He traveled with Stewart again in 1843. In 1849, he and his cousin William Clark Kennerly, joined the gold rush to California. After an unsuccessful stint in the diggings, he worked for a time as a deputy sheriff in Sacramento. His brother-in-law, Stephen Watts Kearny, once characterized him in the following manner: "John has no vices but is a most indolent man." *See* Kennerly. *Persimmon Hill,* 113, 143-49, 210, and 214-16; and Field, *Prairie and Mountain Sketches,* li.

[126] In 1853, Kit Carson, Lucien Maxwell, John Hatcher, Tim Goodale, and others organized a sheep drive from New Mexico to California. The sheep were driven in several herds from Taos to Fort Laramie, and thence along the California-Oregon Trail. The sheep cost less than fifty cents per head in New Mexico, and were sold in California for $5.50 per head, earning the organizers a handsome profit. *See* Carter, "John L. Hatcher," in Hafen, ed., *Mountain Men and Fur Trade,* IV:31-32; Carter, "Kit Carson," *Ibid.,* VI:124; and Murphy, *Lucien Bonaparte Maxwell,* 95-96.

March 3d 1854. Com. clear & windy. Started and went as far as Campo Bonito. Made 20 mile. Bought a Pair of Sock[s] and put them on. Feel quite comfortable about the pedals.

March 4th 1854. Com. clear & pleasant. Started and camped early in consequence of seeing some Indians. Corralled all the Horses and oxen and sent out Scouts to reconnoitre. Kioway & Pelow, our Scouts, returned and informed us that the strangers proved to be Cheyannes.

March 5th 1854. Com. clear & pleasant, wind from S^d^. Made about 13 mile and camped where there was no wood. Asleep all day in the waggon. Had a foot race between a Shawnee Indian belonging to our train and a Mexican of St. Vrain's. The Shawnee beat the Mexican about 20 feet in 150 yds.

March 6th 1854. Com. cloudy with high winds. Passed an Indian village. Made about 10 mile and camped. Several fat Buffalo Cows were killed during the day and we of course enjoyed a luxurious repast. During the night a rain storm came up and [I] found myself afloat. Took shelter in a Robe waggon where I layed snug until Morning.

March 7th 1854. Com. cloudy and drizzling rain. Did not move camp. Sent a waggon in charge of the Mexican for a load of wood.

March 8th 1854. Com. clear & pleasant. Started the trains and camped below Chouteau's Island, so named in consequence of Chouteau who took shelter upon it and built a fort of his waggons when attacked by a Band of Pawnees.[127] The fight lasted for many Days. Shod one of

[127] Chouteau's Island was a well-known landmark on the Santa Fé Trail, situated in the Arkansas River southwest of the town of Larkin in Kearny Co., KS. The island was named for Auguste P. Chouteau. In the autumn of 1815 Chouteau and Jules de Mun

the oxen which had become lame. 8 Lodges of Cheyannes camped on the other side of the river opposite us. Saw several herd of Buffalo.

March 9th 1854. Com. clear & wind[y] with dust flying, which made it exceedingly unpleasant without goggles. Made about 10 mile and camped in a rich bottom. St. Vrain's train camped above us about ¼ of a mile. Bill Garey[128] from the Platte passed our camps on his return from the Kioways and Comanches, where he had been trading for mules. He had 60 head. He reports a big fight on the borders of old Mexico and the total destruction of a town by the savages.

March 10th 1854. Com. clear & pleasant. St. Vrain's train went ahead. We stopped on a/c of trade. Windy & rain during the evening.

March 11th 1854. Com. clear & pleasant. About 200 lodges of Cheyannes, Sue [Sioux] & Apache camped near us. Commenced trade.

---

outfitted an expedition to trade with the Arapaho Indians on the Upper Arkansas. In the spring of 1816, Chouteau and de Mun were heading down the Arkansas after their successful trading venture when they were waylaid by a Pawnee war party. They defended themselves from a wooded island in the river, which thereafter was known as Chouteau's Island. *See* Barry, *Beginning of the West,* 74-76.

[128] William Le Guerrier (variant spellings include Guerrieu and Garriou) was commonly known as Bill Gary in the 1840s and 1850s. He worked intermittently as a trader at Bent's Fort and had an Arapaho wife, but he is most closely associated with trading posts on the North Platte near Fort Laramie. In 1848 he formed a partnership with Seth Ward to trade for buffalo robes on the Arkansas. In 1851 he and Ward bought out John Richard's trading post on the North Platte near modern Torrington WY. In 1852 he operated a ferry on the North Platte and the following year constructed a bridge over the Laramie River at Fort Laramie. In 1856 he obtained a government license to trade with the Sioux, Cheyenne, and Arapaho Indians in Colorado, Wyoming and South Dakota. He was killed in 1858 when ashes from his pipe ignited a powder keg. Guerrier's son, Edmund, married William Bent's daughter, Julia. *See* Hafen, ed., *Mountain Men and Fur Trade,* II:296, 299; III:363-71; V:73-74; VI:155-58; and Barry, *Beginning of the West,* 1148-49.

March 12th 1854. Com. clear & pleasant. Towards night put all the robes & goods in the waggons, it having every appearance of a storm. Played Poker for Tobacco until midnight. Came out ahead 5 plugs.

March 13th 1854. Com. clear & pleasant & very windy during the morning. Caught some small red horse[129] out of the river and had a fry. Greased the waggons and tightened the tires. One of my old Indian friends gave me a mess of side ribs.

March 14th 1854. Com. clear & pleasant. Got up to dinner. Feel very weak. Packed 16 pack of robes, making 20 packs we have traded since here. Made a new journal to date from my twenty-fifth year, which will be tomorrow if God spares me. I have made *so* many good resolutions and departed from them that I am now determined to take advantage of every opportunity to do good. Tim Goodwell & Charley Davidson arrived from the fort, and report that the Cheyannes and Utes had come in Collision, and the latter had run off a number of horses belonging to the former. The Utes were reported to be on the trail of "Oakum hoist" (yellow Wolf)[130] a worthy Cheyanne chief who is on his way to the Cimmeronė to join the Kioways. Wrote to father and expect to send it when we arrive at the crossing of the Arkansas, where we may meet the Santa Fe Mail.

---

[129] Redhorse suckers are of the genus *Moxostoma,* and the family *catostomidae,* which includes more than two dozen American species. *See* American Fisheries Society, *A List of Common and Scientific Names of Fishes,* 27.

[130] Yellow Wolf was prominent on the Southern Plains and the Bent's Fort vicinity from the 1820s until his death in 1864 at the Sand Creek Massacre. James W. Abert, who sketched his portrait in 1845, characterized Yellow Wolf as the "head chief" of the Southern Cheyenne, "a remarkable man" who understood the crisis facing the Cheyenne way of life with the rapid depletion of the buffalo, and who sought ways to help his people adjust to the transition from a hunting economy to farming. *See* Abert, *Western America,* 18; Abert, *Through the Country of the Comanche Indians,* 2-4; and Hoig, *The Peace Chiefs,* 27-34.

March 15th 1854. Com. clear & very pleasant. Moved camp with the Indians about 10 mile below. Tim & Charley started to the fort. Charley to return with all the mules left at the fort to take into the States. The village camped opposite us on the river. 25 years old today. No wood here, consequently we use Bois de Vache[131] to cook with.

March 16th 1854. Com. clear & exceedingly pleasant with light southerly breezes. Got up late, washed my head and combed it, which was quite an undertaking. Several of the party fishing but no luck. My old Cheyanne wife paid me a visit to satisfy a sweet demand. She wanted sugar but I had none to give her. All hands in the camp wanting bleeding but only bled two.

March 17th 1854. Com. cloudy & cool. Mr. Bent sick today. Took his place trading. Trade coming to a close fast. All our mess fishing. Bought a Box of Caps for my pistol, "the only arms which now I have." Bent traded several mules & horses. Feel exceedingly unpleasant in conse quence of having no clean shirt or soap where with to lave with. Innumerable quantities of Duck in the river and the plains literally white with wild geese.

March 18th 1854. Com. clear & cold. Mr. Bent better. Three Cheyannes returned from a war party out of 17 which left two Months since. They are the only Survivors. They report killed in the same Battle 27 Comanches 1 Arrapahoe & 5 Kioways all killed at a small Ranchero near Chihuahua. They report their opponent Shavanoes which if so must be Wild Cat and his band of Seminoles now in

[131] *Bois de Vache* is a French term for buffalo chips, literally "cow wood," or "wood of the cow." *Bois de Vache* was the only source of fuel on much of the treeless plains. Lieutenant Sylvester Mowry wrote to a friend in 1854 from a camp on the Oregon Trail that the *Bois de Vache* burn "to a hard live coal giving out a pleasant odor, and at night, a coal held for a few moments in a tent, effectually 'rubs out' the mosquitoes." *See* Mowry to Bicknall, July 6, 1854 (MS, Utah State Hist. Soc.).

the employ of the Mexican Government.[132] Great mourning in the village in consequence of the loss of their young warriors.

March 19th 1854. Com. with rain & sleet and exceeding ly unpleasant. Had quite a time in cooking breakfast in consequence of the Bois de Vache being wet. Spent most of the day in the waggon ruminating over the many follys of my past life, and laying plans for the future. How I may succeed remains for the sequel. Feel a touch of the Rheumatism in my right leg, which I attribute to the change in the weather. Had fine duck stew for Breakfast. About dark about 20 of the Cavayard were missing, my two horses among them. They wandered off during the storm of Sleet.

March 20th 1854. Com. cloudy. About Meridian cleared off. Old Kioway & Pelow found the horses some distance from Camp. Traded some robes during the day. Wood scarce. Bound to move soon or live on raw meat. Shawnees out ducking. Went over the river after wood. Towards evening windy & misty. The Duckers returned with one Poor Duck.

March 21st 1854. Com. clear & pleasant. Struck Camp and started. Came to[133] at Pawnee fort. The Indians

[132] Wild Cat, whose Seminole name was Coacoochie, was a Seminole chief and scalp hunter who by 1850 lived with his people at San Fernando de Roses (now Zaragoza), Coahuila, about thirty miles southwest of Piedras Negras. Wild Cat, or Gato del Monte as he was known to the Mexicans, signed a treaty with the Mexican Government in which he and his people promised to hunt down and scalp Comanche, Apache, and Kiowa raiders along the Rio Grande and in Northern Mexico. In return, the Mexican Government promised to provide Wild Cat and his people with a land grant in Coahuila, along with Mexican citizenship and other concessions. These Seminole colonies soon became havens for slaves escaping from the United States. Escaped slave warriors, known as mamelukes, helped Wild Cat hunt down and scalp Plains Indian raiders. *See* New York *Daily Tribune,* Aug. 19, 21, 1850; Austin *Texas State Gazette,* Nov. 16, 1850; Smith, "The Mamelukes of West Texas and Mexico," 65-88; and Smith, "The Fantasy of a Treaty to End Treaties," 26-51.

[133] "Came to" is a nautical term meaning "to stop."

camped opposite us on an Island. Found some wood which we treasure. Good grass. Had the misfortune to break my pipe. Charley Davidson arrived from the fort with 8 mules and 12,000 in Gold. Made two new waggon Sheets.

March 22d 1854. Com. clear & pleasant. Pressed 22 pack of robes making in all 227 pack. Expect to make out the 300 with the Commanches and Kioways at Jackson's Grove.[134] Scalded my foot & hand. Applyed the Indian cure. Shot a Cheyanne's dog for being the cause of my Misfortune. It came near raising a row in Camp.

March 23d 1854. Com. clear & pleasant. Pressed some robes and loaded another waggon. Suffered all night with my foot.

March 24th 1854. Com. clear & pleasant. Moved my bed out of the waggon. Moved camp down the river with the Indians. Last day of our trade with the Cheyannes. Camped just above the crossing at the same place I struck the river with Fremont in November last.[135]

March 25th 1854. Com. cloudy & cool. Found that Fremont['s] mare was missing from the Cavayard this morning. All search for her proved unsuccessfull. I fear she has died as she was not worth stealing, she being too

---

[134] Jackson's Grove extended for a quarter mile along the south bank of the Arkansas about ten miles east of Dodge City, KS. It was at this site in 1843 that Captain Philip St. George Cooke of the First U.S. Dragoons encountered Jacob Snively's Texan "Battalion of Invincibles." Bent's train did not find the Kiowa and Comanche camps at Jackson's Grove as expected. *See* Barry, *Beginning of the West,* 478, 619; Hulbert, "Santa Fé Trail," map 27; and Abert, *Western America,* 15.

[135] There were five major crossings of the Arkansas which fed into the Cimarron Cutoff. The Lower Crossing was near Ford, KS at the mouth of Mulberry Creek. A second crossing at "the Caches" was located six miles west of Dodge City and converged with the Mulberry Creek route. The Middle Crossing was situated about twenty miles west of Dodge City at Cimarron, KS. A fourth crossing was at Ingalls, and the Upper Crossing was located at Chouteau's Island. The crossing which the Frémont party used on Nov. 11, 1853, was the crossing near Ingalls.

poor and worn down as well as wounded on the weathers. Was compelled to ride in a waggon in Consequence of my foot. Riding my mule has made it worse and inflamed. Camped near the lower crossing. Greased all the waggons and packed the remaining goods.

March 26th 1854. Com. cloudy & windy. Foot a little better this morning but still very lame and painful. Started and made about 15 mile. Camped about 15 mile from Fort MacKay (Deserted).[136]

March 27th 1854. Com. clear & windy. Travelled about 12 mile and camped near fort MacKay. A number of Commanches came into Camp. The chief embraced Mr. Bent, the usual Indian custom. Gave them a feast. Put up a temporary lodge near us. Corraled horses for the first time on the river. All hands at Quoit's[137] for a feast. An Arapahoe lodge camped near us. Walked to the fort to see what it looked like. Foot painful from the effects of the walk.

March 28th 1854. Com. with cold drizzling rain & cloudy. About noon cleared up pleasant. Started and camped about 5 mile below the fort. Lost $6 at Quoit's. The Commanches and Arapahoe lodge still in Company.

---

[136] While encamped near the Lower Crossing, Bent must have learned that the Comanches, whom he had missed at Jackson's Grove, were encamped about 25 miles to the west up the Arkansas near the site of Fort Mackay. On Mar. 26, Bent and his traders turned around and retraced their route, reaching the Comanche encampment near the site of the abandoned Fort Mackay.

In Sept., 1850, Colonel Edwin V. Sumner selected the site for Fort Mackay. The fort was first known as "New Post on the Arkansas" but was soon named "Fort Mackay." In June 1851, the post was officially named Fort Atkinson. Fort Atkinson was abandoned in Sept. 1853, and briefly re-occupied in 1854. Upon its abandonment, the army destroyed the sod buildings so that Plains Indians could not use the ruins to ambush Santa Fé Trail travelers. Fort Mackay-Atkinson was located on the north bank of the Arkansas about four miles west of Dodge City, KS. *See* Barry, *Beginning of the West,* 965-67; and Hart, *Old Forts,* 75-76.

[137] This Comanche chief cannot be positively identified but may have been Quirts Quip (Elk's Cud), a chief of the Yamparika band. *See* Leckie, *The Military Conquest of the Southern Plains,* 180-181; and Nye, *Carbine and Lance,* 221.

March 29th 1854. Com. cloudy with rain and hail. Got my bed wet. Kioway informed me that the mare lost on the 25 inst. died at the Camp of that date.

Played Monte. Lost my Coat & Blankets.

March 30th 1854. Com. cloudy & misty with rain. Started & came to at Jackson's Grove. My foot getting better. Walked about 8 miles. Cleared off pleasant at mid day. Heavy squall of wind during the night wrecked old Kioway's Lodge. I broke for a waggon to get out of the wind.

March 31st 1854. Com. clear and windy. Did not start Camp. Lost my pistol and won $16 at Monte.

April 1st 1854. Com. clear & pleasant. Started & made about 12 mile. The Commanches left us, crossed the river and went in the direction of Louse creek.[138] Expect to meet the village at Coon creek[139] to trade. Felt the infernal Rheumatism.

April 2d 1854. Com. clear & pleasant. Waiting for the Indians to trade the rest of the goods. The Shawnees shot a number of Geese, & we had quite a feast. A Large Mexican Mule train belonging to the Armijo[140] of New Mexico Camped near us. Two Arapahoe Lodges came over the river & camped near us.

April 3d 1854. Com. clear & pleasant. Shod an ox. Played Poker for Tobacco and lost 13 plugs.

[138] Louse Creek = North Fork of the Canadian River. *See* Gregg, ed., *The Road to Santa Fe: The Journal and Diaries of George Chaplin Sibley,* 261.

[139] Coon Creek heads in Ford Co. It flows to the east-northeast through Ford and Edwards counties and enters the Arkansas in Pawnee Co., about a mile above Garfield, KS.

[140] According to James A. Little, who was traveling with Armijo's train in 1854, Armijo was "a very noted Mexican freighter." The Armijo whom Milligan met cannot be identified precisely. There were several Santa Fé traders from the New Mexican Armijo family. *See* Barry, *Beginning of the West,* 1077 and 1206.

April 4th 1854. Com. clear & pleasant. Started on our road for the "Unidos Estados" direct. Met a large war Party of Kioways with a number of mules and horses they had stolen from a Mexican on the Dry Route.[141] Made about 20 miles and camped early.

April 5th 1854. Com. clear & pleasant. Started before sunrise. Lost my spur trying to head a mule (which we found on the road) from a Band of Buffalo which are plenty today. Nooned on Coon creek. Killed several Buffalo cows and caught a young calf. Bent's Semi-Barbarian Children killed it in mere wantonness while my back was turned. Crossed Coon Creek & camped.

April 6th 1854. Com. clear & pleasant. Started as early as usual and nooned on Pawnee fork. Crossed Ash creek[142] by a near trail and camped at Pawnee Rock.[143] Buffalo Plenty.

April 7th 1854. Com. clear & very windy. Started earlier than usual and nooned about 4 mile from Walnut creek. Crossed it and camped at Big Bend,[144] where we leave the Arkansas. Very windy & exceedingly unpleasant.

April 8th 1854. Com. cloudy with rain. Started about 2

---

[141] The Dry Route (sometimes called Ridge Road) was a shortcut on the Santa Fé Trail which left the Arkansas and the main trail at the mouth of the Pawnee River near Larned, KS. It struck the river again east of Dodge City. The Dry Route avoided the extreme southern bend of the Arkansas. The longer main branch of the trail ran along the north bank of the Arkansas. *See* Riddle, *Records and Maps of the Old Santa Fe Trail,* General Map, sheet 7.

[142] Ash Creek flows in a southeasterly direction through Pawnee County, KS. It flows into the Arkansas about two miles east of Pawnee Rock, KS.

[143] Pawnee Rock is situated about a mile northwest of the town of Pawnee Rock in Barton Co., KS. According to Matt Field, who visited the rock in 1839, the Pawnees believed that the rock contained an evil spirit, and made offerings to it. Field described Pawnee Rock as "a huge wart" rising above "the carpeted green of the prairie." Pawnee Rock is still imposing, although much of it has been quarried to provide building stone. *See* Sunder, ed., *Matt Field,* 100.

[144] The apex of the Big Bend of the Arkansas is at the city of Big Bend in Barton Co., KS. Big Bend marks the point where the Santa Fé Trail first struck the Arkansas.

hours before day. Met the Mail[145] at Cow creek. Passed Plum Butte[146] at Sunrise. Camped on Jarvis creek[147] and shod the oxen which required it. Grass scarce. Buffalo numerous.

April 9th 1854. Com. cloudy & exceedingly windy. Layed by all day on a/c of weather. Jim Swanick,[148] a Deleware Chief, camped with us. He had been up on Pawnee fork trapping for the last 4 months. Learned from him that the Col.'s (Fremont's) mules and horses lost on Salt creek last fall were at Pottawatomie. Had a last feast. Buffalo numerous.

---

145 The east-bound mail stage from Santa Fé was in the charge of Francis Boothe. It reached Independence on Apr. 23, the same day that Milligan arrived at Westport. Newspaper accounts of the mail's arrival in Independence are cited in Barry, *Beginning of the West,* 1204.

146 Plum Butte, also known as Round Mound or Plum Point, is situated midway between Cow Creek and the Big Bend of the Arkansas in Rice Co., KS. Matt Field described Plum Butte as "a beautiful hillock, covered with plum trees, in the middle of a flat Prairie." *See* Sunder, ed., *Matt Field,* 88.

147 Jarvis Creek flows in a southerly direction through Rice Co., entering Cow Creek about a mile southeast of Saxman, KS. Jarvis is a corruption of the Spanish name Chaves. The creek was named for a New Mexican merchant, Antonio José Chavez, who was murdered near the creek by John McDaniel and a gang of Texas bandits. *See* Gregg, *Commerce of the Prairies,* 337-42.

148 Jim Swanock (spelling variations include Swanick, Swanok, Sewanik) was the son of a Delaware chief by the same name. Both were active as hunters and trappers in the Rocky Mountains, the elder Swanock leading a trapping expedition into the mountains as early as 1834. The elder Swanock was reportedly killed in 1844 on the Smoky Hill River by a party of Sioux and Cheyenne warriors, although there is some evidence that he may have survived the attack. In 1845 the younger Jim Swanock signed up as one of twelve Delaware hunters on Frémont's third expedition to California, where he performed creditable service. It is presumably the younger Swanock whom Milligan met on the Santa Fé Trail in 1854.

After returning from California, Swanock spent some time trapping on the Upper Arkansas, for he is mentioned in Alexander Barclay's journal in early 1849. His whereabouts between 1849 and 1854 are unknown. He appears to have spent the years from 1855 to 1860 on the Delaware Reservation in KS, for the names of Jim and his wife Kwa Ese, appear on the reservation ledger books for that period. Swanock was an allottee under the Delaware Allotment Treaty of 1860. *See* Carter, "Jim Swanock and the Delaware Hunters," in Hafen, ed., *Mountain Men and Fur Trade,* VII:293-97; Hammond, *Alexander Barclay,* 65; Hafen, ed., "Boggs Manuscript," 52-54; and Moses Grinter's Ledger Book, Apr. 20, 1855- Oct. 20, 1860, Delaware Reservation, KS (MS, Oklahoma State Hist. Soc.).

April 10th 1854. Com. clear & pleasant. Started, crossed Little Cow creek,[149] Owl creek[150] & Jarvis fork,[151] and nooned at Devil's Hole.[152] Greased waggons. Grass poor & cattle weak. Went out with the Hunter to bring in Meat. The mules run down & killed a young Buffalo Calf. Camped on Little Arkansas.[153]

April 11th 1854. Com. clear & pleasant. Crossed Mud creek,[154] Dry Turkey creek,[155] and nooned on Big Turkey creek.[156] Water thick & muddy in consequence of the late rains. Camped for the night at Little Turkey creek.[157] Let the Horses run out all night. Did not corral.

April 12th 1854. Com. clear & pleasant. Cavayard Scattered from Hell to Halifax. Started at sun-up. Nooned at the Hole where Dodge Swaney & Fillmore killed the Delaware Trapper and his Squaw & then robbed them, for which Dodge & Swaney were hung at St. Louis last July.[158] Camped at Cottonwood and found St. Vrain's train camped

---

[149] Little Cow Creek heads northwest of Lyons, KS. It flows to the southeast through Rice Co. and enters Cow Creek about two miles south of Lyons.

[150] Owl Creek heads about five miles northeast of Lyons, KS. It flows in a southerly direction through Rice Co. and enters Cow Creek about three miles southeast of Lyons.

[151] Jarvis Fork = Jarvis Creek.

[152] Devil's Hole was located on the headwaters of Sand Creek in Rice Co., KS. The name is not mentioned in any of the Santa Fé Trail accounts which we examined and must not have been in common usage.

[153] The Little Arkansas heads in Ellsworth Co., KS. It flows to the southeast through Rice, McPherson, Reno, Harvey, and Sedgewick counties, entering the Arkansas River at Wichita, KS. The Santa Fé Trail crossed the Little Arkansas near its confluence with Lone Tree Creek and Sand Creek in Rice Co., KS.

[154] Milligan's Mud Creek is probably Wolf Creek, which flows through McPherson Co., KS.

[155] Dry Turkey Creek flows in a southerly direction through McPherson Co. past the city of McPherson and enters Turkey Creek about eight miles south of McPherson.

[156] Big Turkey Creek = Turkey Creek, which heads northeast of McPherson. It flows in a southerly direction through McPherson Co., entering the Little Arkansas near Alta Mills in Harvey Co., KS.

[157] Little Turkey Creek = Running Turkey Creek, which flows in a southwesterly direction through McPherson Co. It enters Dry Turkey Creek about eight miles south of McPherson, KS.

there, which left us a month ago on the Arkansas at Jackson's Grove. Rained very hard.

April 13th 1854. Com. with heavy rain. Gov. Merriweather[159] & Doctor Conly[160] in advance of their trains camped near us. Visited his Camp and found him entirely discouraged with the rain. Raining all day. Two mule trains came in and camped near us.

April 14th 1854. Com. with rain & cool. The Cavayard among the missing this morning. Found my mule all right having tied her up during the night. Stormed all day. Wind from the N^{d} & E^{d}.

April 15th 1854. Com. clear & pleasant. Got a late start in consequence of not finding the oxen. Nooned at some holes in the Prairie. Camped at Lost Spring.[161]

---

[158] Joseph Dodge and John Schoen murdered a Delaware trapper at this site in July, 1852. The pair were tried for their crime, sentenced, and hanged in St. Louis on July 22, 1853. *See* Chapter III supra, pp. 65-66.

[159] David Meriwether (1800-1892) was a Kentucky planter and politician, who was territorial governor of New Mexico in 1854. In 1819 Meriwether joined the Yellowstone Expedition as an employee of sutler John O'Fallon. In 1820 he traveled to Santa Fé in hopes of opening up trade relations, but was imprisoned by New Mexican authorties. After his release in 1821, he returned to Kentucky, where he married and settled on a plantation. In 1852 he filled Henry Clay's vacated Senate seat and the following year President Franklin Pierce appointed him to a four-year term as Governor of New Mexico. When Milligan met him, he was traveling in the company of Mrs. Louis Smith (the wife of a Baptist missionary), Dr. Henry Connelly, and a large wagon train belonging to José Francisco Chavez. Meriwether's account of his 1854 journey over the Santa Fé Trail can be found in Meriwether, *My Life,* 176-87. *See* also Horn, *New Mexico's Troubled Years,* 52-69.

[160] Henry Connelly (1800-1866) was a physician from Kentucky who moved to Chihuahua in 1828. Between 1830 and 1848 he ran a store in Chihuahua and operated trade caravans between Mexico and Independence, MO. In 1846 he helped Philip St. George Cooke and James Magoffin negotiate the peaceful conquest of New Mexico with Governor Manuel Armijo. Between 1853 and 1859 he served as a member of the territorial legislature. Abraham Lincoln appointed him Territorial Governor in 1861 and again in 1864. David Meriwether described him as "a large fleshy man." *See Ibid.,* 92-113; and Meriwether, *My Life,* 182.

[161] Lost Spring was near the modern town of Lost Springs in northeastern Marion Co., KS.

April 16th 1854. Com. clear & pleasant. At daylight St. Vrain's train passed us. Met an Emigrant for California on foot and pulling a small waggon after him. Camped near Diamond Spring.[162]

April 17th 1854. Com. clear & pleasant. Started before day. Part of the Cavayard missing. Left some goods at Council Grove.[163] Got 10 dollars from Bent to go to Union Town with Swanick. Nooned at Big John[164] some time to wait for the Cavayard to come up. Pelow arrived late in the evening with the Cavayard and reports 8 animals missing, among them my favourite "Red Eye".

April 18th 1854. Com. clear & pleasant. Started for Caw river in Company with Swanick. My mule, after travelling 10 mile, got the sulks and [I] was compelled to camp in fine grass. Got something to eat & started. Camped all night on Smith's Creek.[165]

April 19th 1854. Com. clear & pleasant. Started at daylight and eat dinner below Union Town. After crossing Caw river, my mule gave out and I had to foot it to Louis Jumbo's, alias Vieux,[166] and Pottowattomie chief having

[162] Diamond Spring was also known as "Diamond of the Plains" and was so named by George C. Sibley during his survey of the Santa Fé Trail in 1825. *See* Gregg, *Road to Santa Fé,* 184.

[163] Council Grove was a favorite stopping place on the Santa Fé Trail. It was situated at the site of the city of Council Grove in Morris Co., KS. George C. Sibley named the grove in Aug. 1825, to commemorate a meeting with Osage chiefs. *See* Gregg, *Road to Santa Fe,* 56-57.

[164] Big John's Spring in Morris Co. was named for "Big John" Walker, who discovered the spring in June 1825, while working on George Sibley's survey of the Santa Fé Trail. *Ibid.,* 185.

[165] Smith's Creek = Mission Creek. Sidney W. Smith operated a Ferry across the Kansas River near the point where Mission Creek empties into the KS. *See* note 22 supra.

[166] Louis Vieux (1809-1872) was a Potawatomi chief of mixed Potawatomi-French ancestry. He was an interpreter, fur trader, and successful businessman who lived on an allotment in Potawatomi Co., KS, just east of the point where the Oregon Trail crossed the Vermillion River. *See* William Smith, "The Oregon Trail Through Potawatomi County," 454-56.

business with this tribe in regard to Col. Fremont's animals. I stayed all night.

April 20th 1854. Com. clear & pleasant. Gave Vieux an order to get all mules belonging to the Col. with directions to advise me upon his success. Started & fell in Company with a waggon returning to Parkville.[167] Rained very hard. Camped on Grasshopper[168] at a deserted house. Saw Solomon's wife, Fremont's interpreter, but could not make her understand me.

April 21st 1854. Com. clear & pleasant. *Hitched* my mule behind the waggon and rode in it for variety's sake, having been on horse & mule-back daily for the last 8 months. Camped on Stranger[169] at a Deserted fish Camp, where I was fortunate enough to find some corn for my mule Billy.

April 22d 1854. Com. clear & pleasant. Arrived at Mr. Findley[170] at Deleware City and gave poor little Billy up, for which I took a receipt. Also took $40 from him on a/c of Fremont.

April 23d 1854. Com. cloudy with rain. Went to Westport in the stage and put up at the Harris House. Disguised myself in a clean shirt and, it being Sunday, I kept sober.

---

[167] Parkville, Missouri, is situated in Platte Co., MO, about ten miles above the mouth of the Kansas River. The town was established by George S. Park. *See* Barry, *Beginning of the West,* 1173 and 1176.

[168] Grasshopper River = Delaware River. The Delaware River flows into the Kansas River from the North a few miles west of Topeka, KS.

[169] Stranger Creek flows south through Atchison Co. and enters the Kansas River in Leavenworth Co. near Leavenworth, KS.

[170] James Findlay was a trader. In partnership with a Shawnee Indian named Joseph Parks, he operated a trading post at the Fort Leavenworth Agency. In Sept. 1850, Findlay became first postmaster of the town of Delaware. Delaware was situated on the Fort Leavenworth-Fort Scott military road at the Grinter Ferry, which crossed the Kansas River near the mouth of the Delaware River in Wyandotte Co., KS. By 1851 Delaware was considered to be the principal trading town for the Delaware Indians. *See* Barry, *Beginning of the West,* 331, 343, 350, 967, 1025, and 1030.

April 24th 1854. Com. clear & pleasant. Bent's train got . . . .[171]

April 26th 1854. Com. clear & pleasant. Went to Kansas and took passage on Board the Polar Star for St. Louis with Jim Sabine[172] and others. Got drunk and liberal. Gave away all my Indian traps and spent all my money.

April 28th 1854. Arrived home after an absence of near 8 months, following a man totally devoid of gratitude.

---

[171] Bottom of page missing in original journal.

[172] James E. Sabine was a trader who was active in the Santa Fé trade in the late 1840s and early 1850s. In Dec. 1850, he brought the mail from Santa Fé to Independence when the scheduled carrier died. He arrived in Independence on the same day that Milligan arrived with the mail from Salt Lake City. It can be assumed that their acquaintance went back at least to that meeting in 1850. *See* Barry, *Beginning of the West,* 885, 904, 956, 976 and 1005.

6

Lt. Milligan of the United States Marine Revenue Service, 1855-1861

and his letter against Frémont in the election of 1856

For nearly a year after his return from the West, James Milligan led an unsettled life. The Treasury Department continued to delay action on his application for a commission in the Revenue Marine Service. Meanwhile, he tried to make do with various jobs. On May 1, 1854, only a few days following his arrival in St. Louis, he records taking a job as a distribution clerk in the Post Office, a position once held by his father. Milligan lasted in this position for just a month and a half, quitting the job on June 16 "in disgust" and leaving with his sister Isabelle to visit their brother Francis in Minnesota. Upon his return to St. Louis, he hired on at his old job as carpenter for the Varieties Theatre, and worked there from September to December. On March 8, 1855, he became 2nd mate on the steamer *Emma Harmon,* which operated on the Osage and Kansas rivers during March and April.

Life began to brighten for Milligan in March 1855. Secretary of the Treasury Guthrie finally granted him a commission as a 3rd Lieutenant on March 10.[1] News of his appointment did not reach him on the *Emma Harmon* until late April, and he was sworn into the Revenue Marine

[1] "Appointment Records-U.S.R.M.S.," Mar. 10, 1855, RG 26, NARS.

Service on April 25, according to one of the few dated entries in his journal after his return from the Frémont expedition. On May 2, Secretary Guthrie ordered Lieutenant Milligan to report for duty to the revenue cutter *William J. Duane* at New Orleans.[2] Upon receiving these orders by telegraph from St. Louis, he took passage on the steamer *Admiral,* arriving at St. Louis on May 15, and then left St. Louis for New Orleans, arriving May 23. He immediately reported to the collector of customs and, after a week's stay in the city, traveled in a towboat downriver to the passes at the mouth of the Mississippi where the *Duane* was on station. Lieutenant Milligan records that he went aboard the *Duane* on May 30, reporting to the Captain, Lieutenant John G. Brushwood, whom Milligan had once known in Norfolk.

Milligan had longed for a commission in the Revenue Marine Service and a chance to return to sea duty, but his tenure in the service coincided with its least prestigious period. The revenue cutters themselves were small and few in number, the pay and morale were low, and organization was bad. To economize after the Mexican War, Congress had abolished the Revenue Marine Bureau and instead placed control of the Revenue Marine Service in the hands of a Commissioner of Customs in the Treasury Department. This official then allowed the district collectors to supervise the cutter service in their area. Describing this situation as "a picnic ground for seaport politicians," one historian of the Coast Guard and its predecessors says that "no longer was there a system of appointments and promotions by examination and merit; rather these became tidbits of political patronage."[3] James Milligan certainly owed his job to patronage, but at least he was qualified for the job by previous naval experience.

---

[2] Guthrie to Milligan, May 2, 1855, "Letters on Revenue Marine and Boats," LS 14/54, RG 26, NARS. Hereafter cited as "Letters Sent-U.S.R.M.S."

[3] Bloomfield, *The Compact History of the United States Coast Guard,* 49.

Lieutenant Milligan seems to have found his new duties, routine as they apparently were, to his liking. Nothing spectacular seems to have happened during his service in the late 1850s. But he did undergo important personal development during this stage of his life. At first he felt rather depressed, as he stated in one of his verses:

My lot is far different from those happy at home
for fate has doomed me a wanderer to roam.

Occasionally he still got drunk and once caught a lecture from the Captain about his intoxicated state. Apparently he decided that if he were to succeed, then he would simply have to largely abandon his former life-style and drinking habits. His commitment to partial sobriety seems to have begun in late 1855. Concurrent with his semi-abandonment of the liquor bottle was his desire to settle down in matters of love and find a wife. He notes in his journal several young women whose company he enjoyed in Louisiana, and there are several examples of his love poems among the random notes at the back of his journal. One of the young ladies he met in August, 1855, was Miss Sarah Lightfoot, who was staying near Pass Christian, Mississippi, with a family whom Lieutenant Milligan had come to visit. Miss Lightfoot was the daughter of a prominent doctor in Norfolk. When the cutter *Duane* was ordered to Norfolk for repairs in October 1855,[4] Milligan had an opportunity to renew his acquaintance with Sally. Their relationship continued to develop into love in Norfolk, and James Fisher Milligan finally took Sarah ("Sally") Colgate Lightfoot[5] as his bride at Christchurch in Norfolk in an Episcopal ceremony on May 1, 1856.[6]

[4] U.S. Coast Guard, *Record of Movements,* II:415.

[5] Her full name is given in a record copied from a family Bible in a certified statement by W.L. Prieur, Jr., Clerk of the Corporation Ct. of the City of Norfolk, Oct. 31, 1940. Document in possession of Robert F. Milligan, Sun City, AZ.

[6] Marriage Register 1, p. 8, line 24, Office of the Clerk of the Circuit Ct., Norfolk.

James Milligan, promoted to 2nd Lieutenant in early June with the support of politicians in Missouri, soon received a new assignment to the cutter *James C. Dobbin* at Wilmington, N.C. He reported for duty on that ship on June 26.[7] He served there until September, when he was granted a month's leave due to illness.[8] The *Dobbin* itself returned to Norfolk for repairs in October, thus allowing Milligan a lengthy stay at home.[9]

Meanwhile the campaign for the election of 1856 was in full swing, and this particular election was bound to have a special fascination for James Milligan. The new Republican Party, born only two years before during the crisis over the possible extension of slavery into the new territories of Kansas and Nebraska, had nominated Milligan's former employer, John C. Frémont, for President. Not only had Milligan developed a profound personal dislike for Frémont on the fifth expedition but also Frémont's association with the "Black" Republicans made his candidacy appear doubly abhorrent to a confirmed Democrat like Milligan.

The Republicans did not nominate Frémont for either his political experience or his demonstrated political leader ship. His only experience in Congress had been as one of California's first senators in 1850, but he had actually served for only a short time. Although Frémont was antislavery, he had not taken a leading role in the formation of the Republican Party following the Kansas-Nebraska Act of 1854. What appealed to Republican leaders about Frémont was his fame as explorer of the West and leader of

[7] Montgomery Blair to Guthrie, May 22, 1856; and William V.N. Bay to P.G. Washington, May 28, 1856, "Applications-R.C.S.," RG 26, NARS; "Appointment Records-U.S.R.M.S.," June 5, 1856, RG 26, NARS; and Milligan to Guthrie, June 26, 1856, "Letters from Officers of Revenue Cutter Service," OL 1856/124, RG 26, NARS. Hereafter cited as "Officers Letters-U.S.R.M.S."

[8] Guthrie to Milligan, Sept. 12, 1856, "Letters Sent-U.S.R.M.S.," 15/70-71, RG 26, NARS.

[9] U.S. Coast Guard, *Record of Movements,* I:202.

the conquest of California in the Mexican War. These traits might prove very attractive to voters, and might divert some attention away from the Republicans' identification with the slavery issue. Against Frémont, the Democrats nominated James Buchanan, a colorless party stalwart whom at least the great majority of Democrats could vote for. The American Party, or Know-Nothings, nominated ex-President Millard Fillmore of New York in hopes of defusing the sectional crisis by rallying voters to the cause of anti-Catholic nativism.

No matter how the parties might try to disguise it, the overriding issue of the election was slavery and its future admission into or exclusion from western territories like Kansas. The Republican Party's central tenet was the exclusion of slavery from the territories. Southerners on the other hand were demanding their right to take slave property into territories. The Northern Democrats were proposing that the people of the territories decide the matter, i.e., the doctrine of popular sovereignty. Many Southerners considered the Republicans to be abolitionists at heart and believed that their ultimate aim was the destruction of slavery in the Southern states, an eventuality which Southerners were prepared to go to war to prevent. Some Southern leaders and newspapers predicted secession by the South if Frémont were elected President, firmly believing that the chief monster of Southern nightmares, Senator William Seward of New York, would be the real power behind the throne and would stop at nothing to destroy slavery.

The day-by-day campaigning in the election of 1856 did not, however, always involve such weighty issues as slavery extension and the possibility of secession. As in other election campaigns, the character of the individual candidates became a subject of minute scrutiny. Even though

Buchanan and Fillmore became targets of character assassination, Frémont was constantly bombarded with one slur after another. Some criticisms were well-founded, especially concerning Frémont's role in the conquest of California, his subsequent court-martial and the disastrous course of Frémont's 1848-1849 winter expedition. Added to these were charges of financial corruption, extravagance with taxpayers' money, illegitimate birth, and even slaveholding. But the charge which Frémont's enemies threw at the voters more than any other was that he was a Catholic. Neither he nor his wife Jessie was a Catholic, but they had been married by a Catholic priest when they had eloped, and the charge that Frémont was Catholic would not die down no matter how fervently and frequently it was denied. Republicans naturally defended their nominee in speeches, songs, articles, and books, portraying him as one of America's greatest explorers and frontier heroes.[10] The laudatory tone of Frémont's campaign biographies led one woman correspondent of the San Francisco *Daily Alta California* to comment:[11]

> Colonel Frémont is treated by his party as a grandmother treats her darling grandson. With them it is what John did when he was a boy; what John's mother thought, and how John's wife felt; and how nobly he appeared on this occasion, and on that, when everybody else would have failed. The field of his life has been laboriously dug over by his political friends. If he is not elected the biographical items will have a ridiculous air.

Among all the subjects regarding Frémont which were argued pro and con in 1856 was his conduct of the 1853-

---

[10] Some good accounts of the 1856 election campaign are: Crandall, *The Early History of the Republican Party, 1854-1856,* 153-288; Barlett, *Frémont and the Republican Party;* Allan Nevins, *Ordeal of the Union,* II:451-514; and Nevins, *Frémont: Pathmaker,* 421-58.

[11] San Fran. *Daily Alta California,* Aug. 3, 1856.

1854 winter expedition. Frémont's father-in-law, Thomas Hart Benton, completed his second volume of *Thirty Years' View* and, even though he was too firm a Democrat to support Frémont's candidacy, included a short statement indicating that the fifth expedition had succeeded in finding a practicable central route for the transcontinental railroad.[12] The most well-known and publicized statement about the fifth expedition during the campaign originated with Solomon Carvalho, the expedition photographer. Carvalho had returned from the expedition in 1854 with a somewhat negative impression of Frémont's character, according to a letter by his nephew,[13] but he had changed his attitude by the time Frémont ran for President. While piecing together notes and letters about the expedition in preparation of his own forthcoming volume, Carvalho allowed John Bigelow to quote extensively from his notes for Bigelow's campaign biography of Frémont.[14] Carvalho's book, *Incidents of Travel and Adventure in the Far West,* and the Carvalho account in Bigelow's campaign biography constitute the only extensive report of Frémont's fifth expedition published prior to the present work. Carvalho even became so enthusiastic about the campaign that he gave a speech at a Republican rally in New York City on September 10 in which he tried to defend Frémont against charges that he had callously left men to freeze to death in the mountains on his last two expeditions. Carvalho detailed Frémont's solicitous efforts on behalf of

---

[12] Benton, *Thirty Years' View,* II:721.

[13] Carvalho's nephew wrote this letter on Sept. 11, just after Carvalho had delivered a campaign speech for Frémont. In part the letter states: "It would astonish you to hear him talk now in favor of Frémont, after having heard his conversation on his return from California. Alas! Money! Money! — He says if Fremont is elected he will have the Office of Collector of the Port of Baltimore, or anything else he wants, . . ." Quoted in Sturhahn, *Carvalho,* 130.

[14] Bigelow, *Life of John Charles Fremont,* 430-42.

poor Oliver Fuller, the only white man to die on the fifth expedition.[15]

Despite Carvalho's unadulterated praise for Frémont, Democratic papers took a jaundiced view of the "Pathfinder's" exploits. The event in Frémont's career which was most easily criticized was the 1848-1849 winter expedition, when ten of Frémont's men perished in the mountains. Many Democratic newspapers in the 1856 campaign published the Richard Kern-James H. Simpson account of the 1849 fiasco.[16] The Cleveland *Plain Dealer* framed a series of political questions for its readers, one of which was: "Who lost more men by his inexcusable rashness in forcing them into snow drifts than all the other explorers to the Pacific? J.C. Frémont."[17] The New York *Daily News* was merciless in its assessment of Frémont's abilities, claiming in a June 30 article that real mountain men and trappers considered Frémont a "fancy amateur tourist" and "over-grown schoolboy playing mountaineer," whom the trappers found ready to believe any tall yarn which they could ply him with. The article pointed to the winter expedition of 1849 as "the correct measure of his merit."[18] This theme was reiterated in that paper a few weeks later in a letter from a trapper at Bent's Fort named Henry Minayell to a friend in New York.[19]

---

15 The only account of Carvalho's speech is in New York *Daily Times,* Sept. 11, 1856. His speech contained virtually the same account of Fuller's death as later printed in Carvalho's book. Carvalho, *Incidents of Travel,* 117-21, 131-35. Carvalho also helped defend Frémont against the charge that he was a Catholic by communicating a long letter from one of Carvalho's friends on the subject to the New York *Daily Tribune,* July 30, 1856.

16 Wash., D.C. *Daily Union,* Aug. 8, 1856; St. Louis *Daily Missouri Republican,* Aug. 14, 1856; Cleveland *Daily Plain Dealer,* Aug. 9, 1856. Kern's account is reprinted in Hafen, ed., *Fremont's Fourth Expedition: A Documentary Account of the Disaster of 1848-1849,* Vol. XI of *The Far West and Rockies Series,* 255-61.

17 Cleveland *Daily Plain Dealer,* Aug. 22, 1856.

18 New York *Daily News,* June 30, 1856.

19 *Ibid.,* Aug. 14, 1856. Letter is reprinted in Wilmington, N.C. *Daily Journal,* Aug. 18, 1856.

> In reply to your inquiries about what I think of Frémont, and what the trappers think of him as a mountaineer and a man, I can only say the general opinion of the boys is that he is a very young beaver — that he is as vain and self-conceited as a young squaw looking at herself in a spring, and as for that last trip of his (the Winter trip) we all feel that no one but a fool would have attempted it at that time of the year, and that none but a cold-hearted, selfish devil would have lost his men and animals in the way he did.

The Kansas City *Enterprise* even jokingly suggest that, if the country wanted a ticket of real explorers rather than an incompetent like Frémont, a better candidate for President would be Kit Carson of Santa Fé, with Tim Goodell of Kansas City for Vice President.[20] An article in the Washington *Daily Union* in September criticized Frémont's supporters for not saying a word "about the great and unnecessary sacrifice of life and property in Col. F's last Rocky Mountain expedition."[21] Toward the end of the campaign, the Albany *Atlas & Argus* questioned Frémont's skills as a surveyor and explorer, stating that the route which Frémont proposed for a railroad to the Pacific had been found utterly impracticable by other engineers. The *Atlas* article pointedly demanded that Frémont prepare an official report of the fifth expedition, which Frémont had promised but had not written in the two years since the expedition, a report which Frémont never did produce.[22]

Almost entirely unnoticed among the 1856 comments about Frémont's qualities was James Milligan's long letter about the fifth expedition, printed in the Norfolk *Southern Argus* in August 1856. Outside of Carvalho's account, the Milligan letter is the only statement about the expedition published by a member of it other than Frémont himself.

---

[20] Kansas City *Enterprise,* quoted in St. Louis *Daily Missouri Republican,* July 8, 1856 and Cleveland *Daily Plain Dealer,* July 26, 1856.

[21] Wash., D.C. *Daily Union,* Sept. 11, 1856.

[22] Albany *Atlas & Argus,* Oct. 23, 1856.

Milligan's letter might have become a more well-known and important campaign document if it had been published by a more prominently known paper. Other Democratic newspapers would then undoubtedly have reprinted it, as they commonly reprinted articles, letters, and other items. But James Milligan's letter about Frémont and the fifth expedition was, as far as the present researchers have found, not reprinted in any other paper. It was only natural for Milligan to send the letter to the *Southern Argus,* since it was in Norfolk that he then resided. But it is also regrettable that the letter appeared in a paper from which other editors were unlikely to reprint.

Locating the published version of James Milligan's letter against the Presidential candidacy of John C. Frémont in the election of 1856 proved a difficult task. The only evidence that such a letter existed was a very rough draft of it inserted at the end of his frontier journal. Luckily the editor of the Norfolk *Southern Argus,* Will Lamb, wrote an 1857 letter in support of a Revenue Marine cutter command for Milligan, a letter in which Lamb cited the Milligan article against Frémont in the press.[23] Unfortunately, collections of the *Argus* issues for the latter part of 1856 are very rare. The only substantial collection of them is in the Library of Congress, and it was among those holdings that the published version of Milligan's letter was finally located. The *Southern Argus* published this article in three separate installments in the issues of August 25, 26, and 27, 1856. However, the Library of Congress has only the latter two issues, and efforts to locate a surviving copy of the August 25 issue with the first installment have proven fruitless.

In comparing the handwritten rough draft with the

[23] Will Lamb to Sec. of the Treas. Howell Cobb, Mar. 6, 1857, "Applications-R.C.S.," RG 26, NARS.

published letter, it becomes obvious that Milligan and/or the *Argus* staff revised the letter extensively. Even supposedly direct quotations from his journal are more elaborate than the journal entries themselves. There are few substantial differences, however, between the existing segments of the published version and those same sections of the rough draft. The following version of the Milligan letter begins with the early parts of the rough draft, followed by the installments as published on August 26 and 27. Where the latter parts of the rough draft include anything substantially different from the published articles, those discrepancies are noted. The Norfolk *Southern Argus* gave the Milligan letter the rather colorful title of "The Pathfinder Picked to Pieces by a Patriot."

U. S. Cutter *Dobbin*

Mr Editor,

As so much has been said and sung by the northern fanatics in regard to the superior merit of John C. Fremont for the Presidency, permit me to give you my ideas of the would be great "Pathfinder." What I say in regard to Fremont has been substantiated long ere this fully to the satisfaction of those who have been particularly associated with him in "his severe trials and hardships." It happened to be my misfortune to volunteer with this overrated individual in question in September, 1853, to accompany him in his expedition to California. I volunteered in no particular capacity but to make myself generally useful, which as far as I accompanied the expedition I flatter myself that I [have] done equally as much for the welfare and success of it as any person in it with one exception, which I shall have occasion to mention hereafter. The object of this expedition as you are no doubt aware was to test the practicability of a route for the Rail Road from the borders of Missouri to California and also to find the relative d[epth] of snow, and other important objects which might prove favourable to the Central Route advocated so strongly by Col. Benton. In regard to the practicability of the route, it is not for me to say having no more idea of it west of the

Pueblos of the Arkan[sas] than "De horse has whistling jigs to a mile stone." Consequently if I were to give an opinion upon it, it would be from what I have heard others say. And I always like to speak from my own experience when not otherwise corroborated. Col. Fremont has seen proper to attribute the disastrous failure of his expedition of 1848 to the incompetency of his guide. Now Mr. Editor let me tell you what all mountain men say in regard to Old Bill Williams' merit as a hunter, trapper, and guide. In regard to the former he had some superiors, as trapper none and as guide, is it not reasonable to suppose that a man who had passed 40 years of his life in the mountains trapping in every stream and creek from the mouth of the Gila to the Dalles of the Columbia and familiar with all the mountain passes knew the country but too well to cross the mountains in that advanced season? He strongly protested telling and predicting the consequences of so rash an act, which alas! the sequel proved, but too fatally fulfilling the prophetic words of Williams. Now sir what ca[used] this great loss of life — Bill Williams' incompetency or Fremont's obstinacy? Echo alone answers for poor Williams has long "gone under" (using one of his own phrases for death), but sir, there are men living who can testify to the truth of all and more than this.[24]

[Here begins the published segment]

I shall endeavor to account for Fremont's success in his several expeditions by a quotation from my Journal, and how, by being the only commentator of his own qualities, he has managed to gull the poor deluded followers of his standard:

"SALINA FORK OF KANSAS RIVER, November 1st, 1853.

Colonel Fremont, at supper, informed us that during his illness in St. Louis, (he turned back shortly after we left Westport in consequence of continued ill health, for medical advice, and anticipating a severe attack, he went to St. Louis, leaving orders for the expedition to proceed to Salt Creek and there await his arrival,) he had seen communications in the newspapers[25] from

---

[24] Milligan apparently based his discussion of the 1848-1849 expedition on the Kern-Simpson accounts published in the 1856 campaign, a clipping of which is tipped in Milligan's frontier journal.

[25] The wording has been changed from Milligan's original journal entry, which mentioned communications "to" the newspapers, to communications "in" the newspapers. *See* chapter IV, note 47.

some gentleman in the camp. I respectfully informed him I was the individual, but was not conscious of having done wrong in so doing. He requested me not to do so again, and I promised him I would not, thereby making a 'virtue of necessity,' for I would not again meet with an opportunity to forward my communications, were I disposed to do so, in consequence of being out of the direct line of communication with the States. He also requested that all journals in the camp should be destroyed; that he had never allowed any person connected with his former expeditions to keep a record, and he would not permit any person of this expedition to infringe upon any rules he had established; and furthermore, it was only customary for the Chief to keep a journal, as 'reports were so contradictory they would invariably conflict,' and it would prove more injurious than beneficial to any expedition where all hands enjoyed the privilege of keeping a journal. Mr. Fuller has complied with his exceedingly modest request. I have deter mined to leave the expedition rather than give up my journal."

SELFISHNESS is the predominant quality with which Col. Fremont appears to be endowed, and I think the request is anything but magnanimous, and fully illustrates the position he wants to assume, viz: The great I AM of the party. I attribute his false position so far before the public to the silence of those whom he has had power over, much to their shame and discredit, and utter want of those God like qualities, magnanimity of soul and a proper degree of independence which all men ought to possess in every station of life. Those who have followed Col. Fremont before, were prevented by policy from making public the Colonel's expeditions; he had the principal men under obligations to him.

How many men have fallen by this great want of independence, the victims of a designing and intriguing man's ambition, backed by strong political patronage. Thus men of capacity, merit, and qualification, generally, have been the "lute a more designing man has played upon," to forward his designs and carry out some political scheme of those who have benefited him with their patronage, and by that put him in positions which may eventually be of great and important service to them. Thus have the men who heretofore accompanied Col. Fremont been robbed of their laurels, and all their talent kept in the dark, to increase the public estimation of Col. Fremont's qualifications, and give him the credit which others so richly deserve.

While favored men have their own way,
Talent lies quiet with nothing to say.

Now what other object could Col. Fremont have in depriving us of our journals but to prevent the public from dividing their opinion between his men and himself. His SELFISHNESS was self evident; he wanted all the glory, and none of the ridicule and infamy to which he is justly entitled. Yes, the infamy which he deserved, if for nothing else but the treatment the poor unfortunate Oliver Fuller met with at his hands, and which I so fortunately escaped by "backing out," and refusing to go farther than Bent's Fort with the expedition.

Listen to his report of Fuller's death, copied from his letter to Col. Benton, dated February 9, 1854, from Parowan Iron county, Utah Territory:

"I lost one Mr. Fuller of St. Louis, Missouri, who died on entering this valley. He died like a man, on horseback, in his saddle, and will be buried like a soldier on the spot where he fell."

How was he buried? Did Col. Fremont attend his funeral rites? No! He lay snug in camp, well wrapped up in his blanket, while the noble Fuller, the night before, lay some distance from the camp, with a single blanket, unable to proceed farther, being overpowered with fatigue and hunger. When found the next morning he was frozen to the waist, and speechless. When the camp moved the next day he was put upon a jaded mule, and there died. So regardless was Fremont of Fuller's condition, and impatient to reach the Mormon settlement of Parowan, that he shoved on, leaving two Delawares behind to stay by Fuller until he died, and then join him in the camp ahead. The brave Delawares were faithful to their trust, and stayed with Fuller until death relieved him from his sufferings. The Indians took his watch and other articles of small value from his person and piled such loose stones as were found convenient upon his corpse, and thus left the gallant Fuller a prey to the vulture and the prowling wolf.[26]

Was this the burial of a soldier? Fremont knew he was but a

[26] This is based on Carvalho's account in Bigelow, *Fremont,* 441, 444.

short distance from the settlement, and why not take the body of Fuller with him, that one so brave and devoted might at least have a Christian burial? This much should have been done, especially when it could so easily have been, to alleviate the torture of a mother's aching heart, and to relieve a fond and devoted sister from many pangs of sorrow. Thus died and was buried Oliver Fuller, whose inestimable virtues endeared him to each and every member of the expedition, and for whose sad fate many deep curses have been heaped upon Fremont's head, curses for his heartless desertion of one so noble in every manly trait of character, and who fell a victim to hunger and exposure rather than complain of his condition.

As to Col. Fremont's power of endurance, it is easily accounted for. Each member of the expedition was restricted to so many pounds weight of clothing, while he had all that comfort could desire in the most inclement weather, or that was necessary for a trip to the North Pole. Col. Fremont has always had the best of hunters engaged with him on all expeditions, but in no one instance do I know of his taking a party through without loss either by hunger or an attack upon his camp. Does this not show at once that he has not used the "precaution, experience, and vigilance," he has had so much credit for possessing?

In regard to his selection of camps, I must say for a man who had travelled so much among the Indians of the plains, his judgment was unpardonable, and would have laid the most veritable green horn on the plains open to ridicule. Any person at a glance would have seen what a favorable chance he afforded an attack from the Indians on the 9th of November, 1853, when encamped upon the Pawnee Fork. Indian signs were discovered; and although his attention was called to it he encamped there, as if determined to give them an opportunity of stealing our animals — that at least some of us would have to go on foot. Next morning, sure enough, seven of our best animals were missing, which, we learned, were stolen by a war party of Cheyennes during the night; and as the old chief TWIST afterwards told me, had it not been for the presence of the Delawares, they might have just as easily taken our scalps — but they were afraid they might have raised the Delawares, and to cross arms with them they had no particular desire.

As a natural consequence, after the loss of our horses, several of us were on foot. Now Col. Fremont did not take this into consideration and moderate his pace until we had become accustomed to walking. No! Why should he? He was well mounted! He left those who were on foot to reach camp as best they could, and this too in an Indian country, upon the war grounds of hostile and barbarous savages.[27] This was a strange way, indeed, for a leader to display his interest in the safety of those whom he had led into the wilderness, and who were obliged to travel on foot through his unskillfulness. After the horses were stolen, until we arrived at the camp below Bent's Fort, contention prevailed in the camp, and even the Indians were becoming dissatisfied with their leader. The subordinates were very insolent, and I got myself suspended from duty for the audacity of striking a Mexican servant who had the insolence to call me a liar. At this stopping place, seeing the state of affairs, I went to Col. Fremont, and told him I could not go further with the expedition; that even if I desired, my feet were so blistered, in consequence of losing my animal, that I could not possibly proceed farther. He detailed me then to remain at Bent's Fort with Dr. Ebers, in charge of a couple of crippled animals. I have ever congratulated myself on being compelled to "back out" at this place, especially as the expedition met with the fate that I could not but foresee.

In conclusion, I would add but a few paragraphs. Had Col. Fremont carried the meat, dried and cured, while encamped at Salt Creek, as any explorer of "experience and vigilance" would have done, his corps would have avoided much suffering which they encountered in the mountains.[28] I venture to say he never suffered much from hunger; — that French vegetable soup

---

[27] After this part of the letter in the rough draft are these statements: "All he cared for was no one and Central Route despite better men's opinions to the contrary. I might not have as good judgment as the man Fremont who was raised by contribution but I've just as good right to the Presidency as he has and a better one, and I am as much fit to be President as the Infernal Regions is a Powder Magazine." Milligan then makes the first of two references to the term 'Thabanequa," which he later describes as "Injin for you 'Great Pathfinder.'" This word, if it is actually an Indian term, has so far defied all efforts to discover its derivation and meaning.

[28] Milligan in the rough draft says that the dried meat was thrown away at Walnut Creek "to make room for instruments scarcely ever used."

which he had with him was a great invention, and no trouble to make when all the rest of the camp except himself and his negro had sunk, weary and hungry, to sleep.[29] For the sake of the Abolitionists, we would say that the Colonel had a favorite negro of whom he made a pet, and defended in the most intolerable insolence to the whites.[30]

It is imagined and asserted by some that Fremont is conversant with several Indian languages, and consequently an interpreter. All the languages I ever heard him speak besides his mother tongue was a smattering of French and Spanish. The whole sum and substance of Col. Fremont's character is ambition and selfishness, and consequently an utter disregard for the feeling of others. He is not half as well fitted for the Presidency as Davy Crockett would be.

Yours truly,
J. F. M.
U. S. Revenue Service

The impact of Lieutenant Milligan's letter on the 1856 Presidential campaign was undoubtedly negligible, given the very limited audience who read it — Virginians in and around Norfolk who would not have voted for Frémont under any circumstances anyhow. In November, Democrat James Buchanan defeated Frémont and Fillmore. Frémont faded from the limelight until the Civil War,

[29] In the rough draft, the statement is: "French soups put up in small canisters are exceedingly convenient to make after all hands are at rest. The Nigger and him have I expect had many a sly mess together." This information about the canisters of soup appears only in Milligan's 1856 letter. Carvalho makes no mention of it. Did Frémont actually have such canisters with him? Probably so. Milligan would have been in a position to have known of their existence since he had charge of the mules and packs. As for Frémont eating these soups while his men starved, this is probably nothing more than very biased conjecture on Milligan's part, since he was not with the expedition in the mountains. Carvalho's statement that Frémont sometimes ate alone in his tent may have inspired Milligan's conjecture. Bigelow, *Fremont*, 440. As for the canisters of soup, it is impossible to tell what really may have happened to them.

[30] A bit earlier in the rough draft is the statement: "In fact general dissatisfaction pervaded the Camp, caused by a Pet Darkey the Colonel had with him. Mr. Darkey came near losing his hair at Bent's Fort for insulting one of the Delawares." Milligan then cites the "Darkey's" attitude as one reason he backed out of the expedition.

when as a Union general, he suffered a series of frustrations in Missouri and West Virginia which finally led him to resign his commission.

James Milligan remained a Lieutenant in the Revenue Marine Service until the outbreak of the Civil War in 1861. He apparently endured some personal trials in his relationship with his wife Sally during these years, as evidenced by one of the poems in the back of his journal. One source of discord was Milligan's Irish background. He was proud of his heritage and abhorred the prejudices of the Know-Nothings and other nativists against the Irish, as he made clear in some of his verse. Sally's family was of English extraction, and she apparently resorted to some anti-Irish comments when she got into an argument with her husband. James Milligan responded, at least in verse, by calling her a "Small specimen of a presumptuous race/ Ugly old Briton monkey face" who should not "slander refined people and call them trash" or "open...[her] mouth to display...[her] ignorance." He further criticized her for thinking only of her own comfort and extravagance while she kept "poor Brick's nose to the stone." Whatever misunderstandings troubled the early years of their marriage, however, James and Sally Milligan, like many other young couples, were able to overcome the difficulties and remain together.

Lieutenant Milligan did keep his "nose to the stone." While awaiting orders in Norfolk for his next assignment and taking a leave of absence due to illness, Milligan attempted to secure a command for himself on one of the new cutters being built for service on the Great Lakes. Despite the efforts of *Southern Argus* editor Will Lamb on his behalf, Milligan did not receive such a command.[31] In

[31] Lamb to Cunningham, Oct. 28, 1856; and Lamb to Cobb, Mar. 6, 1856, "Applications-R.C.S.," RG 26, NARS.

late April, 1857, Milligan was assigned to his former ship, the *William J. Duane*, and was able to remain at his home port of Norfolk for the next several years.[32] Not until April 1860, did he receive a new duty station, this time on the cutter *Isaac Toucey* at Michilimackinac on the Great Lakes, where he remained for the rest of that year.[33] In January 1861, during the secession crisis prior to the Civil War, Milligan was promoted to First Lieutenant and transferred back to the *Duane* at Norfolk.[34]

Besides his duties as a Revenue Marine officer during the late 1850s, Milligan found time occasionally to correspond with newspapers. A rough draft of one of these letters is preserved in the back of Milligan's journal, and probably dates from late 1856 or early 1857, although there is no date on it and no indication given of which newspaper it may have been published in. The letter is a vigorous attack on Senator Stephen Mallory of Florida, Chairman of the Senate Naval Affairs Committee, for disparaging remarks made by him concerning the qualifications necessary for a revenue officer. Milligan refuted Mallory's contention that revenue officers did not really need to be skilled seamen.

Much of Lieutenant Milligan's correspondence was printed in the St. Louis *Daily Morning Herald*, beginning in 1857. He preserved clippings of some of these letters in his journal, and several other letters are to be found in the only extensive collection of *Herald* issues at the Missouri Historical Society in St. Louis. Milligan apparently

[32] Acting Sec. of the Treas. P.C. Clayton to Milligan, Apr. 27, 1857, "Letters Sent-U.S.R.M.S.," LS 15/305, RG 26, NARS; and Milligan to Clayton, Apr. 29, 1857, "Officers' Letters-U.S.R.M.S.," OL 1857/29, RG 26, NARS.

[33] Cobb to Milligan, Apr. 23, 1860, "Letters Sent-U.S.R.M.S.," OL 1860/136, RG 26, NARS.

[34] "Appointment Records-U.S.R.M.S.," Jan. 5, 1861, RG 26, NARS; and Sec. of the Treas. Philip F. Thomas to Milligan, Jan. 9, 1861, "Letters Sent-U.S.R.M.S.," LS 18/68, RG 26, NARS.

switched his allegiance from the *Missouri Democrat* to the *Herald* when the latter became the chief proponent of the Democratic Party in St. Louis; the *Democrat* was gradually turning Republican.

Several of these letters concerned revenue marine and naval matters. In 1857 letters Milligan damned the contractors who had built the cutter *Dobbin* only three years before in such a shoddy fashion that the ship had to be completely overhauled.[35] He lambasted Commodore Perry for his "Great Big Nothing treaty with the Japanese" and especially for his use of the Naval Retiring Board to get rid of good Naval officers whom Perry did not like.[36] He condemned the government's use of machinery — earlier rejected by merchant steamers — in U.S. steam warships,[37] and described the recent capture of a slave-trading ship by the Africa Squadron in the Congo River.[38] Two of his letters in early 1858 criticized the U.S. Navy, particularly Commodore Hiram Paulding, for their role in intercepting and halting the filibuster William Walker's second expedition against Nicaragua. Milligan stated his belief in these letters that the whole continent would one day be "one glorious confederacy" and that Central America desired U.S. colonization.[39] Later in 1858 Milligan ridiculed the U.S. naval expedition to Paraguay and especially its commander, Flag Officer William B. Shubrick. This expedition was designed to punish the Paraguayans for having fired on and damaged an American naval steamer there. Milligan did not think much of the

---

[35] Milligan to editor of St. Louis *Daily Morning Herald,* Feb. 14, 1857. Clipping in Milligan journal.

[36] Milligan to editor, Nov. 10, 1857, St. Louis *Daily Morning Herald,* Nov. 17, 1857.

[37] *Ibid.*

[38] Milligan to editor, Dec. 21, 1857, *Ibid.,* Dec. 29, 1857.

[39] Milligan to editor, Jan 11, 1858, *Ibid.,* Jan. 19, 1858; and Milligan to editor, Jan. 29, 1858, *Ibid.,* Feb. 4, 1858. Walker's second expedition and the controversy over Paulding's interference with it is covered in May, *The Southern Dream of a Caribbean Empire, 1854-1861,* 111-26.

twenty or so vessels in the expedition, stating that "the way our mosquito fleet of chartered egg shells will be knocked 'convex and concave' will be a sin to modern warfare." But Milligan's opinion of Shubrick was even worse — that old Shubrick was unqualified for such a command due to his lack of military experience and that the only reason for Shubrick's senior rank was his own machinations while President of the Naval Retiring Board (which Milligan called the "Inquisitorial Board of fifteen"). Despite Milligan's opinion, Shubrick and his squadron performed their mission without serious difficulty.[40]

In other letters to the *Herald,* James Milligan addressed himself on a multitude of subjects. In February 1857, he criticized the British consul at Norfolk for becoming upset when Norfolk authorities punished two free Negroes from a British ship according to Virginia law.[41] Milligan, in two of his letters, vigorously supported the development of Southern maritime trade with Europe, in order to prevent the North from completely garnering all the benefits of this trade, and he felt that Norfolk, with its natural harbor advantages, should take a leading role in this process.[42] After hearing a lecture in Norfolk by ex-Mormon John Hyde, Jr., Milligan wrote a letter to the *Herald* vigorously condemning the sect and warning Erastus Snow, "the king devil of the Mormon Church in St. Louis," that Hyde was on his way to St. Louis to expose the barbarities of the sect.[43] On the other hand, Milligan just as vigorously defended the Irish Catholics from whom he traced his

[40] Milligan to editor, Nov. 8, 1858, St. Louis *Daily Morning Herald,* Nov. 13, 1858. The story of the difficulties with Paraguay and the expedition sent to resolve them is in Warren, *Paraguay,* 194-95.

[41] Milligan to editor of St. Louis *Daily Morning Herald,* Feb. 18, 1857. Clipping in Milligan journal.

[42] Milligan to editor, *Ibid.,* Mar. 26, 1857 and Aug. 28, 1858. Clippings in Milligan journal.

[43] Milligan to editor, Dec. 4, 1857, *Ibid.,* Dec. 10, 1857.

heritage after the St. Louis German paper *Anzeiger des Westens* had editorially assaulted them.[44] On occasion Milligan reported on events in Norfolk, such as an altercation between some soldiers and civilians, and the Seaboard Agricultural Fairs of 1857 and 1858.[45] Some of the letters expressed Milligan's political opinions, for example, against the Republicans ("Seward and his white niggers"),[46] or in support of Democrats like Senator Trusten Polk of Missouri,[47] Secretary of War John Floyd,[48] and Governor John Letcher of Virginia.[49] Numerous other topics are mentioned in these letters.

Besides writing to the *Herald,* Lieutenant Milligan became a fairly regular correspondent of the Washington, D.C. *States,* which changed its name in late 1859 to the *States and Union.* Unlike his letters to the *Herald,* which Milligan signed "J.F.M.", his letters to the *States* were signed with his old nickname "Bricks." Also, while most of his letters to the *Herald* date from 1857 and 1858, most of his letters to the *States* are from the 1859-1861 period. There is a stronger emphasis on local Norfolk subjects and a more frequent sprinkling of Milligan's own verse in the *States* letters. Only one "Bricks" letter was sent from outside the Norfolk area, a letter which Milligan wrote to the *States* while stationed in Michigan in 1860.

Some themes pursued by Milligan in his *States* letters were similar to those in the *Herald.* Several concerned ships in and out of Norfolk port.[50] One letter reported on the feudal tournament and ball at the Seaboard Agricul-

---

[44] Milligan to editor, July 19, 1858, *Ibid.,* July 23, 1858.

[45] Milligan to editor, Sept. 4, 1857, *Ibid.,* Sept. 11, 1857; Milligan to editor, Nov. 13, 1857, *Ibid.,* Nov. 19, 1857; and Milligan to editor,Nov. 8, 1858, *Ibid.,* Nov. 13, 1858.

[46] Milligan to editor, Nov. 8, 1858, *Ibid.,* Nov. 13, 1858.

[47] Milligan to editor, Aug. 2, 1858, *Ibid.,* Aug. 6, 1858.

[48] *Ibid.*

[49] Milligan to editor, Nov. 8, 1858, *Ibid.,* Nov. 13, 1858; and Milligan to editor, *Ibid.,* Feb. 22, 1859, clipping in Milligan journal.

tural Fair of 1858.[51] Another vigorously supported the establishment of rail connections between Norfolk and other commercial centers and an increasing role for Norfolk port in transatlantic trade with the French.[52]

Milligan's *States* letters touched on numerous other topics as well. Several reported on ordnance testing near Old Point Comfort by the military.[53] One letter gave a detailed account of a Jewish wedding ceremony in Norfolk.[54] Another described a meeting of a group of the Knights of the Golden Circle, an organization in favor of slavery expansion, in Norfolk.[55] In another letter, Milligan favorably recounted the efforts of his friend Will Lamb, editor of the Norfolk *Southern Argus,* to root out political corruption in Norfolk.[56] While stationed in Michigan in 1860, Milligan wrote a letter opposing the organization of a Negro militia unit in that state, saying that this would lead to racial amalgamation and intermarriage, a thought quite abhorrent to Milligan's mind. In the same letter he indicated that the Mackinac area of Michigan would vote for Stephen Douglas for President, and Milligan appears also to have favored him rather than the extreme Southern Democratic candidate John Breckinridge.[57] Milligan's Democratic unionism fitted perfectly with the sentiment of the *States and Union,* which was a firm pro-Douglas paper, and was also quite typical of a Southerner whose life

[50] Milligan to editor, Feb. 15, 1858, Wash., D.C. *States,* Feb. 18, 1858; Milligan to editor, Oct. 17, 1859, *Ibid.,* Oct. 21, 1859; and Milligan to editor, Dec. 5, 1859, *Ibid.,* Dec. 8, 1859.

[51] Milligan to editor, Nov. 12, 1858, *Ibid.,* Nov. 20, 1858.

[52] Milligan to editor, Feb. 24, 1858, *Ibid.,* Mar. 3, 1858.

[53] Milligan to editor, July 18, 1859, Wash., D.C. *States and Union,* July 21, 1859; Milligan to editor, July 28, 1859, *Ibid.,* Aug. 2, 1859; Milligan to editor, Aug. 18, 1859, *Ibid.,* Aug. 22, 1859; and Milligan to editor, Dec. 5, 1859, *Ibid.,* Dec. 8, 1859.

[54] Milligan to editor, Mar. 1, 1860, *Ibid.,* Mar. 5, 1860.

[55] Milligan to editor, Mar. 21, 1860, *Ibid.,* Apr. 23, 1860.

[56] Milligan to editor, July 28, 1859, Wash., D.C. *States,* Aug. 2, 1859.

[57] Milligan to editor, June 19, 1860, Wash.,D.C. *States and Union,* June 29, 1860.

had been spent in the border states of Missouri and Virginia.

More than any other single subject, the "Bricks" letters discussed, in the most glowing terms, a favorite "watering-place" at Old Point Comfort called the Hygeia Hotel. He seems to have frequented the place often, and he became a propagandist for the Hygeia and its facilities.[58] The most interesting of these letters is one in which Milligan mentions himself in third-person fashion as a guest at a fancy costume ball, held at the Hygeia in early August 1859. Almost all the fancy ladies and fine gentlemen came dressed as royalty or other important personages — not Milligan though. As "Bricks" wrote of his own appearance, "Lieutenant M———n, U.S.R.S., as Paddy Miles' Boy, was the character of the evening; he acted his part, stick and all."[59] This incident is fairly revealing about Milligan's character. He came to a fancy dress ball costumed as a poor Irishman, a character quite below the status to which the other participants were pretending. James Milligan, as much as he wished to mix with fine society of predominantly English heritage, never forgot his Irish heritage. His performance at the ball, in a way, shows what deep-seated contempt he harbored, as an Irishman, for the English, attending the ball of mostly wealthy English descendants costumed in finery, and proclaiming his social equality with them, though comparatively clad in rags.

The last of James Milligan's letters to this paper appeared in early April 1861, just prior to the beginning of the Civil War. In this letter, Milligan analyzed the rather

---

[58] Milligan to editor, July 5, 1859, Wash., D.C. *States,* July 8, 1859; Milligan to editor, July 18, 1859, *Ibid.,* July 21, 1859, Milligan to editor, Aug. 1, 1859, *Ibid.,* Aug. 3, 1859; Milligan to editor, Aug. 3, 1859, *Ibid.,* Aug. 10, 1859; Milligan to editor, Aug. 16, 1859, *Ibid.,* Aug. 18, 1859; Milligan to editor, Mar. 21, 1860, Wash., D.C. *States and Union,* Apr. 23, 1860; and Milligan to editor, June 19, 1860, *Ibid.,* June 29, 1860.

[59] Milligan to editor, Aug. 3, 1859, Wash., D.C. *States,* Aug. 10, 1859.

confusing state of Virginia politics in the secession crisis. He described the change that had occurred in sentiment since the election campaign:[60]

> During the Presidential campaign, every man you met, no matter what party he advocated, looked as if he bore all the responsibilities of a statesman upon his own particular shoulders. But, alas! a change has come o'er the spirit of their dreams. Since the inauguration of President Lincoln, all now are warriors in behalf of their own individual cause.

Milligan then related how the secessionists were trying to circulate a petition to have Norfolk's delegate to the state convention instructed to vote for secession, how the unionists had already petitioned the delegate to stand by the Union, and how others who had voted against Lincoln were now "doing all they [could] to sustain their points for official favor from the very man they so heartily opposed."[61] Milligan finished with a statement of his own ambivalent feelings:[62]

> I hope the sequel will best develop, that after this rather prolonged political squall has blown over, reason and moderation may again be restored, with a greater prospect of stability. To tamper much longer with the tranquil masses, may prove dangerous. Virginia is moving now in earnest, and unless the proper concessions are made for the incontrovertible protection of her institutions, she will be driven to seek security with her sister States who sympathize more cordially with her integrity of sentiment.

---

[60] Milligan to editor, Apr. 3, 1861, Wash., D.C. *States and Union,* Apr. 5, 1861.

[61] *Ibid.*

[62] *Ibid.*

7

Major Milligan of the C.S.A. Independent Signal Corps

The sectional crisis over slavery and slavery expansion, which had been gradually building throughout the 1840s and 1850s, finally boiled over into civil war after the election in 1860 of Abraham Lincoln of Illinois as President. Several slaveholding states, believing that Lincoln and his Republicans from the North would use their power to destroy slavery and thereby the basis of Southern society, began the process of seceding from the Union. Efforts at compromise failed, and by the time Lincoln was inaugurated on March 4, 1861, seven states had left the Union, and others were threatening to. President Lincoln refrained from aggressive action against the seceded states themselves, but became determined to maintain a shadow of Federal sovereignty in the South by holding onto and resupplying those few Federal installations not yet possessed by the secessionists. The most prominent and vulnerable of these positions was Fort Sumter in the harbor of Charleston, South Carolina. Despite Southern threats to attack this fort if Lincoln would not surrender it, the President carried out what he felt to be his constitutional duty and attempted to resupply Fort Sumter. The Confederates did not wait for that event to take place. Southern artillery began a massive bombardment of Fort Sumter on

April 12, 1861, and forced the fort to surrender on April 13. At news of this, President Lincoln, on April 15, called for 75,000 volunteers to put down the rebellion in the Southern states. With Lincoln's final resort to force, four more states seceded, making eleven Confederate States. The Civil War had begun.

Given James Milligan's oft-expressed pro-Southern feelings in the previous years, it came as no surprise that he finally chose to serve the Confederate cause, despite the efforts of his father and of Francis P. Blair, Jr., of Missouri to secure him a position in the Federal service.[1] The Milligans thus became another of many families with divided allegiance among their members in the war. On April 15, 1861, two days before Virginia's convention voted to secede, Lieutenant Milligan sent in his resignation from the U.S. Revenue Marine Service at Norfolk to the new Secretary of the Treasury, Salmon P. Chase:[2]

> Sir
>
> As I believe the principles of coercion to be subversive to the Constitution of the United States, and as it would be incompatible with my moral convictions of right to sustain a government who no longer recognizes the Equality of Rights, as enunciated and set forth by the immortal Jefferson and Madison in the Virginia and Kentucky resolutions of 98 & 99, *I hereby most respectfully resign my position as a First Lieutenant in the United States Revenue Service.* In doing so I feel within me a peace above all earthly dignities, a still and quiet conscience, consoled with the proud assurance that I have ever and at all times done my duty to the best of my ability and never under any circumstances

[1] Milligan to Maj. Gen. S.G. French, Dec. 6, 1862, "Compiled Service Records of Confederate Soldiers in Organizations Raised Directly by the Confederate Government," M258, reel 119, RG 109-War Dept. Coll. of Confederate Records, NARS. Hereafter cited as "CSR — Milligan."

[2] Milligan to Chase, Apr. 15, 1861, "Officers' Letters — U.S.R.M.S.," OL 1861/133, RG 26 NARS.

have *I* violated any Federal trust reposed in me by the Constitutional obligations required of me upon being sworn into office, I am yours most respectfully
Jas. F. Milligan

Secretary Chase received the letter and drafted a short reply, also dated April 15, stating that Milligan's services were no longer required and that his name was dropped from the rolls of the service.[3]

Upon leaving the U.S. Revenue Marine, Milligan immediately accepted a commission as lieutenant in the Virginia State Navy and immediately assumed command of the steamer *Empire* at Norfolk.[4] After the Confederates took over the Norfolk Magazine and Navy Yard, Milligan and the *Empire* became engaged in various harbor duties, such as towing vessels loaded with ballast into position to obstruct the channel between the forts guarding the harbor.[5] After commanding the *Empire* for almost a month, on May 15, 1861, Milligan was ordered by Commodore Forrest of the Norfolk Navy Yard to signal duty and to report to Brigadier General Walter Gwynn of the Virginia State Forces. On May 18, Lieutenant Milligan was ordered by General Gwynn to "arrange, perfect and establish a system of signals, and to call into . . . (his) service the men necessary to carry them into effect."[6] Milligan's naval experience had familiarized him with marine signals, and

---

[3] Chase to Milligan, Apr. 15, 1861, "Letters Sent — U.S.R.M.S.," LS 18/182, RG 26, NARS.

[4] Milligan to French, Dec. 6, 1862, "CSR — Milligan," RG 109, NARS.

[5] U.S. Dept. of the Navy, Official Records, Ser. I, vol. IV:405. This order refers to Milligan as Captain but that simply refers to his command position on the *Empire* rather than his actual rank. The *Empire* was later transformed into a gunboat named *Appomattox* and sent to North Carolina. Porter, *A Record of Events in Norfolk County,* 310.

[6] Milligan to Adj. Gen. Samuel Cooper, Jan. 29, 1863, "CSR — Milligan," RG 109, NARS.

he worked out a system for use in the Norfolk area. He would be on signal duty for the remainder of the war.

Military signalling was an ancient art, but an efficient system of signals for the U.S. Army had begun to be developed just prior to the Civil War by Dr. Albert J. Myer, an army surgeon. At the beginning of the war, several different signal systems were utilized, such as the marine signals of the type employed by Milligan in the Norfolk area. These marine signals entailed the use of poles on which flags and colored balls were hung, the various combinations of which indicated various phrases. Milligan's system at Norfolk was apparently successful enough that General John B. Magruder sent a member of his staff, William Norris, to study Milligan's operation in preparation for establishment of a signal system on the peninsula and across the James River. Norris had had nautical experience himself and so was already familiar with the marine signals. Milligan assisted Norris and gave him a book of signals he was using at Norfolk. Norris utilized this system on the peninsula, but the marine signals were simply not adequate for general use in land warfare. Therefore the Myer system was soon adopted generally by both armies. The officer most responsible for introducing Myer's signals into the Confederate army was Captain (later General) Edward P. Alexander of General Beauregard's staff. Alexander had learned this system under Myer himself before the war.[7]

The Myer system of signals was a sign language using flags by day and torches by night. The flags measured about 4 feet by 2½ feet, and in the center of each flag was a square of a different color than the border of the flag.

---

[7] *Ibid.;* Gaddy, "William Norris and the Confederate Signal and Secret Service," 171, 174; Marshall, "The Confederate Army's Signal Corps," 65, 67; Cummins, "The Signal Corps in the Confederate States Army," 93-94.

Whichever flag showed up best in a particular terrain or against a particular background was the one employed in the situation (i.e., a scarlet flag in snow-colored terrain, a white flag against a dark background, etc.). Various combinations of right and left waves of the flag or torch communicated certain letters of the alphabet (hence the system was known as "wigwag"), and an entire message could be communicated quickly from station to station by skillful signalmen. Flag codes (i.e., the left/right combinations) were often changed to protect message security. Signal stations were not very far apart, but usually each station had to read the messages sent to it by using binoculars or a telescope. Some messages would travel by flag signals for some distance and then be carried to the final destination by telegraph where available.[8]

Both sides sent their messages at least partly in code or cipher in order to prevent the enemy from reading their messages. The Confederates used what was known as the "court cipher," and an excellent description of it was provided in an early article about the Confederate Signal Corps by Edmund H. Cummins:[9]

> A key-word or phrase is agreed upon by the parties who intend to communicate in cipher. The message is written under the key. Suppose, for example, the key to be "In God we trust;" and the message, "Longstreet is marching on Fisher 's Hill." It will be written thus:

```
I n G o d w e t r u s t i n G o d w e t r u s t i n G o d w e t r
L o n g s t r e e t i s m a r c h i n g o n F i s h e r s H i l l
```

[8] Taylor, "The Signal and Secret Service of the Confederate States," 303-304.

[9] Cummins, "Signal Corps," 101-102.

The Alphabet is written out in a square, thus:

A B C D E F G H I J K L M N O P Q R S T U V W X Y Z
B C D E F G H I J K L M N O P Q R S T U V W X Y Z A
C D E F G H I J K L M N O P Q R S T U V W X Y Z A B
D E F G H I J K L M N O P Q R S T U V W X Y Z A B C
E F G H I J K L M N O P Q R S T U V W X Y Z A B C D
F G H I J K L M N O P Q R S T U V W X Y Z A B C D E
G H I J K L M N O P Q R S T U V W X Y Z A B C D E F
H I J K L M N O P Q R S T U V W X Y Z A B C D E F G
I J K L M N O P Q R S T U V W X Y Z A B C D E F G H
J K L M N O P Q R S T U V W X Y Z A B C D E F G H I
K L M N O P Q R S T U V W X Y Z A B C D E F G H I J
L M N O P Q R S T U V W X Y Z A B C D E F G H I J K
M N O P Q R S T U V W X Y Z A B C D E F G H I J K L
N O P Q R S T U V W X Y Z A B C D E F G H I J K L M
O P Q R S T U V W X Y Z A B C D E F G H I J K L M N
P Q R S T U V W X Y Z A B C D E F G H I J K L M N O
Q R S T U V W X Y Z A B C D E F G H I J K L M N O P
R S T U V W X Y Z A B C D E F G H I J K L M N O P Q
S T U V W X Y Z A B C D E F G H I J K L M N O P Q R
T U V W X Y Z A B C D E F G H I J K L M N O P Q R S
U V W X Y Z A B C D E F G H I J K L M N O P Q R S T
V W X Y Z A B C D E F G H I J K L M N O P Q R S T U
W X Y Z A B C D E F G H I J K L M N O P Q R S T U V
X Y Z A B C D E F G H I J K L M N O P Q R S T U V W
Y Z A B C D E F G H I J K L M N O P Q R S T U V W X
Z A B C D E F G H I J K L M N O P Q R S T U V W X Y

The first letter in the key is "I" and the letter under it is "L." Take "I" in the top horizontal column and run down the "I" vertical column until it intersects the "L" horizontal column. The letter at the intersection is "T." This is substituted in the message for "L" in Longstreet. The other letters are converted in the same way, and the message will read thus:

t b t u v p v x v n a l u n x q k e r z f h x b a u k f v d m e c

Sometimes the small words were run into the contiguous large ones, and sometimes no division into words is made, as in the above example. The last is the best plan. If the words are separated, or if a part of the message is written in plain language, a chance is given to guess at some of the words, of which an expert is not slow to avail himself.

The cipher, if properly used, was almost impossible for enemy signalmen to translate correctly, since they would be helpless without the key word or phrase. However, given the frequency with which Union and Confederate signalmen intercepted messages, it is apparent that too many messages, or parts thereof, were sent in plain language. Sometimes, of course, it was fully intended that the enemy should intercept certain messages designed to deceive the enemy, and thus hopefully lead them to disaster. The Confederate signalmen normally used a key word or phrase of fifteen letters, and changed it regularly by sending a special messenger to the various departments with the new key. This word or phrase would then be communicated orally to the signal officers and men in that area, but was never written down. A handy device for enciphering and deciphering signals was developed during the war by Captain William Barker, who had been trained in signals by Captain Alexander. The alphabet square was pasted on a cylinder which revolved under a bar with a sliding pointer enabling the user to find, conveniently and quickly, the point of intersection between the horizontal and vertical columns. This Barker device became widely used by Confederate signalmen.[10]

Just when James Milligan adopted the Myer system instead of the marine signals is not clear, but probably he had done so by early 1862. In those early days of Milligan's signal duty, his particular status in the rebel forces was rather unclear, not very surprising given the general problems of organizing a relatively new type of service in an entirely new army. Milligan's rank remained that of Lieutenant in the Virginia State Navy until October 7, 1861 when he received a commission as 2nd Lieutenant in the Artillery Corps with a brevet (temporary) rank of Captain. He regularly referred to himself in dispatches as Captain and Signal Officer in the Department of Norfolk in late 1861.[11] Just how many men were serving him in 1861 is impossible to determine. The men needed for

[10] *Ibid.*, 102; Marshall, "Signal Corps," 73-74.

[11] U.S. Dept. of War, *War of the Rebellion,* Ser. I, Vol. IV:719 (hereafter cited as *Official Records);* and Milligan to Pres. Jefferson Davis, Mar. 30, 1862; Milligan to French, Dec. 6, 1862; Milligan to Cooper, Jan. 29, 1863, "CSR — Milligan," RG 109, NARS.

signal duty were detached from other commands temporarily, and they probably found Milligan to be a strong disciplinarian and an effiicient instructor in the arts of signalling and observation. Although he later claimed that he had an organized corps authorized in August 1861, the official status of his unit appears to have been less clear in the eyes of Confederate leaders than in Milligan's estimation.[12] Whatever status his unit had, it performed the extremely valuable service of keeping watch over the important Union fleet movements in Hampton Roads at the mouth of the James River and kept Richmond apprised of these activities.[13]

The Confederate government did not officially organize a separate Signal Corps until early 1862. Major General Benjamin Huger, Commander of the Department of Norfolk and appreciative of Captain Milligan's services on his staff, recommended to Secretary of War Judah Benjamin that a separate signal unit be organized in his department. This authority was granted on February 22, 1862, almost two months before the creation of the Confederate Signal Corps by law on April 19, 1862.[14] In early March, the Adjutant and Inspector General's Office ordered that all those detailed from other units to serve on signal duty in the Norfolk area were being transferred to the new signal company being formed by Captain Milligan.[15] The first company of the "Independent Signal Corps and Scouts" was officially mustered into service by Major Bradford, the inspector general for the Department of Norfolk, on April 25, 1862, composed of 73 men under the

---

[12] Milligan to Maj. Gen. Arnold Elzey, Aug. 11, 1863, "CSR — Milligan," RG 109, NARS.

[13] For some early Milligan dispatches in Oct. and Nov. 1861 and Mar., 1862, *see Official Records,* Ser. I, IV:701-702; VI:297; XI:pt. III, 388, 389, 403.

[14] *Ibid.,* XI: pt. III, 628; Milligan to Cooper, Jan. 19, 1863, "CSR — Milligan"; Muster roll, Independent Signal Corps, Mar. 15, 1863, Box 641, RG 109, NARS.

[15] Porter, *Record of Events,* 304.

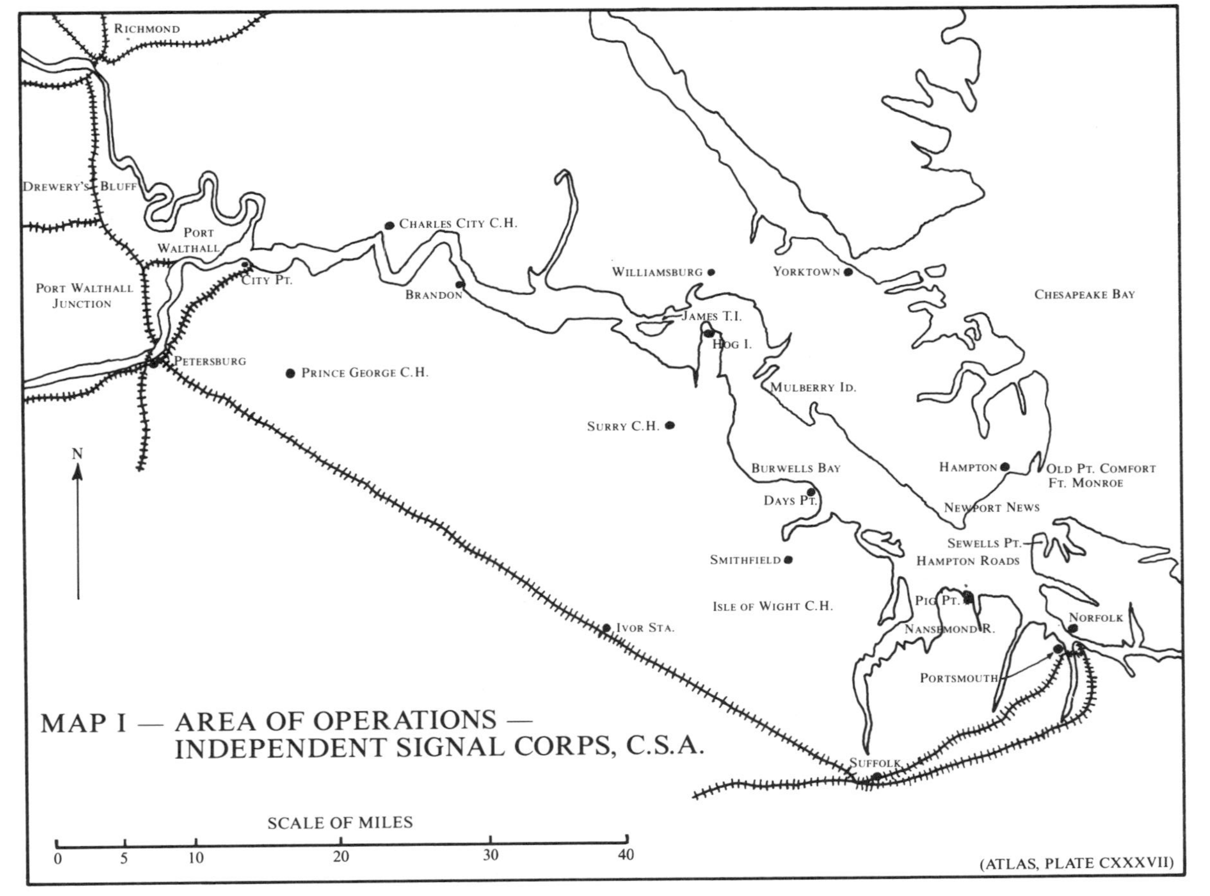

MAP I — AREA OF OPERATIONS — INDEPENDENT SIGNAL CORPS, C.S.A.

immediate command of Lieutenant Nathaniel W. Small of Norfolk, and under the overall command of Captain James Milligan.[16]

But Milligan was showing reservations about remaining on signal duty. Man of action that he was, signal duty must have appeared pretty tame to him. Already on March 30, 1862, he had written to President Jefferson Davis detailing his service and devotion to the cause in his request for a position as First Lieutenant in the Cavalry or the Artillery. As he then stated it, "I am exceedingly desirous to enter the army [it] being better suited to my temperament &c." Then, as the Confederate government undertook the process of establishing a regular Signal Corps in the Confederate Army during April 1862, Milligan apparently felt that he might stand a good chance for a command position in the new branch, given his signal experience. He accordingly applied to the new Secretary of War, George W. Randolph, for an appointment as Captain in the new Signal Corps, an application which was not acted upon and which Milligan withdrew some time later. These letters began a long process of frustration in Milligan's hopes for the kind of promotion and command which he felt he deserved.[17]

When the Confederate Congress acted on April 19, 1862, to establish the Signal Corps, James Milligan was curiously overlooked among the ten officers named to the organization. Why is not exactly clear. Possibly his letter to the President on March 30 requesting a different type of service created reservations in the minds of authorities about Milligan's commitment to signal duty. Or possibly

---

[16] *Official Records,* vol. XI:pt. III, 628. *See* also muster roll for Small's Co., M258, reel 116, RG 109, NARS.

[17] Milligan to Davis, Mar. 30, 1862; Milligan to Sec. of War George W. Randolph, Apr. 14, 1862, "CSR — Milligan," RG 109, NARS.

the generals whom Milligan worked for did not have the degree of influence which other generals, whose signal officers did gain appointment in the regular Signal Corps, did. Milligan's lack of formal education and social standing may also have influenced his failure to become an officer in the regular Signal Corps. In any case, Milligan felt "overslaughed," and firmly believed that he had more seniority than other officers on signal duty and should therefore have been given top command of the Confederate Signal Corps.[18]

Certainly Milligan had been on signal duty since the second month of the war, no matter how unclear his status, and had probably done that service longer than any other Confederate officer, except possibly Major E. Porter Alexander. From the experience standpoint, it is easy to understand Milligan's inability to comprehend why, after Alexander had refused to head the Signal Corps, the Confederate authorities did not appoint Milligan himself to the job. But experience is one thing and rank is another. James Milligan, a second lieutenant and brevet captain, was not the senior signal officer after Alexander. Senior in rank to Milligan was Yale-educated Captain William Norris, signal officer on General Magruder's staff, whom Milligan had assisted in the early days of the war and whom Alexander had since instructed in the use of the Myer system. And it was Norris who was promoted to Major and given command of the Confederate Signal Corps with headquarters in Richmond. Milligan, throughout 1862 and 1863, continued to claim seniority to Norris and carried on a running feud with him, but to no avail. But at least if Milligan could not have Norris' job and command, he became absolutely determined that his own

[18] "CSR — Milligan," RG 109, NARS. Almost every letter in "CSR — Milligan" concerns his complaints about being "oversloughed."

Independent Signal Corps would remain as fully independent of Norris' authority as possible. To signify this, Milligan sent his official reports directly to Adjutant General Cooper, not to Norris. In the summer of 1863, one of Milligan's lieutenants brought charges against Norris for being drunk on duty and giving away signals to the enemy. A court of inquiry found these charges to be groundless, and, while there is no proof, it is quite possible that Milligan may have at least encouraged his subordinate to bring the charges in an effort to discredit his rival.[19] Even after being promoted to major of cavalry, a rank virtually equal to Norris', in July 1863, Milligan continued to complain about Norris' attempts to extend authority over the Independent Signal Corps; the only authority Milligan would tolerate over the I.S.C. was his own.[20] Major Milligan did not begin to get along well with the commander of the regular Signal Corps until Captain William Barker took over temporary command from Norris in 1864 while Norris inspected the Signal Corps units in the various departments of the Confederacy.[21]

Even though there was considerable squabbling between the regular Signal Corps and the I.S.C., basically they both performed the same function in the Confederate war effort — intelligence-gathering and communication of this information to headquarters. This function included signalling, scouting, sending men behind Union lines on secret missions, and gathering information both from Confederate sympathizers in Yankee territory and from Northern newspapers. The activities of the Signal Corps headquartered at Richmond were much more wide-ranging than those of Milligan's Independent Signal

---

[19] Gaddy, "Norris," 172, 174-175. Mr. Gaddy provided the authors with much helpful advice on this chapter.

[20] Milligan to Elzey, Aug. 11, 1863, "CSR — Milligan," RG 109, NARS.

[21] Gaddy, "Norris," 176, 182.

Corps, which confined itself almost entirely to battlefield intelligence.[22]

Milligan's area of operations quickly grew to encompass much more than the Norfolk and Hampton Roads area. His report of July 1, 1862, details the increasing scope and dangers of the I.S.C. operations, especially after the fall of Norfolk to the Union in early May and the establishment of Milligan's new headquarters at Petersburg:[23]

> In obedience to General Orders, No. 40, May 29, 1862, Adjutant and Inspector General's Office, I beg leave to report the number and organization of the signal corps of this department and its general operations during the quarter ending June 30, 1862.
>
> The corps which I command is composed of one company, organized by authority of the honorable Secretary of War upon recommendations of General Huger, commanding Department of Norfolk, February 22, 1862, and is composed of 1 captain, 3 lieutenants, and 114 non-commissioned officers and privates.
>
> . . . Since its organization 41 men have entered the corps by enlistments and transfers. My posts in the Department of Norfolk extended from Harden's Bluff, by the south side of James River, to headquarters in Norfolk; distance between posts varying from 2 miles to 7, according to the facilities for connection and view.
>
> The posts on James River, as far down as Pig Point, fell back after our evacuation of our fortification at Harden's Bluff and Fort Boykin. After the evacuation of Mulberry Island the posts were used to pass the steamers up and down the river by private signals.
>
> On the 10th of May the post at Sewell's Point came very near being cut off by the enemy. Our forces, leaving at 4 a.m., gave no notice to the Signal Corps of their movement. They never left their posts until 7 p.m., and then only when ordered to do so from headquarters in Norfolk.
>
> After our retreat from Norfolk and falling back upon this place I was ordered to report to the honorable Secretary of War for

[22] *Ibid.*, 173; H.V. Canan, "Confedertate Military Intelligence," 46.

[23] *Official Records*, XI:pt.III, 628-29.

further orders by Maj. Gen. Benjamin Huger. I reported accordingly, and received verbal orders from the honorable Secretary of War to establish communication on the James River and Appomattox, which I have accordingly done, as follows: One post at Drewry's Bluff, communicating with Chaffin's Bluff, thence down the river to Gregory's farm, where there is a good view of the river for 15 miles. I found it impossible to get communication lower in consequence of the sinuous character of the river. The posts on the Appomattox are from Rhea's farm, on the western side of the Appomattox, to Blanfield, on the eastern side of the river; thence to Cobb's farm, between Point of Rocks and Port Walthall, on the western side of the river; thence to Clifton, on the same side of the river, at the obstructions, amid the fortifications covering them; thence to Old Blanford Church, near Petersburg; from thence to McIlwain's building, on Sycamore street, near the custom-house, the headquarters in Petersburg; making in all six stations between the mouth of the Appomattox and headquarters.

I have each post doubled, in order to transmit messages with the least possible delay. I can get communication with Rhea's farm, the lower post on the Appomattox, to headquarters, a distance of 15 miles, and pass through six posts, in twenty minutes. The river is exceedingly hard to communicate by, in consequence of its sinuous character and dense timber upon its banks.

On the 26th ultimo the posts of Rhea's farm, Blanfield, and Cobb's were shelled out by a fleet of gunboats, which ascended the river rather suddenly, but which returned on the 27th, after burning one of their vessels, which had grounded in the Appomattox channel.

The discipline of the corps is good, and the men drilled by sight and sound. All are sworn to secrecy, and apply themselves to their duty with commendable zeal. The men not being armed, I would most respectfully recommend to the honorable Secretary of War to arm them with army revolvers or light carbines, that they may have some means of protecting themselves in case of a sudden attack.

In addition to the men who are stationed at the several posts herein mentioned, I keep a reserve at the Halfway Station, on the Richmond and Petersburg Railroad, with a complete outfit for

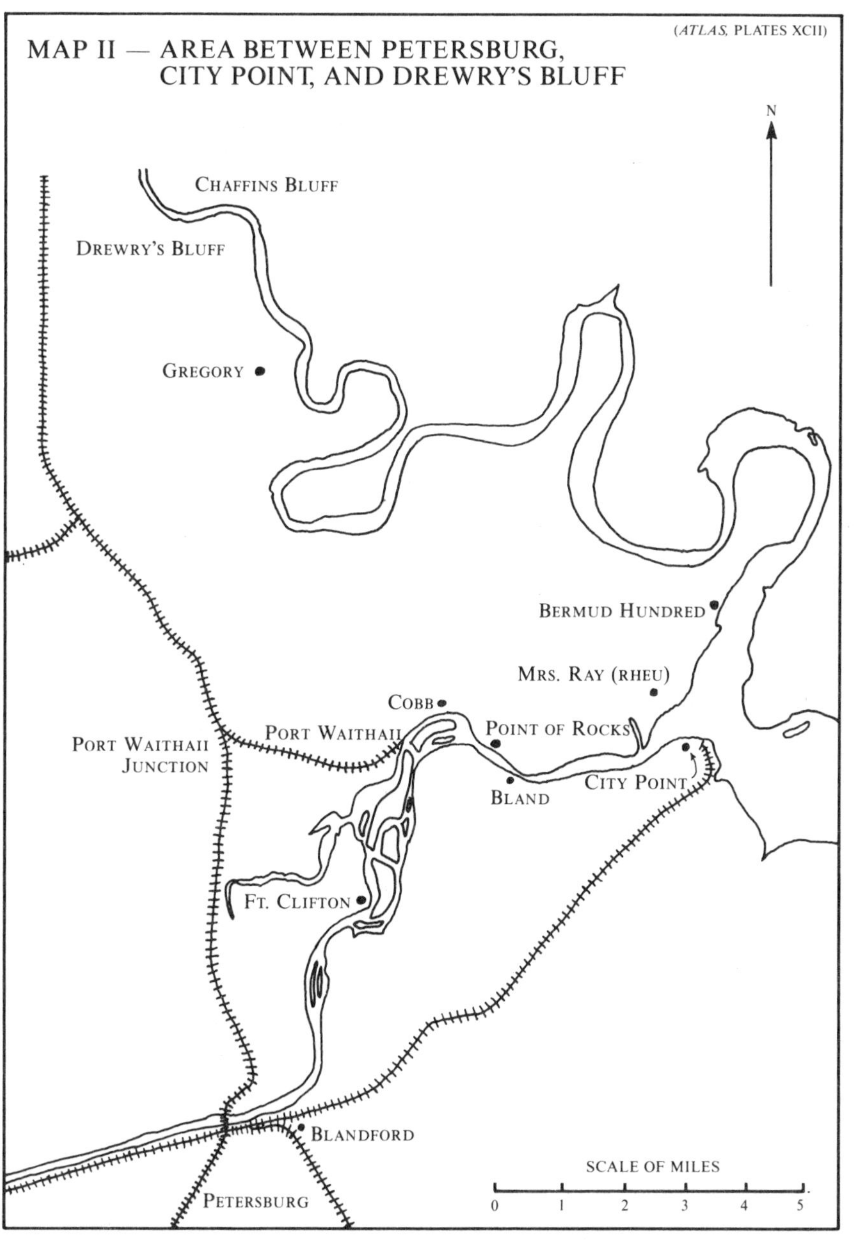
(ATLAS, PLATES XCII)
MAP II — AREA BETWEEN PETERSBURG,
CITY POINT, AND DREWRY'S BLUFF
N
Chaffins Bluff
Drewry's Bluff
Gregory
Bermud Hundred
Mrs. Ray (rheu)
Cobb
Port Waithaii
Port Waithaii
Junction
Point of Rocks
Bland
City Point
Ft. Clifton
Blandford
Petersburg
SCALE OF MILES
0 1 2 3 4 5

any emergency or demand that circumstances may require. I have a complete and good outfit for fifteen posts, in addition to an outfit sent to Major Alexander for twelve posts.

I have the honor to be, with great respect, your obedient servant,

JAS. F. MILLIGAN,
Captain and Signal Officer,
Department of the Appomattox.

July 7, 1862

Respectfully referred to Colonel Gorgas to know if the arms asked for on the third page of this letter can be conveniently supplied.

S. COOPER
Adjutant and Inspector General

July 10, 1862

Respectfully returned. No pistols or carbines on hand. Shotguns may be supplied perhaps.

J. GORGAS,
Chief of Ordnance.

Milligan's concern over the arming of his men brought another message from him to the Adjutant General at the end of August 1862: "Is there no possible means of arming the signal corps, at least with revolvers? I understand the Navy Department has a number."[24] The troop strength of the I.S.C. remained fairly constant throughout 1862, returns toward the end of the year disclosing only a few more than Captain Milligan's July report showed.[25]

While most men in the I.S.C. hailed from the Norfolk-Portsmouth area, some of the unit's most notable recruits were from Georgia, namely the famous future Southern writer, Sidney Lanier, and his brother Clifford. The Laniers joined the I.S.C. in Petersburg in July 1862, following the tremendous Confederate defense of Richmond against General George McClellan in the Battle of Seven Days. As Sidney Lanier later reminisced, "While in Camp there, I, with Cliff and two friends, obtained a

[24] *Ibid.*, XVIII:741.
[25] *Ibid.*, 750, 788.

transfer to Maj. (then Capt.) Milligan's Signal Corps; and becoming soon proficient in the System, attracted the attention of the Com'd'g Off. who formed us into a mounted Field Squad and attached us to the Staff of Maj. Gen. French."[26] The Laniers were fascinated by their new commander, this rough and tumble plainsman and seafarer who shared a love for music, poetry, and literature with the Lanier brothers. It is from two of Sidney Lanier's letters to his father in late 1862, describing his situation, that we have a most engaging portrait of Milligan, in the midst of wartime enjoying a friendly camaraderie with some favored privates:[27]

Petersburg Va. Sept 10th"/62-

My Dear Pa:

. . . We have each engaged a uniform suit of the Corps, consisting of gray double-breasted frock coat, vest, and pants, for Thirty Dollars a piece: also a pair of shoes for Ten Dollars — The Suit is by far the cheapest one we could procure: we are confident it will be a good investment, as it is made of very thick gray cloth, which was purchased by one of our Lieutenants for the Corps, in the mountains of Virginia-: and is at least thirty Dollars cheaper than any other suit that could be obtained- The shoes are less than half what we would have to pay for them in Petersburg: they are to be made by one of the Corps who was at our station, and got detached to go to his home at Salem, (above Lynchburg) for the purpose of making shoes for the Corps. So that, in the course of ten days, we shall need at least Forty Dollars apiece —

You cannot imagine, My dear Pa, with how much reluctance

---

[26] Sidney Lanier to Milton Northrup, June 11, 1866, in Anderson, gen. ed., *Works of Sidney Lanier,* VII: 226 (hereafter cited as Anderson, ed., *Lanier's Works*). The "two friends" were William A. Hopson and Charles K. Emmell. They and the Laniers had been in Company B, 2nd Georgia Battalion.

[27] Sidney Lanier to Robert S. Lanier, Sept. 10, and Oct. 5, 1862, *Ibid.*, 60-65. Lanier also stated in the letter of Sept. 10 that Milligan had just been made commander of the entire Confederate Signal Corps. This is simply a bit of misinformation. General S.G. French also mentions Lanier's escapades. French, *Two Wars,* 157. Lanier Letters reprinted by permission of Johns Hopkins Univ. Press.

we call upon you for so much money — You would doubtless be amused if I could record for you the proceedings of the innumerable councils of War which Cliff and I have held on the subject: the investigations we have instituted as to prices, and the calculations we have made: with the thousand wild projects, successively named and abandoned, for making the money ourselves — We had to give it up, at last, however, in despair: and write you for the money — The only consoling reflection is, that after we are fitted out with winter clothes we will have no further occasion to call on you for a long time — We have been as economical in our selection as possible: as it is, I do not know what we shall do this winter, without overcoats: but Forty Dollars, which is the lowest price for which one can be obtained here, is out of the question —

Events have followed each other in such rapid succession, here, that I am dazzled, and under the influence of exultant feelings, can hardly form a sober opinion in regard to the future — Jackson, Longstreet, A.P. Hill, and D.H. Hill, with their respective corps, are across the Potomac, and are reported, in this morning's papers, at the Relay House — In the same report, Lee is said to occupy Arlington Heights — These are only well-founded rumors: but our brave fellows have accomplished such astonishing things lately, that unbounded credulity in regard to their rumored exploits seems to be, on the whole, about as safe a policy as the most captious skepticism — If the two reports which I have just mentioned be true, the fall of Washington is inevitable — And after the fall of Washington —? Perhaps Peace! I somehow feel a presentiment of great events: at any rate, I had as lief utter, nowadays, the wildest and most visionary prophecy, as the most guarded speculation: for the former has at least the charm of daring, and is as likely of fulfillment as the latter —

Apropos of the fall of Washington I managed to rig out two guitars, the other day, one for Cliff, and the other for Hopson: for three days I kept them steadily thrumming, "from Morn til dewy Eve," and at the end of that time I had them tolerably proficient in the accompaniments to several tunes — In the meantime I wrote off some Second parts for Charlie Emmell, who had just received his flute, and who singularly enough is utterly unable to play the simplest tune without the notes before him — All preliminaries being arranged, accompanied by Lieut. Cannon, we sallied out, night before last, armed with instruments, and the Station Lantern (which we lit up, at every house, for Charlie to see his notes by) — Amongst other places we serenaded Capt. Milligan — At the third tune, the burly Chief appeared, in nightshirt and slippers: "Walk in, Boys!" Loud enough, and cordially enough, for us to have been his children and all deaf — We "walked in" both the house, and the Decanter to which he conducted us, on the piano in the parlor — We then chatted: he told us, amongst other characteristic remarks that he was expecting shortly to establish a Signal Station on the dome of the Capitol at Washington: "but," said he, "them damned ten-inch Shells from the gunboats in the Potomac! That's the devil of it! Tho' I'll swear," (with a most comical earnestness) "I'd risk about Six of 'em to wave a message from that position!"

He's a singular Chap — Profane to an alarming extent: keeps open house: yet never touches a drop of liquor in any shape . . .

Our Serenade, by the way, was a magnificent Success — In the narrow streets of Petersburg, brick-built and rock-paved, the Music, which was intrinsically fine, sounded ravishingly: and our first tune, every time, would be followed by a simultaneous hoisting of windows and protruding of night-Caps, on both sides of the Street, as far as we could see by the moonlight; insomuch that we came nigh to waking up by far the greatest part of the good city's inhabitants — We came back to our quarters laden with bouquets: we were invited in at several places: and, to crown the whole, we received yesterday afternoon, a nice note from Miss Dimitry (a splendid-looking woman, daughter of the Spanish Consul: has travelled, and heard fine Music, and sings gloriously) highly complimentary, especially to the "solo flutist" — I regret that for want of some clothes I can't "follow-up" that last "success" — . . .

Petersburg, October 5th"/62-

My Dear Pa:

I got, yesterday, your letter written from Knoxville: but our trunk has not yet arrived- These Expressmen are wretchedly slow: monopolizing all transportation facilities, and being amenable to nobody, they manage to make a pretty high-handed thing out of it-

We have no War-news: the only triumphs occurring, now, are those which "the Four Georgians" have been achieving, recently, not only over the affections of the Women of this Good City, but also those of the burly Chief of the Signal Bureau, in addition (to cap the climax) to those of the General commanding this Department together with his whole Staff!

The interpretation whereof is as follows:- Capt. Milligan sent us a message a few days ago, requesting us to come in and go with him to serenade Gen'l French- Of course, we went: Met Capt. M. at our Head-Quarters: and, about Eleven O'Clock, sallied forth, led by the Chief, and attended by Capt. Small, Lieut. Cannon, our Orderly Sergeant Benson and Commissary Jenkins — Our old Chief fairly lit up the route with witty coruscations: I have never seen him so brilliant and so good-humored — Arrived at the Gen'l's house, we played some select pieces: shortly appeared one of his Staff, who flung wide the doors and conducted us into a finely-furnished parlor, the centre-table, whereof groaned under various good things —, and then the General and the rest of the Staff made their appearance — Capt. M. introduced us individually to the Gen: I, however, had met the Gen. as well as some of his Staff, (in Wilmington) before: after the handshaking, which I thought would be interminable, we all "proceeded to business"— I, like the wine, "circulated freely" amongst the company, trying to find out the best man in it: which, accordingly, I did in the person of one Capt. Baker, of North Carolina — He was the finest-looking man I ever saw: a perfect Antinous, very tall, and muscular, and looked as if he were about to step into the Olympic Arena, indifferent whether to wrestle physically or mentally — I found he had travelled in Greece, and other countries: and so I had a good time with him — To cut a long story short—: we stayed there about an hour and a half: and when we left, we carried General and Staff with us, until we had finished serenading — A brave party of Troubadours, wasn't it? One General, Six Captains, One Lieutenant, and four privates!

The whole affair constitutes one of the most brilliant successes of the war — Captain Milligan has officially announced that the four Georgians are to be retained at this post, to constitute his field-Staff: so that unless he is ordered to field, we will winter in

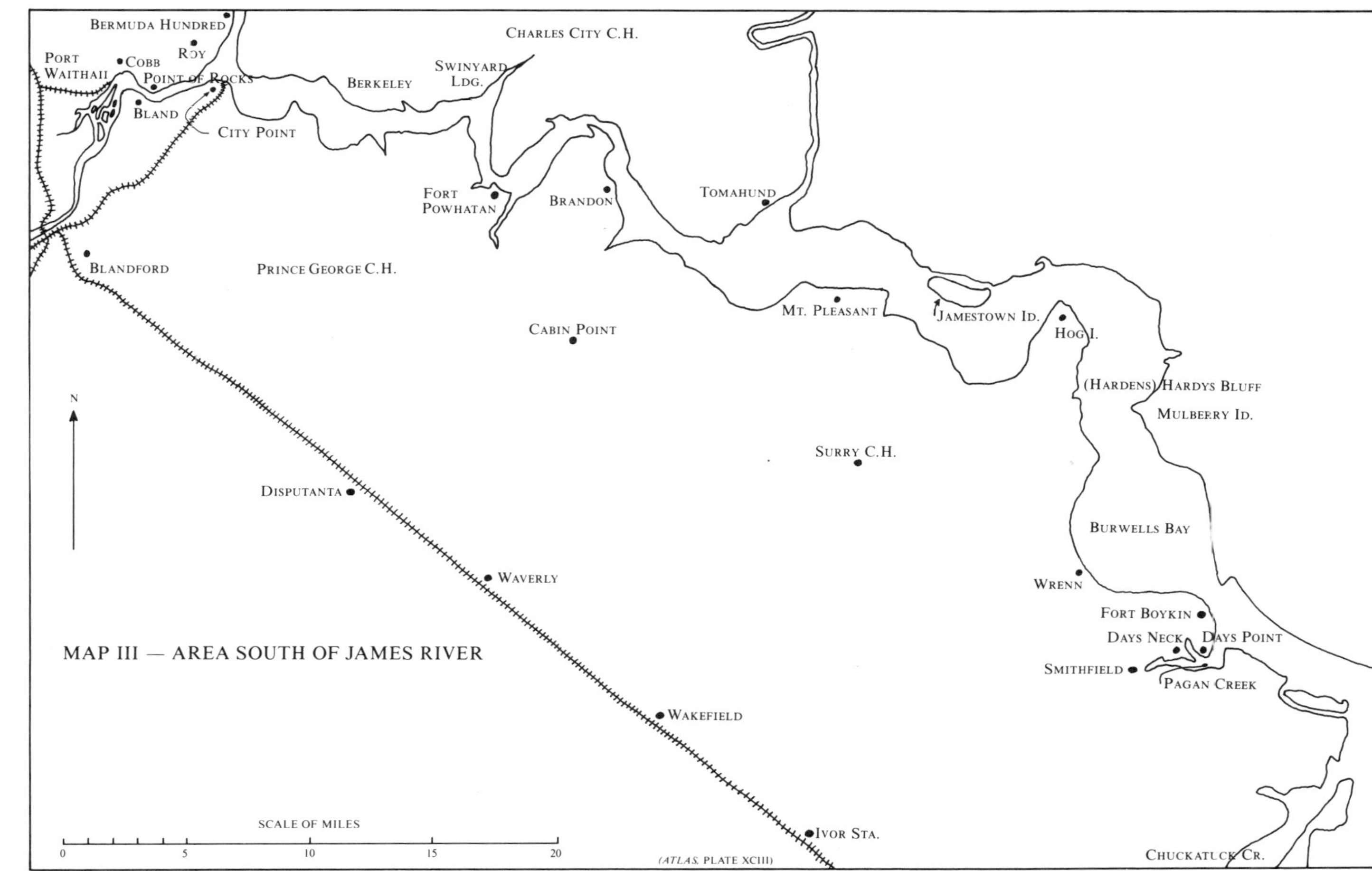

MAP III — AREA SOUTH OF JAMES RIVER

> Petersburg — You cannot imagine how proud he is of us: he boasts of us as the Roman Matron did of her children: "these are my Jewels!"—
>
> I had a dispatch the other day from Uncle Sid and Washburn in relation to his (W's) joining our Corps— I immediately went in and saw Capt. M. about it: he said he could not possibly receive another man, now, as the Corps was completely crammed, and he had a long list of applications for membership which he was unable to grant— He has, however, made an application to the Sec'y of War for permission to increase the Corps by twenty-five men, which is not decided yet— If Washburn wishes me to try and get him in, in case of the Success of Capt. M.'s application, I think I may succeed— Tell this to Uncle Sid: I telegraphed Washburn the other day— . . .

James Milligan must have rejoiced in those rare chances for merriment which Lanier described. Milligan's attention was usually riveted on his first priority — the operations of the Independent Signal Corps. During 1863 the I.S.C. set up signal stations all the way down the James River to the Smithfield area with another communication system to Suffolk through Ivor on the railroad south of Petersburg. Milligan's I.S.C. was also enlarged to two companies, and he himself received his long sought after rank of Major on July 17. The strength, area of operations, and actions of the I.S.C. in 1863 are best seen in Milligan's report of July 3:[28]

> I respectfully submit the following report as to the numbers and organization of the independent signal corps under my command, and its general operations since my last report:
>
> The corps consists of two companies, respectively commanded by Capt. N.W. Small and E.G. DeJarnette, each company having 1 first and 2 second lieutenants, 5 sergeants, and 4 corporals, with 75 privates in each company. They are stationed from Drewry's Bluff to Day's Neck, along the line of the James River and the Appomattox; in all, twenty-three stations. The

[28] *Official Records,* XXVII: pt. III, 964-65. Appointment as Major is in "CSR —Milligan."

line is busily employed, and the men are upon continuous duty. Being only 6 at each post, the duty is particularly heavy in cases of sickness, &c.

The line from Fort Powhatan to Day's Neck was opened by order of General Longstreet on the 11th of April, Captain (J.H.) Manning, of the Signal Corps, C.S. Army, rendering hearty co-operation in carrying out the orders of the commanding general. On the 14th, Captain Small took the posts from Upper James River, and, according to orders, ran a line from Ivor to General Longstreet's headquarters, near Suffolk. On the 24th, the telegraph being opened, Captain Small ran a line along our front at Suffolk, which rendered valuable and efficient service. The field corps, consisting of 14 mounted men, rendered able and efficient service in acting as scouts, guides, and couriers, and were highly complimented for their general utility by Maj. Gen. S.G. French, under whom they personally served.

On the 5th of June, the post of Hog Island had a skirmish with a barge of the enemy sent over to reconnoiter their post from King's Mill Wharf. Lieutenant (R.A.) Mapp, in command of the post, fired into her, and has no doubt that 2 of the Yankees were severely wounded.

On the 11th of June, the enemy ascended the river with three iron-clads and two gunboats, accompanied by several transports. They shelled every signal station from Hog Island to Tomahund: two iron-clads anchored directly under Mount Pleasant Station, and shelled it vigorously for about twenty minutes, nearly demolishing the house at which it was located. This station was under command of Sergt. J.B. Smith, who deserves great credit for his coolness in finishing a message under a heavy fire. I therefore most cordially recommend him to the consideration of the Department.

As the enemy showed every disposition to land a large force at Dillard's Wharf, on the south side of the river, from Jamestown Island, I took 2 of my own men and a detachment of the Third North Carolina Cavalry, and burned it on the night of the 11th instant. Connection was only broken four hours on the line.

On the night of the 24th of June, Captain DeJarnette, under my orders, crossed James River, and burned the enemy's wharf at Jamestown Island; this wharf was very serviceable to them, as they used it to embark and disembark troops upon their raids up the James and Chickahominy.

The line as a general thing is reliable and efficient. Occasionally mistakes occur, which I attribute more to the want of system on the part of telegraph lines than to the signal corps proper. When mistakes occur on the signal line, they are easily detected and the offenders punished; but when a dispatch goes out of their jurisdiction I see no remedy for the punishment of delinquencies, as they are beyond my control

Milligan ended this report with an example of mistaken signals and a vigorous complaint about army commanders at certain posts interfering with the transmission of messages through the signal stations located there. Despite these occasional difficulties, Milligan's units continued to keep Richmond posted on Union activities in the James River-Hampton Roads area.

While the Confederacy had to cope with the news of the twin disasters of Gettysburg and Vicksburg in July 1863, Milligan's health took a turn for the worse. Apparently he contracted "James River malaria." On July 27 Lieutenant Forbes of the I.S.C. reported that "Major Milligan is very sick," and on August 11 a medical board recommended that Milligan take a twenty-day furlough to recuperate. Though the major was reluctant to leave his duties, his weakness left him no choice. The malaria also put many of his men on the sick list.[29]

By October and November 1863, Major Milligan was again back on duty. His dispatches then concerned the outcome of Northern elections, prospects for Union raids in North Carolina, the possibility of mining the Nansemond River to interrupt Union troop movements on the river, and other matters. Milligan showed special concern for the welfare of his men in a November dispatch after

[29] *Official Records,* XXVII: pt. III, 1043; Milligan to Elzey, Aug. 11, 1863, "CSR—Milligan," RG 109, NARS.

receiving reports that Union General Ben Butler was planning to execute Milligan's scouts captured behind Union lines: "I would respectfully ask to be officially informed if it is General Butler's purpose to put to death our scouts caught within his lines, uniformed as soldiers of the Confederacy. My scouts are everywhere in the locality, often visiting Norfolk, Old Point, and Yorktown. Such a threat I deem against the laws of Christian warfare, and not sustained by the laws of war or nations."[30] Major Milligan kept a careful watch on Butler's troop movements during the early months of 1864, gathering information not only from his scouts and signal stations but also from a woman informant on the north side of the James River.[31]

The enemy attempted to disrupt Milligan's intelligence network on several occasions, but failed to do much damage, and Milligan's men continued to harass the Yankees whenever they got the chance, as reported by the I.S.C.'s commander on April 5, 1864:[32]

> In accordance with orders, I herewith most respectfully submit the first quarterly report of 1864, ending March 31, of the number, organization, and operations of the Independent Signal Corps, under my command: The First Company, commanded by Capt. N.W. Small, consists of 4 commissioned officers, 9 non-commissioned officers, and 109 privates, making a line of signals from Drewry's Bluff to City Point, on the James River, thence via the Appomattox River to Petersburg, Va. The Second Company, commanded by Capt. E.G. DeJarnette, consists of 4 commissioned officers, 9 non-commissioned officers, and 110 privates, forming a line of signals on the James River from Berkeley to Fort Boykin. The corps acts as pickets along the line of James and Appomattox Rivers, and detachments under the command of reliable and efficient officers do scout duty within the lines of the enemy upon the lower James and Nansemond

---

[30] *Official Records,* XXIX:pt. II, 849-50.

[31] *Ibid.,* XXIX: pt. II, 787-788, 849-950; XXXIII:1122, 1175-176, 1293.

[32] *Ibid.,* LI: pt. II, 849-50.

Rivers. Therefore, the Department will readily perceive that the whole duty of this corps is not confined to that of signals. It also often occurs that the posts on lower James are attacked by the enemy from their gun-boats, which so far have been successfully resisted, and invariably with loss to the enemy. The corps has never been regularly armed, and I would most respectfully call to the attention of the Department the fact that my repeated efforts to have it armed have so far been unavailing. We are sadly in need of arms of a uniform caliber, and I most truly hope I may be gratified in yet meeting with success. On the night of the 24th of January the enemy, with three gun-boats and one transport, came up the James River and landed a large force at Brandon under cover of darkness and the opposite shore. Post K was in communication with Post I, back of Brandon, sending on a message. At about 7:30 a.m. on the 25th of January a detachment of the enemy, numbering about 200, were seen emerging from the woods in the rear of Station I, a short distance off, at a double quick. At the time Sergeant Joiner and Private Cartwright were at the glass taking a message from K, north side of James River; Private Marks on the waving stand, sending it on to Post G. Upon discovering the enemy Marks immediately gave the alarm, jumped from the platform, and made good his escape. Sergeant Joiner only had time to conceal the record book when the house was entirely surrounded and all the post taken, with the exception of Marks, Ruffin, and Kuykendal; the latter two absent on leave. Lieutenant Forbes, commanding the district, only escaped capture by being absent visiting his post at headquarters. Lieutenant Mapp, commanding the Swynyard district, north side of James River, promptly sent over two men from his district, and connection was broken but about one hour.

The negro blacksmith at Brandon was secured as a guide by the enemy, who, by a circuitous route, guided them to the rear of the station. Had the picket, which it was customary to have kept at Brandon, been at his post, the occurrence would not have happened; but this picket was removed upon application of Doctor Richie, residing at Brandon, to General Jenkins. Post I was an isolated post upon the farm of Doctor Orsborn, with no view of the river but that of continuity with Post K on the north side of James River. The approach of the fleet was duly announced ascending the river by courier to Ivor, thence to Petersburg by telegraph; also by signals. The enemy, after accomplishing their designs, made a hasty retreat with their booty, taking Doctor Richie and his overseers prisoners. The scouts on Chuckatuck Creek, commanded by Sergeant Norsworthy, and a detachment of North Carolina troops under Lieutenant Bowen, fired into the Federal steamer Flora Temple on Saturday, the 30th day of January, killing and wounding, by the enemy's own account, all but four men on board. On Sunday, the 31st day of January, the enemy with the steamer Smith Briggs, landed a force at Smithfield in order to flank the scouts at Chuckatuck. They were met at Scott's Mills and driven back to Smithfield. Sergeant Rooney had his horse shot under him. On February the 1st Captain Sturdivant met and gloriously defeated the enemy, capturing the whole party and destroying the gunboat. Lieutenant Woodley, commanding field squadron, Independent Signal Corps, co-operated with Captain Sturdivant from the west side of Pagan Creek, rendering most efficient service, capturing ten prisoners and securing one 12-pounder howitzer. I most respectfully refer with pride and satisfaction to the official report of Captain Sturdivant. On Monday, the 28th of March, the enemy attempted to land in two barges manned by negroes and white officers from the Federal steamer Stepping Stones, at Day's Neck, just below old Fort Boykin. They were repulsed, with the loss of a white officer and one negro, by the pickets and signal men at Fort Boykin. At about 11 a.m. the enemy returned with three gun-boats and shelled the fort and point vigorously for about one hour and proceeded up James River as far as Fort Powhatan, where they shelled indiscriminately, doing no harm, but expending a very large amount of ammunition.

The overall picture for the Confederacy was bleak in 1864, much worse than one perceived in Milligan's reports of minor engagements in the James River area. Lieutenant General Ulysses Grant, after winning impressive victories further west at Vicksburg and then Chattanooga, had come East to launch the great Union offensive in Virginia in 1864. Against Grant's army of 120,000 men, General

Robert E. Lee would have to repel their advance against Richmond with about 65,000. But Grant's army was not the only weapon to be used. Another attack was to be launched by General Ben Butler from Fortress Monroe up the James River with over 30,000 men to attack Richmond from the South. The Confederates were expected to have difficulty mustering any sizable force to oppose this move by Butler. As Grant's army marched into the Wilderness to begin its campaign in early May 1864, Butler took his army up the James River in transports and disembarked them at Bermuda Hundred on May 5.

Butler's offensive provided the only recorded occasion on which Major James Milligan was able to become involved in a real battlefield action against the Yankees. Milligan had done a very efficient job with his Independent Signal Corps, but he still possessed an instinctive urge for action and a good fight, neither of which a signal command offered much chance for. So Milligan became part of the desperate Confederate attempt to hold Butler's army at bay. If Butler had moved decisively in force from Bermuda Hundred, there was little that could have prevented him from at least cutting the railroad which linked Richmond and Petersburg. He might even have linked up with Grant to destroy Lee's army and end the war quickly, as Grant hoped. However, decisiveness was demanded in this situation, and Butler proved cautious and incompetent, thus giving the Confederates a chance to build some defensive forces against the Union attack. Even then the Confederates could muster only a few thousand men, but Butler obliged them by launching piecemeal, inadequate attacks against the railroad. One of those attacks came on May 7 and resulted in the Battle of Port Walthall Junction.

Whatever General George Pickett, the overall Confederate commander, lacked in quantity of troops was partially compensated for by their quality. General Beauregard ordered three brigades from his old Charleston command, and two regiments of them arrived just in time to stop Butler's first probing attack against the railroad on May 6. General Bushrod Johnson, a tough fighter, then arrived with his Tennessee brigade from up at Drewry's Bluff to throw back the Union assault. That evening, as the Confederates dug in to defend against the next day's expected attack, more of the South Carolinians arrived, a brigade commanded by General Johnson Hagood. On May 7 the Confederate force totalled about 3000 men defending Port Walthall Junction under the commands of Johnson, Hagood, and the veteran fighter General D.H. Hill. Among these Confederates were men scraped from various units, and James Milligan was one of them. Whether or not he was ordered to help in the front lines that day is not clear.

The only record of Milligan's presence at Port Walthall Junction on May 7 is in Sidney Lanier's first novel, *Tiger-Lilies*. In the story Major Milligan rousted two of his men out of bed on the morning of May 7 by sending a messenger with a note for them, one of whom was Lanier. The two joked about the Major's phraseology, noting how he began it "You damned lazy hounds . . . I want you! &c. &c." They dressed quickly since "Major M-" was "fuming, being the most restless of mortals." "'Mount, boys!' cried the major, as the two young men descended the steps. 'Haygood's out on railroad, and he's going to have a devilish hard time of it this morning'." The three rode off toward the junction, and heard the cannon and musket fire begin. "'Haygood's having a rough time of it. Let's get there hearties! It'll be three more of us, anyhow,' said the major, sticking spurs to his horse."[33] Lanier's pen then recounted his strongly felt impression of the battlefield and the progress of the battle:[34]

> There lies a man, in bloody rags that were gray, with closed eyes. The first hailstone in the advancing edge of the storm has stricken down a flower. The dainty petal of life shrivels, blackens: yet it gives forth a perfume as it dies; his lips are moving, — he is praying.
>
> The wounded increase. Here is a musket in the road: there is the languid hand that dropped it, pressing its fingers over a blue-edged wound in the breast. Weary pressure, and vain, — the blood flows steadily.
>
> More muskets, cartridge-boxes, belts, greasy haversacks, strew the gound.
>
> Here come the stretcher-bearers. They leave a dripping line of blood. "Walk easy as you kin, boys," comes from a blanket which four men are carrying by the corners. Easy walking is desirable when each step of your four carriers spurts out the blood afresh, or grates "the rough edges" of a shot bone in your leg.
>
> The sound of a thousand voices, eager, hoarse, fierce, all speaking together yet differently, comes through the leaves of the undergrowth. A strange multitudinous noise accompanies it, — a noise like the tremendous sibilation of a mile-long wave just before it breaks. It is the shuffling of two thousand feet as they march over dead leaves.
>
> "Surely that can't be reserves; Haygood didn't have enough for his front! They must be falling back: hark! there's a Yankee cheer. Good God! Here's three muskets on the ground, boys! Come on!" said the major, and hastily dismounted.
>
> The three plunge through the undergrowth. Waxen May-leaves sweep their faces; thorns pierce their hands; the honey-suckles cry "Wait!" with alluring perfumes; guarded oak-twigs wound the wide-opened eyes.
>
> It is no matter.
>
> They emerge into an open space. A thousand men are talking, gesticulating, calling to friends, taking places in rank, abandoning them for others. They are in gray rags.
>
> "Where's Haygood?"

[33] Anderson, ed., *Lanier's Works,* V:129-32.

He is everywhere! On the right flank cheering, on the left flank rallying, in the centre commanding: he is ubiquitous; he moves upon the low-sweeping wing of a battle genius: it is supernatural that he should be here and yonder at once. His voice suddenly rings out, —

"Form, men! We'll run 'em out o' that in a second. Reinforcements coming!" . . .

The Federals, having driven the small Confederate force from the railroad, stop in their charge as soon as they have crossed the track. Behind their first is a second line. As if on parade this second line advances to the railroad, and halts. "Ground Arms!" Their muskets fall in a long row, as if in an armory-rack. The line steps two paces forward. It stoops over the track. It is a human machine with fifty thousand clamps, moved by levers infinitely flexible. Fifty thousand fingers insert themselves beneath the stringers of the road. All together! They lift, and lay over, bottom upwards, a mile of railroad.

But, O first line of Federals, you should not have stopped! The rags have rallied. Their line is formed, in the centre floats the cross-banner, to right and left gleam the bayonets like silver flamejets, unwavering, deadly; these, with a thousand mute tongues, utter a silent yet magnificent menace:

"Charge! Steady, men!"

The rags flutter, the cross-flag spreads out and reveals its symbol, the two thousand sturdy feet in hideous brogans, or without cover, press forward. At first it is a slow and stately movement; stately in the mass, ridiculous if we watch any individual leg, with its knee perhaps showing through an irregular hole in such pantaloons!

The step growns quicker. A few scattering shots from the enemy's retiring skirmishers patter like the first big drops of the shower.

From the right of the ragged line now comes up a single long cry, as from the leader of a pack of hounds who has found the game. This cry has in it the uncontrollable eagerness of the sleuth-hound, together with a dry harsh quality that conveys an uncompromising hostility. It is the irresistible outflow of some fierce soul immeasurably enraged, and it is tinged with a jubilant tone, as if in anticipation of a speedy triumph and a satisfying

[34] *Ibid.*, 133-35. Account reprinted by permission of Johns Hopkins Univ. Press.

> revenge. It is a howl, a hoarse battle-cry, a cheer, and a congratulation, all in one.
>
> They take it up in the centre, they echo it on the left, it swells, it runs along the line as fire leaps along the rigging of a ship. It is as if someone pulled out in succession all the stops of the infernal battle-organ, but only struck one note which they all speak in different voices.
>
> The gray line nears the blue one, rapidly. It is a thin gray wave, whose flashing foam is the glitter of steel bayonets. It meets with a swell in the ground, shivers a moment, then rolls on.
>
> Suddenly thousands of tongues, tipped with red and issuing from smoke, speak deadly messages from the blue line. One volley? A thousand would not stop them now. Even if they were not veterans who know that it is safer at this crisis to push on than to fall back, they would still press forward. They have forgotten safety, they have forgotten life and death: their thoughts have converged into a focus which is the one simple idea, — to get to those men in blue, yonder. Rapid firing from the blue line brings rapid yelling from the gray.
>
> But look! The blue line, which is like a distant strip of the sea, curls into little waves; these dash together in groups, then fly apart. The tempest of panic has blown upon it. The blue uniforms fly, flames issue from the gray line, it also breaks, the ragged men run, and the battle has degenerated to a chase.

Butler had attacked Port Walthall Junction with four brigades, between 6000 and 8000 men, and had outnumbered the Confederates by at least two to one. The main attack had come at 2 P.M. on the Confederate left flank and threatened to overrun their position. But the Confederates retreated back from the railroad in good order, and General Hagood and other officers rallied and reorganized the men. Meanwhile, Union troops busied themselves tearing up a few hundred yards of track, some telegraph lines, a bridge, and a sawmill. The Confederates then mounted the counterattack which Lanier so well described, threw back the Union forces, and won the day. Butler made another weak assault on May 9 before suffering a bad defeat in his attacks on the Confederate position at Drewry's Bluff on May 13-16. After that, the outnumbered rebels bottled up Butler's army at Bermuda Hundred, removing this threat and permitting the Confederates to put almost all their resources into the struggle against Grant's Wilderness campaign.[35]

Major Milligan had played his small part in frustrating Butler's offensive, but even Confederate victories proved unable to stop the Yankee juggernaut from grinding inevitably onward. Lee's army stood valiantly against Grant in the Wilderness, at Spottsylvania, North Anna, and Cold Harbor, costing Grant dearly in casualties, but there were always more Union soldiers to fill the ranks. Grant thereupon maneuvered his army south of the James River, and in June 1864 forced Lee's army into the defenses of Petersburg itself. The Confederates anxiously attempted to keep their supply lines open and requisitioned men for duty on ships to run through the Union blockade of Southern ports.

Like the rest of the army, Milligan's Independent Signal Corps was largely confined to duty in the Petersburg defenses now. The War Department requested Major Milligan for signalmen to go on blockade-running duty. Probably feeling that such duty would be a welcome relief from the perilous situation at Petersburg, Milligan tabbed his two favorites, the Lanier brothers, and some others to become crewmen on blockade-runners, which were to run from Wilmington, N.C., the only Confederate port still open, to Nassau or Bermuda. Milligan informed the

[35] On the Battle of Port Walthall Junction, except for *Ibid.*, *see* Foote, *The Civil War*, III:256-257; Catton, *Never Call Retreat*, 348; Hagood, *Memoirs of the War of Secession*, 219-27. For some detailed official reports of the action, *see Official Records*, XXXVI: pt. II, 73-75, 84-85, 87-88, 101-102, 124-25, 240-42, 251-53.

Laniers of their new mission in July 1864, although their orders did not come through until August 2.[36] Clifford Lanier portrayed this scene of Milligan's giving out the new assignment in his postwar novel *Thorn-Fruit,* describing Milligan as "an old oak roughened with the winds of all varieties of rough life, with a genuine jewel of a heart in the right place."

Lanier wrote:

> "Late in the summer he informed them that, in his opinion, they had been campaigning enough for one year. 'I have an order, boys, to send five of you to Wilmington for blockade duty. No more pork and hard-tack. Two hundred dollars a trip in gold — in gold; think of that! And cotton to make money on hand over fist — worse'n h-l beating tanbark!'"

Lanier then expressed the belief that "Old Sinner" Milligan would acquire some boots and other articles from these blockade-runners for "his covetous, now nearly bare limbs." Thus Milligan and the Laniers parted. Unfortunately for Sidney Lanier, his blockade-runner was captured, and his stint in a Union prison had a detrimental effect on his health for the rest of his life.[37]

Back in the Petersburg defenses, Milligan's men earnestly maintained their signal stations along the lines. Major Milligan himself even found time to devise a new signal system, which was never widely adopted. It was basically a different flag code using abbreviations and contractions. The operations of the I.S.C. were not entirely limited to Petersburg, though. Lt. Joseph Woodley and a small band of dauntless scouts were still active on the south side of the James River and managed to send regular reports to Petersburg, despite strong Union efforts to capture them.

---

[36] Clifford Lanier to Gertrude Lanier, July 27, 1864; Sidney Lanier to Robert S. Lanier, Aug. 2, 1864, Anderson, ed., *Lanier's Works,* VII: 157, 162.

[37] Lanier, *Thorn-Fruit,* 57-58; Starke, *Sidney Lanier,* 62-65.

Milligan's last official report of January 1, 1865, describes these activities, displaying his deeply felt appreciation for the services rendered by his men and also his contempt for black Union soldiers who operated against his scouts on the lower James River.[38]

> In accordance with orders, I beg leave to submit the following report for the quarter ending December 31, 1864:
>
> The Independent Signal Corps consists of two companies. The First Company consists of 119 men, rank and file, on duty as follows: At Drewry's Bluff, 1 sergeant and 5 men; at Chaffin's Bluff, 1 sergeant and 6 men; at Battery Brooke, 1 sergeant and 4 men; at Battery Semmes, 5 men; at Battery Dantzler, 5 men; on special duty in deciphering enemy's signal messages, 2 men. The above men form a signal line from Drewry's Bluff to Battery Dantzler, on James River, and co-operating with our fleet under Commodore Mitchell. This district is under command of Lieut. J.B. Smith of the Second Company, Lieut. S.C. Wells of the First Company having tendered his resignation in consequence of continued ill health. In connection with the above men there are fourteen men of the company on duty upon the James River fleet and under command of Corporal Handy. In Pickett's front, from Battery Dantzler to Swift Creek, there are twenty-two signalmen, stationed at various points, who watch and report the movements of the enemy from lookouts. This duty is extremely arduous and not without much danger. The men perform it cheerfully and with much satisfaction and information to General Pickett. This line is in command of Sergeant Rooney, of the First Company. On the Nansemond and lower James River there are sixteen men under Lieutenant Woodley (in charge of the scouts of this department). These men watch and report the movements of the enemy and their peculiarities along the lower James and Nansemond; cross to the north side of the James and get information from Old Point, Newport News, Yorktown, and Williamsburg. This is an important connection, and great care and caution are necessary to keep it up. The scouts upon this service are able and true men, and have performed their duties with credit to themselves and the satisfaction of the various generals commanding this department. The importance of their

services has been duly appreciated, and credit accorded to them for their operations by General Lee, which will be referred to in this report under the head of these operations. Stable guard, 1 man; signal office, 5 men; an adjutant, commissary, clerk, and couriers; courier-line between Petersburg and Fort Boykin, 3 men; forage detail, 1 man; quartermaster department, 1 man; sick, 3 men; prisoners of war, 2 men. On furlough by War Department, 1 officer, Lieutenant Cannon; on furlough by Navy Department, 2 men; on furlough from headquarters Army of Northern Virginia, 3 men. Detailed by order of War Department, 22 men.

The Second Company consists of 117 men, rank and file, on duty as follows, Lieut. R.A. Mapp commanding the company: The First Signal District, Lieut. R.A. Forbes commanding, consists of four posts, viz: At the customhouse, in Petersburg, 1 sergeant and 4 men; post I, at Blandford, 1 sergeant and 5 men; post G, at General A.P. Hill's headquarters, 5 men; post L, at General Ransom's headquarters, in the trenches, 3 men. The Second Signal District, along the immediate front of Petersburg, consists of 4 posts: Post K, at Dunn's Hill, 6 men; post D, at Whitehead's, Chesterfield County, Va., 7 men, an important post, as it reports all movements of the enemy's train in the rear of their defenses from City Point to the Weldon railroad; post E, at Cumming's battery, 3 men; post B, at Fort Clifton, 9 men; stable guard, 3 men; headquarters — as clerk and acting assistant surgeon, 2 men. On courier-line, 3 men; teamster, 1 man; scouts with Lieutenant Woodley and Sergeant Emmell, 20 men. Absent with leave, 4 men; absent without leave, 2 men; absent sick, 9 men. Detailed by order of War Department, 12 men. Prisoners of war exchanged but not reported, 1 officer, Captain DeJarnette, and 4 men; prisoners of war, 10 men. The Second Company for the last quarter have been performing signal duty in our front at Petersburg and extending to General Pickett's right in Chesterfield. Connection has been at all times kept up between the posts; the number of men performing this duty is 46, and the majority are excellent operators. This company, since the 8th of October, have been furnished, as well as the First Company, with clothing complete, with the exception of overcoats, which have never been issued to the corps as an organization, about forty having been drawn in all upon special requisition.

The arms and equipments of the corps are good, but owing to the exchanged prisoners not having been furnished, and the arms of the sick having been turned over last summer, the corps lacks some ten Enfield rifles in the Second Company and some few Austrian rifles in the First Company. The corps has been at all times prepared to render able and efficient services in the trenches or wherever else called upon to do duty as soldiers. As operators and signal men, they stand on their own merits, and can compare favorably with the best in the service. Feeling a deep interest in the success and utility of the signal organization and its deportment, if I find a man worthless as an operator I report it at once and request his transfer to some other branch of the service, where he can be made more efficient to the public interest. The men detailed upon the blockade-runners from Wilmington from the Independent Signal Corps are highly spoken of for efficiency and ability by Lieutenant Wilmer, in charge of marine signals (stationed at Wilmington). This is highly gratifying, and conclusively proves that where harmony prevails duty and co-operation are appreciated. It affords me infinite pleasure to record the courtesy and laudable interest of the Signal Bureau in Richmond, under charge of Captain Barker, Signal Corps, C.S. Army, who shows at all times a lively interest in the utility of the service by suggesting and perfecting improvements of great service to its successful operation, both in the field and the security of our communications from the scrutiny of the enemy.

On 1st of October I introduced a new system, with an entire change of alphabet, which, experience has developed, works with ease and satisfaction to all concerned. The system consists in a series of arbitrary abbreviations, contractions, and combinations, which have the advantage of speed and security from the enemy. By a slight preconcerted signal agreed upon every message can be sent by a different key-word or letter. I have, therefore, fully demonstrated the fact that abbreviations do not sacrifice certainty to speed, and I feel confident of proving it to any intelligent mind in the signal service not blinded by prejudice or incapable of judging upon the merit of the system by success. The operations of the scouts of the Independent Signal Corps in this quarter have been confined to the lower James and Nansemond Rivers; their duties have been dangerous and onerous; onerous from the fact that their movements have to be concealed; no fixed abode or camp; crossing James River at great personal risk of capture from the guard and picket-boats, and engaging parties of the enemy purposely landed to capture and break them up but without success. These scouts are under the command of Lieut. J.R. Woodley, of the First Company, Independent Signal Corps, a man of cool and collected courage, untiring in energy and zeal for the cause, prudent and cautious, keeping up his connections and performing his duties under the most trying circumstances to the satisfaction of all, forwarding regularly tri-weekly to headquarters his report of the enemy's movements and the result of his scouts' observations, both along James River and about Old Point, Newport News, and wherever else occasion may offer an opportunity to collect information for the information of the commanding general and the department. On the 12th of November Lieutenant Woodley, with a party of scouts, left Day's Neck for Surry County, by my orders, to endeavor to suppress the unlicensed marauding of the negroes and white-livered vandals of the Federals, whose depredations upon the unarmed and defenseless inhabitants of that once happy region cried aloud for help. The wily foe did not attempt to come while the lieutenant and his gallant party were on their track.

On the 14th of November Lieutenant Woodley returned from Surry to Isle of Wight just before day; the moon shining bright, his suspicions were aroused by noticing a number of tracks as he crossed the road coming up from the mill at Burwell's Bay. Taking the trail along the road leading toward Fort Boykin by Wrenn's, upon the main road, he found that the party had kept on as if toward Wrenn's Mill; having but seven of his men with him, the rest being on other duty, he took a short cut through Wrenn's field to head the party off if they purposed visiting Fort Boykin. Just this side of Fort Boykin, at Mr. Bourne's house, he dismounted his party, cached his horses, and waited for them to come up, which they did in a short time, and throwing out a long line of skirmishers and flankers, swept the woods and took the horses of the party. Another party coming up from Fort Boykin totally surrounded Woodley and his party. "Every man for himself," was the order silently passed, "and, as you get out, rendezvous at our camp." The signal men got out with the exception of one man, who disobeyed the lieutenant's orders and was taken; the night, or rather morning, being very cold and the party being up all night in Surry looking for the vandals, he slipped into Bourne's kitchen to warm, and when the enemy came up was thus captured. As the signal men got out of the "surround" and rallied under orders of their lieutenant, they were determined to retrieve their misfortune, no matter what force the enemy were in. This gallant band of Woodley's, consisting of nine men all told (three having joined the lieutenant from camp), ambuscaded the enemy in their triumphs and recaptured every horse but one, which was killed in the action; took 5 prisoners and killed 1; the rest took flight and embarked under heavy fire for their gun-boats. The force of the enemy was 150 men, landed at three points from as many gun-boats, viz, at Burwell's Bay, Rock Wharf, and Day's Neck. The commanding general, R.E. Lee, complimented Lieutenant Woodley for his gallantry in retrieving the misfortunes of the day.

On the 4th of December a detachment of signal scouts, getting information that a band of Yankees and negroes would cross from the north shore to the south side for the purpose of plunder, repaired to Lyon's Creek, under Sergeant Dilworth. About midnight four boats entered the creek loaded with negroes; the sergeant let the two leading boats pass, and then opened upon the boats with a preconcerted signal. One boat was sunk, two captured, and 18 negroes were killed, wounded and captured, and two white men were afterward found dead, who, no doubt, were in company with the negroes. Sergeant Dilworth, being some distance from camp, with the enemy raiding through the country in detached parties, deemed it advisable to give his negro marauders lynch parole. This summary treatment has had a very good effect. That portion of Surry County has been quite quiet, and the marauders, who are nothing more than villainous negroes, have been pretty shy how and where they land. The lower portion of the James River is patrolled by steamers attached to Graham's naval brigade. They are a dastardly and villainous set, and are easily whipped with a determined party. The enemy have used every means to capture Lieutenant Woodley and his party that subterfuge could invent. They have landed at various points and scouted the country with cavalry, but have never taken but one signal man of the scouting party under Lieutenant Woodley, and had he obeyed orders he would not have been taken.

Although Major Milligan gave no indication of the truly desperate state of the Confederate cause in his report, their situation steadily deteriorated in early 1865 as the Petersburg defenses stretched further and further, and manpower to defend them grew thinner and thinner. By February 10, Milligan's corps had fallen to a duty strength of 7 officers, 153 men.[39] Grant finally massed troops on the Confederate right and, after attacks which failed on March 31, General Philip Sheridan broke through the Confederate position manned by Pickett's men at Five Forks on April 1. This cut the last railroad supply line for the Confederates, forcing the evacuation of Richmond and forcing the remainder of Lee's army to retreat out of the Petersburg defenses northwest to Amelia Courthouse.

The Independent Signal Corps fled along with Lee's army. They would have liked to remain signalmen, but very reluctantly became infantry. As one of them on the last march commented:[40]

> We have dreaded the infantry. Your true signal man is essentially a stationary animal, not gregarious like your infantryman, but he likes a quiet retreat — ladies, &c. — far from the turmoil and dangers of battle fields — near good pastures where buttermilk is plenty — and neighbors kind — and being turned over to the infantry has ever been his great bug bear.

Signalmen tried standing around, looking important with their now useless equipment, but to no avail:[41]

> As usual the Signal men claimed exemption from any kind of duty except their specialty. One produced a spy glass — another a copper torch — & some one thing and some another — but Maj. Bridgeford [Bridgford] the Provost Marshal Gen. of the Army of N.Va. was inexorable — and the redoubtable flag

---

[38] *Official Records,* XLII: pt. I, 867-70.

[39] *Ibid.,* XLVI: pt. I, 387.

[40] Harwell, ed., *A Confederate Diary,* 12-13.

[41] *Ibid.,* 11-12.

floppers were much to their chagrin & disgust turned into infantry.

This same diarist recorded Major Milligan still exercising authority as he characteristically commanded his men on April 6: "Come Bullies get up — rise Bullies."[42]

But there were few days left for men to rise as Confederates. The Union forces now converged for the kill, out-racing Lee to his last supplies at Appomattox Station on April 9. Virtually surrounded, Lee did the only thing possible and surrendered to Grant at Appomattox Courthouse that same day. On April 22 Major James Milligan signed his parole at Richmond and received permission to take his wife, who apparently had been at Petersburg with him during the war, to Norfolk with his horses and private property. Permission for the journey was granted by the Provost Marshal General Patrick to allow Milligan to collect his scouts on the lower James River, presumably Woodley's men, and have them paroled.[43]

The Civil War was over at last. James Milligan had performed a significant role in the Confederate war effort, as many others had also. He had not originally wanted to be tied down on signal duty, but, when that became his fate, he organized a corps which became Richmond's eyes in the whole James River area, and he performed his duty well. Richmond authorities must be given some credit for handling Milligan the way they did, and thus securing the valuable services of this volatile personality. The authorities would neither let Milligan have his way in his feud with Norris over seniority nor give Milligan control of the regular Signal Corps over Norris. But they did leave

[42] *Ibid.*, 13.

[43] Milligan's parole and the order giving him permission to proceed to Norfolk are in "CSR — Milligan."

Milligan's I.S.C. virtually independent of Norris' authority, and they did permit Milligan to have nearly absolute control over his corps and its operations. In seeing that the mission of the I.S.C. was performed efficiently, James Milligan proved to be a fine leader. He had always detested having a subordinate position, especially one beneath those he did not like. Richmond authorities therefore showed good judgment in utilizing this man's abilities to their fullest extent in the service of the Lost Cause.

8

James Milligan in the Postwar Years

Following the end of hostilities, James and Sally Milligan again took up residence in Norfolk. Milligan at the time was only 36 years old. He and his wife finally started a family with the return of peace, and in subsequent years five children were born to them: Charles S. Milligan, born December 25, 1866; Mary Louise Milligan, born January 31, 1870 (later Mrs. Jessie Price); Robert Tunstall Milligan, born October 10, 1872 (the father of Robert F. Milligan of Sun City, Arizona); Maude Lightfoot Milligan, born February 16, 1875; and Susie Lee Milligan, born December 8, 1876.[1]

James Milligan's search for a postwar career led him back to somewhat familiar territory — the newspapers. Milligan had written letters to newspapers for years and now decided to get into the business itself. In 1866, while he boarded with his family at 118 E. Main Street, Milligan became a reporter for the Norfolk *Post,* and the next year became a reporter and acting local editor on the *Virginian.* In subsequent years he also worked on the *Journal,* the *Day Book,* the *News and Courier,* and in 1889 became

[1] Record of births copied from a family Bible in a certified statement by W.L.Prieur, Jr., Clerk of the Corporation Ct. of the City of Norfolk, Oct. 31, 1940. Document in possession Robert. F. Milligan, Sun City, AZ.

editor of the *Norfolk Advocate*. A city directory of 1877-1878 also listed him as a real estate agent.[2]

James Milligan published a few postwar directories himself. "Jas. F. Milligan and Co., Solicitors and Advertising Agents" published Norfolk directories for 1869 and 1870. In 1872 Milligan and A.J. Dalton were listed jointly as the publishers. That directory was Milligan's last venture along these lines.[3]

Milligan's political affiliations after the war did not remain consistent with his Democratic loyalties of the prewar years. Political party labels became very hazy, anyway, in reconstruction Virginia. Whites of different political persuasions joined in a coalition known as the Conservative movement led by John Baldwin in 1868-1869. James Milligan joined this effort to overthrow Radical Republican reconstruction and supported Conservative Gilbert Walker in his successful campaign for governor in 1869. When this Conservative coalition then became transformed into the Democratic Party in Virginia one might have expected James Milligan to remain loyal to it.[4]

But James Milligan did not remain a Democrat. He did the unthinkable after reconstruction ended in Virginia and became a Republican. His anti-Negro attitude over the years might make this course of action seem strange, especially given the abhorrence of most southern whites for Republicans. However, Milligan's change of party

---

[2] On Milligan's newspaper activities after the war, consult the newspapers themselves and the various Norfolk city directories at the Norfolk Public Lib. *See* also Stewart, *History of Norfolk,* 293, 295; David W. Gaddy, "James F. Milligan," (unpublished article, 1971); and Chambers and Shank, *Salt Water & Printer's Ink,* 128. The last-named work gives the fullest history of newspapers in Norfolk during the late nineteenth century.

[3] These directories are in the Sargeant Memorial Room of the Norfolk Public Lib., Norfolk, VA.

[4] Norfolk *Virginian-Pilot,* Mar. 23, 1899.

loyalty did make some sense, as it did for the handful of other white southerners who remained or became Republicans in the Gilded Age. Milligan and many other Republicans of the same type were anxious for office. That was probably their single most important rationale for being Republicans. While being Republicans precluded such people from having much power in a southern state itself, they were quite suitable for appointment to Federal jobs in their states by the Republican Presidents who usually occupied the White House in the postwar era. As a Republican, James Milligan received several such Federal appointments in his area, working in the customs department in Norfolk from 1873 to 1885, in addition to his newspaper work. In 1879 he was appointed revenue inspector and inspector of hulls for Norfolk, with his office in the Customs House. He remained in that position until 1885 when Democrat Grover Cleveland took over the White House. After Republican Benjamin Harrison won the election of 1888 over Cleveland, James Milligan received another Federal appointment, this time as inspector of hulls for Norfolk, a position which he held until 1894 when he retired from political office.[5]

Becoming a Republican did not mean that Milligan repudiated his old Confederate sympathies. James Milligan remained very active in the United Confederate Veterans as a member of the Pickett-Buchanan Camp of that organization in Norfolk. He was a member of their Memorial Day Committee in 1885 and was a member of the Norfolk UCV delegation in 1887 which attended the

[5] *Ibid.* This newspaper obituary notice states that it was Milligan's earlier Whig Party affiliation that led him to become a Republican. We have found no evidence of any party affiliation except Democratic before the war. For Milligan's offices, *see* Norfolk city directories in the Norfolk Public Lib.; Norfolk *Landmark,* Mar. 23, 1899; and Norfolk *Dispatch,* Mar. 22, 1899.

laying of the cornerstone for the equestrian statue of General Robert E. Lee at Richmond.[6]

As the years passed, the ranks of the veterans were steadily thinned by death, and in 1899 death came to James F. Milligan. In late February he became ill with a kidney infection which, given his age, steadily weakened him. After he had been ill about four weeks, his heart failed, and he died on March 22 at 5 A.M. in his home at 18 North Street. He was seventy years old. Friends were received at his residence by Milligan's family when they came to offer condolences, and, except in one case, these friends were welcomed. Milligan in later years had cultivated friendship with a number of Catholics including some priests. When one of these priests came to the house, a strongly prejudiced member of the family grabbed a broom and drove the priest from the house. Some family members apparently wanted no reminder of Milligan's earlier faith. And apparently they wanted no reminder that he was of Irish background, either, because, in the obituary printed in the Norfolk *Virginian-Pilot,* they portrayed him as Scots-Irish. The funeral for Milligan was conducted the day after his death by two Episcopal ministers. Family, friends, and Confederate veterans attended the flower-bedecked casket to its final resting place in Elmwood Cemetery.[7]

A man who had participated in some of the more momentous events of the 19th century was laid to rest. James Milligan was an intelligent and articulate man, but many such men never advance very far in society. Milligan was determined to attain a respectable position, and did so, depending in large part, as his father had before him, on

---

[6] Gaddy, "Milligan".

[7] Norfolk *Public Ledger,* Mar. 23, 1899; Norfolk *Landmark,* Mar. 23, 1899; Norfolk *Dispatch,* Mar. 22, 1899; and Norfolk *Virginian-Pilot,* Mar. 23, 1899. The story about the priest's being ejected from the house is in a letter from Robert F. Milligan to the authors.

political patronage. He accepted the spoils system of the 19th century as a route of advancement for himself in life, and he performed his duties competently. Milligan was stubborn, romantic, egotistical. His was not a saintly life, but a credibly human one. Ultimately, after a youth spent searching for his place in the sun, James Milligan settled down, married, and raised a family. Following his service to the "lost cause" of the Confederacy, he turned his earlier interest in corresponding with newspapers into a long newspaper career in Norfolk in the postwar era. But the most memorable thing about Milligan's life must remain his wonderfully honest account of Frémont's fifth expedition, an eyewitness, day-by-day record of an event in western history about which there exists very little information.

Appendix, Bibliography & Index

APPENDIX

Some Dramatis Personae of the Fifth Expedition

WILLIAM PALMER

William H. Palmer was a brother of Joseph C. Palmer of the San Francisco firm of Palmer, Cook and Company. Although the reason for his association with the fifth expedition is conjectural, William H. Palmer acquired an interest in Frémont's California property, and the Palmer bank was heavily involved in financing Frémont's real estate speculation in California. Frémont carried a letter of credit from Palmer, Cook and Company with him on the fifth expedition and used it in Utah to purchase horses and mules. Frémont's relationship to the bank was an election issue in his 1856 presidential campaign. William Palmer died in 1857. We are indebted to Mary Lee Spence for this information. *See* Almon W. Babbitt to editor, Mar. 14, 1854, San Francisco *Daily Herald,* Mar. 15, 1854; and campaign pamphlet entitled: "John C. Fremont! Is he Honest? Is he Capable?" (Pamphlet collection, Wisconsin State Hist. Soc., Madison), 6-7.

ALBERT LEA

Albert Lea was Frémont's free mulatto servant. He was reared in Senator Thomas Hart Benton's household, where his mother was employed. According to Jessie Benton Frémont, Lea was "just grown" when he joined the expedition. Although a San Francisco newspaper referred to Lea as Fremont's "valet," Jessie insisted that he was Frémont's "brave companion in danger," a "faithful nurse" during Frémont's convalescence in Kansas, and a man who shared Frémont's tent because he did not smoke. Lea remained at Frémont's side throughout the entire fifth expedition, and was in his employ in California. Lea married Meline Paullier in San Francisco. He subsequently murdered his estranged wife in that city on July 9, 1859. Lea was tried, found guilty, and hanged for murder on Mar. 1, 1861. *See* San Francisco *Daily Alta California,* Feb. 26, 27, and Mar. 2, 1861.

FREDERICK W. VON EGLOFFSTEIN

Frederick W. von Egloffstein, also known as Freiherr von Egloffstein (the German equivalent of Baron Egloffstein), was a skilled cartographer, artist, and topographer. Although most accounts indicate that he was born in Prussia, his fellow German artist-adventurer, Balduin Möllhausen, stated that he was a native of Bavaria. He emigrated to the United States sometime before 1850, for his name appears in the 1850 St. Louis County census schedules along with that of his German-born wife, Pomgard. By 1853 he was a partner in the surveying and topographical firm of "Egloffstein and Zwanziger." Eminent St. Louis botanist George Englemann apparently recommended him to Frémont. We do not know the exact terms of his employment, but know that in Aug. 1854, Frémont forwarded from New York through George Englemann the last hundred dollars due von Egloffstein for service on the fifth expedition.

Frémont made an excellent choice in selecting von Egloffstein. Although none of his topographical work dating from the fifth expedition appears to have survived, he went on to become one of the West's great nineteenth century map makers, and he was an artist and illustrator in his own right. His sketch of the Black Canyon of the Gunnison River is one of the few surviving visual records of the fifth expedition. It was printed as a colored lithograph in volume II of the *Reports of Explorations and Surveys.*

Frémont was disappointed when exhaustion forced von Egloffstein to leave the expedition in Utah. He characterized the German topographer as a man of "many good qualities," but not robust enough for western duty. Von Egloffstein soon disproved that assessment, establishing a reputation as a seasoned and daring explorer.

After recuperating in Salt Lake City, he joined Captain Edward G. Beckwith's survey of the 42nd parallel railroad route, replacing Edward Kern. Kern, John W. Gunnison and several other members of the railroad surveying party had been killed in an Indian attack in Utah in Oct. 1853. Von Egloffstein sketched beautiful if somewhat romantic panoramas of the route across the Great Basin, and helped draw the map of the route. Beckwith best summarized von Egloffstein's eye for meticulous detail and his dedication to duty when he stated: "I cannot speak too highly of the fidelity, zeal, and ability with which Mr. Egloffstein always performed these onerous labors."

In 1857 he joined Lieutenant Joseph C. Ives' survey of the Lower Colorado River and Grand Canyon. He proved to be an enthusiastic, competent explorer and an outstanding cartographer. Although he has been criticized for the Doresque views of the Lower Granite Gorge in Grand Canyon, he also sketched a number of large pen and ink panoramas of the Grand Canyon. These panoramas are the first accurate views of the Grand Canyon published in the United States.

In preparing maps of the Colorado Plateau, he invented a method of applying acid to the printing plate which produced a map showing a relief as though light were falling on it at an oblique angle.

In 1862 he joined the 103d New York Infantry Regiment and served in the Civil War. After suffering a serious wound, he left the army with the brevet rank of brigadier general. In 1864 he established the Geographical Institute in New York City, and in 1865 invented the half-tone process.

See "7th U.S. Census, 1850," M432, Reel 418, p. 405, RG29, NARS; St. Louis *Daily Missouri Democrat,* Sept. 2, 1853; Balduin Möllhausen, *Reisen in die Felsengebirge Nord-Amerikas,* II:19; *Reports of Explorations and Surveys,* II:4 and Appendix D, 125-27; 36th Cong., 1st Sess., House Executive Doc. No. 90, *Report Upon the Colorado River of the West, Explored in 1857 and 1858 by Lieutenant Joseph C. Ives,* 107-108; Carl I. Wheat, *Mapping the Trans-Mississippi West,* IV:143; Taft, *Artists and Illustrators,* 263-64; and Frémont to George Englemann, Aug. 20, 1854 (MS, Missouri Botanical Garden, St. Louis). We are indebted to Mary Lee Spence for information contained in the Frémont-Englemann letter.

SOLOMON NUNES CARVALHO

Solomon Nunes Carvalho (1815-1897) was a talented painter, author, and inventor who helped pioneer photography in the United States. Born and reared in Charleston, South Carolina, Carvalho pursued a successful career as an artist and photographer in Charleston, Philadelphia and Baltimore during the 1840s. Frémont met him in New York City in Aug. 1853, and employed him to make photographs on the fifth expedition. Apparently Carvalho had never entertained the idea of going West prior to meeting Frémont. His magnetic personality was a major factor in Carvalho's decision. "I know of no other man to whom I would have trusted my life, under similar circumstances," he admitted. "I impulsively, without even a consultation with my family, passed my word to join an exploring party, under command of Col. Frémont, over a hitherto untrodden country, in an elevated region, with the full expectation of being exposed to all the inclemencies of an arctic winter." After purchasing a daguerreotype camera and photographic supplies, he left New York City on Sept. 5 for a rendezvous with Frémont in St. Louis. *See* Sturhahn, *Carvalho;* and Carvalho, *Incidents of Travel,* 17-18.

OLIVER FULLER

Little is known about the life of Oliver Fuller beyond the material Milligan presents in his journal and the scattered references in Carvalho's *Incidents of Travel.* He was von Egloffstein's assistant. According to Carvalho, he was an "assistant engineer." More is known concerning his controversial death in the mountains of Utah in 1854. He was one of two casualties of the expedition, the other being John Smith, a Delaware hunter who died in 1854 aboard a Mississippi River steamer while en route home to Kansas.

Fuller was a resident of St. Louis. However, the only Oliver Fuller listed in the 1850 St. Louis census schedules was a thirteen year old son of Cornelius Fuller, a musician in the U.S. Dragoon Band at Jefferson Barracks. The Oliver Fuller from Jefferson Barracks would have been 16 in 1853, too young to fit the description of the Oliver Fuller on Frémont's fifth expedition. Carvalho noted that "Mr. Fuller was the strongest and largest man in the camp when we left Westport, and appeared much better able to bear the hardships of the journey than any man in it." An 1856 Frémont campaign pamphlet described Fuller as "a tall, large and powerful looking man, who had already crossed the plains to California, principally on foot." Fuller was highly regarded by those who knew him. His death came as a great tragedy. Frémont wrote to Benton that Fuller died "like a man, on horseback in his saddle, and will be buried like a soldier on the spot where he fell."

See "7th U.S. Census, 1850," M432, Reel 415, p.269, RG29, NARS; [William F. Bartlett], *Life of Col. Fremont* (New York, 1856), 27-28; Carvalho, *Incidents of Travel,* 19, 118, 134-35; J.C. Frémont to Thomas Hart Benton, Parawan, Utah Territory, Feb. 9, 1854, Wash., D.C. *National Intelligencer,* Apr. 12, 1854; and Almon W. Babbitt to editor, Mar. 14, 1854, San Francisco *Daily Herald,* Mar. 15, 1854.

THE DELAWARES

Frémont drew up a formal contract with the ten Delaware Indians at Westport on Sept. 16, 1853: "I have this day made an agreement through Jim Secondi, Delaware Chief, by which ten Delaware hunters, good men, are to accompany me on my journey to California and back to this country. The ten Delawares are to furnish their own animals and are each to be paid two dollars a day. They are to provide themselves with good animals, and if any of their animals should die upon the way I am to pay for the loss. They will, of course, be furnished to them by me at my own cost."

In addition to the seven Delaware hunters Milligan named, Frémont also employed George Washington, Caperessis, and John Johnnycake.

Apparently Frémont never made good on his contract for payment. In 1886 George Washington filed a claim with the Office of Indian Affairs for payment. Washington's claim was denied on the grounds that Frémont's survey was a private venture, not a government expedition.

John W. Gunnison employed John Moses as guide and Wahone as hunter as he traveled through Kansas in June 1853. The Delawares joined Gunnison at Uniontown on June 29, and remained with the railroad surveyors as far as Walnut Creek, where Gunnison dismissed them on July 12.

Solomon Everett (also spelled Eviet or Aviet) was a veteran of Frémont's third expedition and saw service in California during the Mexican War. John Johnnycake left the expedition on Oct. 30, 1853. John Smith was the only Delaware casualty. He died aboard a Mississippi River steamer near Diamond Point, Arkansas, in 1854 while en route home from California. Seven of the eight remaining Delawares returned to St. Louis in company with Max Strobel on June 5, 1854.

See 61st Cong., 1st sess., Senate Doc. 134, *Delaware Indians,* 6-9 for copies of Frémont's agreement with the Delawares as well as correspondence relating to George Washington's claim; the St. Louis *Daily Missouri Republican,* June 6, 1854; *Reports of Explorations and Surveys,* II:15, 19; Barry, *Beginning of the West,* 1168; and "Delaware Census for Feb. 15, 1862" (MS, Mary Witcher Coll., Oklahoma Hist. Soc.), which contains information on James Harrison, Jacob Enis (Eneos), George Washington, John Johnnycake, John Moses, Wahone, and Wolf. The Wyandot Census of June 3, 1872 (MS, Mary Witcher Coll., Oklahoma Hist. Soc.), lists John Brown and the Cotters, whose name Milligan misspelled.

MAX STROBEL

Max Strobel was employed in May 1853, as an artist on Isaac Stevens' survey of the 49th parallel railroad route. He was to assist artist John Mix Stanley in making sketches of the scenery along the route for use in Stevens' *Report.* Strobel made some sketches of the St.

Paul area and the Minnesota River. A lithograph based upon his sketch of St. Paul has survived, but apparently no original works are known to exist. According to Robert Taft, Strobel was unable or unwilling to keep up with the rapid pace which Stevens established, and resigned shortly after the expedition's departure from St. Paul. The New York *Daily Tribune* reported that Strobel and several other employees had "abandoned" Stevens' expedition in response to Stevens' "severe and arbitrary conduct."

According to Carvalho, Frémont was reluctant to employ Strobel because he already had a full roster. Frémont finally "yielded to his continued entreaties" and agreed to allow Strobel to accompany the expedition as an unpaid volunteer. When von Egloffstein's poor health forced him to resign from the expedition in Utah, Frémont put Strobel on the payroll as topographer and paid him about $700 for his services. Strobel returned to St. Louis on June 5, 1854, accompanied by seven of Frémont's Delaware hunters.

Strobel later managed the mines on Frémont's Mariposa estate in California and prepared a map of the property which Frémont used in marketing his estate to British investors. Strobel remained in the West where he was active in mining in Nevada and California.

See Reports of Explorations and Surveys, XII:33-39; Carvalho, *Incidents of Travel,* 29; New York *Daily Tribune,* June 3 and Aug. 3, 1853; St. Louis *Daily Missouri Republican,* Aug. 29, 1853; John C. Frémont to George Engelmann, Aug. 20, 1854 (MS, Missouri Botanical Garden); and Robert Taft, *Artists and Illustrators,* 273-74. We are indebted to Mary Lee Spence for information concerning Strobel's mining activities in California.

DR. A. EBERS

Dr. A. Ebers is listed as a homeopathic physician in the 1853-54 *Saint Louis Business Directory.* According to Frémont's wife, John C. Frémont had great confidence in Dr. Ebers because he was experienced in providing medical treatment under field conditions. The doctor had served in the Russian Army in Russia's victorious war against Turkey in 1828. The Saint Louis *Weekly Tribune* characterized Dr. Ebers as "a gentleman of deservedly high repute as a scientific man and skillful physician." Carvalho noted that he was "an immense man on an immense mule," a fact borne out by Julia Ann Stinson, who met him when Frémont's party stopped at her husband's trading house near present-day Topeka. "The doctor was very odd," she noted. "He rode on a great pillow, he sank way into it, it came up high in front of him. I asked Frémont why the doctor rode on a featherbed. He said 'Oh that's a pillow. He is a very odd man.'" Ebers stayed at Frémont's side until he was fully recovered. He remained behind with Milligan at Bent's New Fort. We are indebted to Mary Lee Spence for providing us with information contained in Jessie Benton Frémont's letter to Elizabeth Blair, Oct. 14, 1853 (MS, Blair-Lee Papers, Princeton University).

See also William L. Montague, *The Saint Louis Business Directory for 1853-4* (St. Louis, 1853), 49; St. Louis *Weekly Tribune,* Oct. 21, 1853; Carvalho, *Incidents of Travel,* 59; and "Statement of Mrs. Julia Ann Stinson," Apr. 15, 1914 (MS, Stinson Coll., Kansas State Hist. Soc.).

Bibliography

Documents and Manuscripts

Bancroft Library, University of California, Berkeley, CA:
Early Utah Records
Jessie Benton Frémont, "Great Events During the Life of Major General John C. Frémont"
Jenkin Family Papers

Bent's Old Fort National Historic Site, CO: James Larkin Memorandum Book

Bureau of Vital Statistics, St. Louis, MO: Death Certificate — Edward Milligan

Circuit Court of the City of Norfolk, Norfolk, VA: Marriage Register I

City Hall, St. Louis, MO: Marriage Records, Vol. 05

Denver Public Library, Denver, CO: Bent Papers

David W. Gaddy: Typescript — "James F. Milligan"

Jefferson Medical College, Philadelphia, PA: List of Graduates

Kansas State Historical Society, Topeka, KS: Stinson Coll.

Knox County Courthouse, Edina, MO: Land Records — Books A, B, C

Lewis County Courthouse, Monticello, MO: Land Records — Book D

Robert F. Milligan, Sun City, AZ:
Journal of James F. Milligan, 1846-1848
Journal of James F. Milligan, 1853-1856
Letter of James F. Milligan to Commissioner of Pensions, Sept. 1, 1853
Statement of W. L. Prieur, Oct. 31, 1940

Missouri Botanical Garden, St. Louis, MO: Frémont letter, 1854

Missouri Historical Society, St. Louis, MO:
Hiram H. Baber MS
County Court Papers, 1844, 1845

National Archives, Washington, DC:
Record Group 24:
Letters Sent Relating to Officers' Appointments, Orders, and Resignations, 1842-1895
Ships' Logs — USS *Albany, Scorpion, John Adams, Portsmouth, Porpoise*
Record Group 26:
Applications for Positions in the Revenue Cutter Service, 1844-1880
Appointment Records — U.S.R.M.S.
Letters from Officers of Revenue Cutter Service
Letters on Revenue Marine and Boats
Letters Received — Revenue Cutter Service, 1836-1910
Record Group 29:
Population Schedules of the Fifth Census of the United States, 1830. Microfilm M-19
Population Schedules of the Seventh Census of the United States, 1850. M-432
Record Group 45:
Index to Letters Received, 1823-1866
Letters from Officers Acknowledging Receipt of Commissions and Warrants and Enclosing Oaths of Allegiance, 1804-1864
Letters from Officers Commanding Squadrons, 1841-1866. M-89
Letters from Officers of Rank Below That of Commander, 1802-1884. M-148
Letters of Resignation from Officers, 1803-1877
Letters to Officers, 1798-1886. M-149
Miscellaneous Letters Received, 1801-1884. M-124
Miscellaneous Letters Sent, 1798-1886. M-209
Register of Applications for Appointment as Midshipmen, 1840-1857
Record Group 49:
Land Entry Papers of the General Land Office

Military Bounty Land Warrants and Related Papers
Record Group 75:
Documents Relating to Negotiations of Ratified and Unratified Treaties, 1801-69
Records of the Bureau of Indian Affairs
Record Group 109:
Compiled Service Records of Confederate Soldiers in Organizations Raised Directly by the Confederate Government. M-258

Naval Historical Center, Washington Navy Yard, Washington, DC: Biographical File — James F. Milligan

Northamptonshire Record Office, Northampton, England: Charles William Wentworth Fitzwilliam Letters

Oklahoma Historical Society:
Mary Witcher Coll.
Moses Grinter's Ledger Book

Perkins Library, Duke University, Durham, NC: Samuel Breese Papers

St. Louis Society for Medical and Scientific Education, St. Louis MO: List of Early Members

Sargeant Memorial Room, Norfolk Public Library, Norfolk, VA: Norfolk Directories Coll.

Scotland County Courthouse, Memphis, MO: Land Records — Book A

Sheffield City Libraries, Sheffield, England: Charles William Wentworth Fitzwilliam Letters

Smithsonian Institution Archives, Washington, DC: Frederick Kreutzfeldt Journal

State Historical Society of Colorado, Denver: Henry Chatillon to Denver *Evening Post*, letter

University of Southern Illinois at Edwardsville: Journal of Paul Wilhelm, Duke of Württemberg

Utah State Historical Society: Lt. Sylvester Mowry letter, 1854

Wisconsin State Historical Society, Madison, WI: Campaign Pamphlet Coll.

NEWSPAPERS

Albany *Atlas & Argus*
Austin *Texas State Gazette*
Charleston *Mercury*
Cleveland *Daily Plain Dealer*
Kanesville, Ia. *Frontier Guardian*
Mexico City *Daily American Star*
New Orleans *Bee*
New Orleans *Daily Picayune*
New York *Daily News*
New York *Daily Times*
New York *Daily Tribune*
Norfolk *American Beacon and Norfolk and Portsmouth Daily Advertiser*
Norfolk *Dispatch*
Norfolk *Landmark*
Norfolk *Public Ledger*
Norfolk *Southern Argus*
Norfolk *Virginian-Pilot*
St. Joseph *Adventure*
St. Joseph *Gazette*
St. Louis *Daily Evening News*
St. Louis *Daily Missouri Democrat*
St. Louis *Daily Missouri Republican*
St. Louis *Daily Morning Herald*
St. Louis *Intelligencer*
Salt Lake City *Deseret News*
San Francisco *Daily Alta California*
San Francisco *Daily Herald*
Washington, D.C. *Daily Union*
Washington, D.C. *National Intelligencer*
Washington, D.C. *States/States and Union*
Wilmington, N.C., *Daily Journal.*

BOOKS, ARTICLES, AND DISSERTATIONS

Abert, James W. *Report . . . of His Examination of New Mexico, in the Years 1846-47.* House Ex. Doc. 41, 30th Cong., 1st Sess.

________. *Through the Country of the Comanche Indians in the Fall the Year 1845.* Ed. by John Galvin. San Francisco: 1966.

________. *Western America in 1846-47: The Original Travel Diary Lieutenant J. W. Abert.* Ed. by John Galvin. San Francisco: 1966.

American Fisheries Society. *A List of Common and Scientific of Fishes from the United States and Canada.* Bethesda:

Anderson, Charles R., gen. ed. *The Centennial Edition of the of Sidney Lanier.* 10 vols. Baltimore: 1945.

Barry, Louise. *The Beginning of the West: Annals of the Kansas to the American West, 1540-1854.* Topeka: 1972.

Bartlett, Ruhl. *Frémont and the Republican Party.* Columbus:

[Bartlett, William F.] *Life of Col. Fremont.* New York: 1856.

Bauer, K. Jack. *Surfboats and Horse Marines: U.S. Naval in the Mexican War, 1846-48.* Annapolis: 1969.

Benton, Thomas Hart. *Thirty Years' View; or, a History of the of the American Government for Thirty Years, from 1820 1850*. 2 vols. New York: 1854-1856.

Berthrong, Donald J. *The Southern Cheyennes.* Norman: 1963.

Bloomfield, Howard V. L. *The Compact History of the United Coast Guard.* New York: 1966.

Bodson, Robert L. "A Description of the United States Occupation of Mexico as Reported by American Newspapers Published in Vera Cruz, Puebla, and Mexico City, September 14, 1847 to July 31, 1848." Unpublished Ed.D. diss., Ball State Univ., 1970.

Bonner, Thomas D. *The Life and Adventures of James P. Beckwourth.* Lincoln: 1972.

Bridge, Horatio. *Journal of an African Cruiser.* Ed. by Nathaniel Hawthorne. New York: 1853.

Brown, A. Theodore. *Frontier Community: Kansas City to 1870.* Columbia: 1963.

Brown, T. Allston. *A History of the New York Stage from the First Performance in 1732 to 1901.* New York: 1964.

Caldwell, Martha B. *Annals of Shawnee Methodist Mission and Indian Manual Labor School.* Topeka: 1939.

Canan, H.V. "Confederate Military Intelligence." *Maryland Historical Magazine,* (Mar. 1964), LIX:34-51.

Carson, William G.B. *The Theatre on the Frontier: The Early Years of the St. Louis Stage.* 2nd ed. New York: 1965.

Carvalho, Solomon N. *Incidents of Travel and Adventure in the Far West.* New York: 1857.

Catton, Bruce. *Never Call Retreat.* Vol. III of *The Centennial History of the Civil War.* 3 vols. New York: 1965.

Chambers, Lenoir and Shanks, Joseph E. *Salt Water and Printer's Ink: Norfolk and its Newspapers, 1865-1965.* Chapel Hill: 1967.

Chappell, Philip E. "A History of the Missouri River." *Transactions of the Kansas State Historical Socety,* (1905-1906) IX:237-94.

Chaput, Donald. *Francois X. Aubry: Trader, Trailmarker and Voyageur in the Southwest, 1846-1854.* Glendale, CA: 1975.

Christopher, Adrienne. "The Old Vogel Saloon." *Westport Historical Quarterly,* (1970) V:10-12.

Coad, Oral S. "Joseph M. Field." Vol. III of *Dictionary of American Biography*. Ed. by Allen Johnson and Dumas Malone. 12 vols. New York: 1958.

Coel, Margaret. *Chief Left Hand, Southern Arapaho*. Norman: 1981.

Conner, Philip S.P. *The Home Squadron Under Commodore Conner in the War with Mexico*. Philadelphia: 1896.

Crampton, C. Gregory. *Standing Up Country: The Canyon Lands of Utah and Arizona*. New York: 1964.

________. "Utah's Spanish Trail." *Utah Historical Quarterly*, (Fall, 1979) XLVII:361-83.

Crandall, Andrew W. *The Early History of the Republican Party, 1854-1856*. Gloucester: 1960.

Cummins, Edmund H. "The Signal Corps in the Confederate States Army." *Southern Historical Society Papers*, (1888) XVI:93-107.

Custer, George A. *My Life on the Plains*. Norman: 1962.

Delaware Indians. Senate Doc. 134. 61st Cong., 1st Sess.

DeVoto, Bernard. *Across the Wide Missouri*. New York: 1964.

Egan, Ferol. *Fré*mont: Explorer for a Restless Nation. Garden City: 1977.

Ellicott, John M. *The Life of John Ancrum Winslow, Rear Admiral, United States Navy*. New York: 1902.

Field, Matthew C. *Prairie and Mountain Sketches*. Ed. by Kate L. Gregg and John F. McDermott. Norman: 1957.

Foote, Andrew H. *Africa and the American Flag*. New York: 1854.

Foote, Shelby. *The Civil War: A Narrative*. 3 vols. New York: 1958-1974.

Frazer, Robert B. *Forts of the West*. Norman: 1965.

Frémont, John C. *Memoirs of My Life*. Chicago: 1887.

French, Samuel G. *Two Wars: An Autobiography*. Nashville: 1901.

Gaddy, David W. "William Norris and the Confederate Signal and Secret Service." *Maryland Historical Magazine*, (Summer, 1975), LXX:167-88.

Garraghan, Gilbert J. *The Jesuits of the Middle United States*. 3 vols. New York: 1938.

Garrard, Lewis H. *Wah-to-Yah and the Taos Trail*. Vol VI of *The Southwest Historical Series*. Ed. by Ralph P. Bieber and LeRoy R. Hafen. 12 vols. Glendale: 1931-1943.

Ghigliazza, Manuel M. *Invasión* Norteamericana en Tabasco, 1846-1847. Mexico: 1848.

Goff, William A. *Old Westport.* n.p: 1977.

Gregg, Josiah. *Commerce of the Prairies.* Ed. by Max L. Moorhead. Norman: 1954.

Gregg, Kate L., ed. *The Road to Santa Fé: The Journal and Diaries of George Chaplin Sibley.* Albuquerque: 1952.

Griffis, William E. *Matthew Calbraith Perry: A Typical American Naval Officer.* Boston: 1890.

Grinnell, George Bird. "Bent's Old Fort and its Builders." *Collections of the Kansas State Historical Society,* (1919-1922) XV:28-91.

———. *The Cheyenne Indians.* 2 vols. Lincoln: 1972.

———. *The Fighting Cheyennes.* Norman: 1955.

Gudde, Erwin G. and Elisabeth K. *Exploring with Frémont: The Private Diaries of Charles Preuss.* Norman: 1958.

Hafen, LeRoy R., ed. "The W.M. Boggs Manuscript about Bent's Fort, Kit Carson, the Far West and Life among the Indians." *Colorado Magazine,* (Mar. 1930) VII:45-69.

———. *Broken Hand: The Life of Thomas Fitzpatrick, Mountain Man, Guide and Indian Agent.* Denver: 1973.

———. and Ann W., eds. *Frémont's Fourth Expedition: A Documentary Account of the Disaster of 1848-1849.* Vol. XI and Heap and Beale, *Central Route to the Pacific.* Vol. VII of *The Far West and Rockies Series.* 15 vols. Glendale, CA: 1954-1961.

———. *The Mountain Men and the Fur Trade of the Far West.* 10 vols. Glendale: 1965-1972.

———. *The Overland Mail, 1849-1869: Promoter of Settlement, Precursor of Railroads.* Cleveland: 1926.

———. *Ruxton of the Rockies.* Norman: 1950.

Hagood, Johnson. *Memoirs of the War of Secession.* Columbia: 1910.

Haines, Aubrey L. *Historic Sites along the Oregon Trail.* St. Louis: 1981.

Hamersly, Lewis R., comp. *The Records of Living Officers of the U.S. Navy and Marine Corps. . .* Philadelphia: 1870.

Hammond, George P. *The Adventures of Alexander Barclay, Mountain Man.* Denver: 1976.

Hanson, Charles E., Jr. "Robe and Fur Presses." *Museum of the Fur Trade Quarterly,* (Summer, 1967) III:3-6.

Hart, Herbert M. *Old Forts of the Southwest.* New York: 1964.

Harwell, Richard B., ed. *A Confederate Diary of the Retreat from Petersburg, April 3-20, 1865.* Atlanta: 1953.

Heap, Gwinn Harris. *Central Route to the Pacific.* Philadelphia: 1854; *see also* above Hafen reprint edition.

History of Lewis, Clark, Knox, and Scotland Counties, Missouri. St. Louis: 1887.

Hodge, Frederick Webb. *Handbook of American Indians North of Mexico.* B.A.E., Bulletin 30. 2 vols. Washington: G.P.O., 1907-1910.

Hoig, Stan. *John Simpson Smith: Frontiersman, Trapper, Trader, and Interpreter.* Glendale, CA: 1974.

_______. *The Peace Chiefs of the Cheyenne.* Norman: 1980.

Honig, Louis O. "Map of the Town of Westport in 1855." Kansas City: ca. 1942.

Horn, Calvin. *New Mexico's Troubled Years: The Story of the Early Territorial Governors.* Albuquerque: 1963.

Hyde, George E. *Life of George Bent Written from His Letters.* Norman: 1968.

Inman, Henry. *The Old Santa Fé Trail.* New York: 1897.

Ives, Joseph. C. *Report Upon the Colorado River of the West Explored in 1857 and 1858.* House Ex. Doc. 90, 36th Cong., 1st Sess.

Jackson, Donald and Spence, Mary Lee, eds. *The Expeditions of John Charles Frémont.* 3 vols. and supplements. Urbana: 1970-84.

Johannsen, Robert W. *Stephen A. Douglas.* New York: 1973.

Jones, Charles C., Jr. *The Life and Services of Commodore Josiah Tattnall.* Savannah: 1878.

Kappler, Charles M., ed. *Indian Affairs: Laws and Treaties.* 7 vols. Washington: 1904-1979.

Karnes, Thomas L. *William Gilpin: Western Nationalist.* Austin: 1970.

Keemle's St. Louis Directory for 1840-1841. St. Louis: 1840.

Kennerly, William Clark. *Persimmon Hill: A Narrative of Old St. Louis and the Far West.* Norman: 1948.

Lanier, Clifford. *Thorn-Fruit.* New York: 1867.

Lanier, Sidney. *Works. See* Anderson, C.R., ed.

Lass, William E. *From the Missouri to the Great Salt Lake: An Account of Overland Freighting.* Lincoln: 1972.

Lavender, David. *Bent's Fort.* Garden City: 1954.

Leckie, William H. *The Military Conquest of the Southern Plains.* Norman: 1963.

Lecompte, Janet. *Pueblo, Hardscrabble, Greenhorn: The Upper Arkansas, 1832-1856.* Norman: 1978.

Lowe, Percival G. *Five Years a Dragoon.* Ed. by Don Russell. Norman: 1956.

Ludlow, Noah M. *Dramatic Life as I Found It.* St Louis: 1880.

Luebers, H.C. "William Bent's Family and the Indians of the Plains." *Colorado Magazine,* (Jan. 1936) XIII:19-22.

Majors, Alexander. *Seventy Years on the Frontier.* Chicago: 1893.

Marshall, David J. "The Confederate Army's Signal Corps." in *The Story of the U.S. Army Signal Corps.* Ed. by Max L. Marshall. New York: 1965.

Mattes, Merrill. *The Great Platte River Road.* Lincoln: 1969.

May, Robert E. *The Southern Dream of a Caribbean Empire.* Baton Rouge: 1973.

MacNamara, Charles. "The First Official Photographer." *Scientific Monthly,* (1936) LXII:68-74.

Meriwether, David. *My Life in the Mountains and on the Plains.* Ed. by Robert A. Griffen. Norman: 1965.

Möllhausen, Balduin. *Reisen in die Felsengebirge Nord-Amerikas.* 2 vols. Leipzig: 1861.

Montaignes, Francois de. *The Plains.* Ed. by Nancy Alpert Mower and Don Russell. Norman: 1972.

Moore, Jackson W., Jr. *Bent's Old Fort: An Archaeological Study.* Denver: 1979.

Morison, Samuel E. *"Old Bruin:" Commodore Matthew C. Perry, 1794-1858.* Boston: 1967.

Morrison's St. Louis Directory for 1852. St. Louis: 1852.

Mumey, Nolie. *Old Forts and Trading Posts of the West: Bent's Old Fort and Bent's New Fort on the Arkansas River.* Denver: 1956.

Murphy, Lawrence R. *Lucien Bonaparte Maxwell.* Norman: 1983.

A Naval Encyclopedia, Comprising a Dictionary of Nautical Words and Phrases, Biographical Notices, and Records of Naval Officers. Philadelphia: 1881.

Nevins, Allan. *Frémont: Pathmarker of the West.* New York: 1955.

Newhall, Beaumont. *The Daguerreotype in America.* n.p.: 1961.

Nye, W.S. *Carbine and Lance: The Story of Old Fort Sill.* Norman: 1937.

Parker, William H. *Recollections of a Naval Officer, 1841-1865.* New York: 1883.

Porter, John W. H. *A Record of Events in Norfolk County, Virginia, from April 19, 1861 to May 10, 1862.* Portsmouth: 1892.

Powell, Peter J. *Sweet Medicine: The Continuing Role of the Sacred Arrows, the Sun Dance and the Sacred Buffalo Hat in Northern Cheyenne History.* Norman: 1979.

Ray, P. Orman. *The Repeal of the Missouri Compromise: Its Origin and Authorship.* Cleveland: 1909.

Reed, Nelson. *The Caste War of Yucatan.* Stanford: 1964.

Reports of Explorations and Surveys. Vols. II, XII. House Ex. Doc. 91, 33rd Cong., 2nd Sess.

Riddle, Kenyon. *Records and Maps of the Old Santa Fé* Trail. Raton: 1949.

Rolle, Andrew. "Exploring an Explorer: Psychohistory and John Charles Frémont." *Pacific Historical Review,* (1982), LI:135-63.

Ross, Edith C. "The Old Shawnee Mission: The Pioneer Institution of Christian Civilization in the West." *Collections of the Kansas State Historical Society,* " (1926-1928) XVII:417-35.

Ross, Marvin C. *The West of Alfred Jacob Miller.* Norman: 1968.

Rudisill, Richard. *Mirror Image: The Influence of the Daguerreotype on American Society.* Albuquerque: 1971.

Russel, Robert R. *Improvement of Communication with the Pacific Coast as an Issue in American Politics, 1780-1864.* Cedar Rapids: 1948.

Saint Louis Business Directory for 1853-1854. St. Louis: 1854.

Sands, Benjamin F. *From Reefer to Rear Admiral.* New York: 1899.

Scarne, John. *Encyclopedia of Games.* New York: 1973.

Schultz, George A. *An Indian Canaan: Isaac McCoy and the Vision of an Indian State.* Norman: 1972.

Seger, John H. *Early Days Among the Cheyenne and Arapahoe Indians.* Ed. by Stanley Vestal. Norman: 1979.

Semmes, Raphael. *Service Afloat and Ashore During the Mexican War.* Cincinnati: 1851.

Slavens, J.S.L. "Historical Atlas Map of Jackson County, Missouri." Philadelphia: 1877.

Smith, Ralph A. "The Fantasy of a Treaty to End all Treaties." *Great Plains Journal,* (Fall, 1972) XII:26-51.

_______. "The Mamelukes of West Texas and Mexico." *West Texas Historical Association Yearbook,* (1963) XXXIX:65-88.

Smith, William. "The Oregon Trail Through Pottawatomie County." *Kansas State Historical Collections,* (1926-1928) XVII:435-64.

Spence, Mary Lee. "David Hoffman: Frémont's Mariposa Agent in London." *Southern California Quarterly,* (1978) LX:379-403.

_______. "The Frémonts and Utah." *Utah Historical Quarterly,* (1976) XLIV:286-302.

Starke, Audrey H. *Sidney Lanier: A Biographical and Critical Study.* Chapel Hill: 1933.

Stewart, William H. *History of Norfolk, Virginia, and Representative Citizens.* Chicago: 1902.

Sturhahn, Joan. *Carvalho, Artist-Photographer-Adventurer-Patriot: Portrait of a Forgotten American.* Merrick, N.Y.: 1976.

Sunder, John E., ed. *Matt Field on the Santa Fé Trail.* Norman: 1960.

Taft, Robert. *Artists and Illustrators of the Old West, 1850-1900. New York: 1953.*

_______. *Photography and the American Scene: A Social History, 1839-1889.* New York: 1984.

Taylor, Charles E. "The Signal and Secret Service of the Confederate States." *Confederate Veteran,* (Aug.-Oct. 1932) XL:302-305, 338-40.

Taylor, Fitch W. *The Broad Pennant: or, A Cruise in the United States Flag Ship of the Gulf Squadron During the Mexican Difficulties.* New York: 1848.

Trenholm, Virginia Cole. *The Arapahoes, Our People.* Norman: 1970.

Tyler, Daniel. *Sources for New Mexican History, 1821-1848.* Santa Fé: 1984.

U.S. Coast Guard. *Record of Movements — Vessels of the United States Coast Guard, 1790-Dec. 31, 1933.* 2 vols. Washington: n.d.

U.S. Department of the Navy. *Official Records of the Union and Confederate Navies in the War of the Rebellion.* 30 vols. Washington: 1894-1927.

U.S. Department of War. *War of the Rebellion: A Compilation of the Official Records of the Union and Confederate Armies.* 128 vols. Washington: 1880-1901.

Unrau, William H. *The Kansa Indians: A History of the Wind People, 1673-1873.* Norman: 1971.

Walker, Henry P. *The Wagonmasters: High Plains Freighting From the Earliest Days of the Santa Fé Trail to 1880.* Norman: 1966

Warren, Harris G. *Paraguay: An Informal History.* Norman: 1949.

Weber, David J. *Richard H. Kern: Expeditionary Artist in the Far Southwest, 1848-1853.* Albuquerque: 1985.

Wheat, Carl I. *Mapping the Trans-Mississippi West.* 6 vols. San Francisco: 1957-1963.

Wheelock, Walt. "Following Frémont's Fifth Expedition." *Westerner's Brand Book.* Los Angeles: 1966.

———. "Frémont's Lost Plates." *Westerner's Brand Book.* San Diego: 1971.

Index